THE LANGUAGE OF POETRY: CRISIS AND SOLUTION

STUDIES IN MODERN POETRY OF FRENCH EXPRESSION, 1945 TO THE PRESENT

edited by

MICHAEL BISHOP

Printed in the Netherlands
ISBN: 90–6203–681–3

ACKNOWLEDGEMENTS

I should like to express my thanks to James Lawler and James Brown for their support and advice during the preparation of this volume; to all other contributors whose ideas, enthusiasm and patience have helped me greatly; to Mr. Fred van der Zee for his kindness and efficiency; to the Research Development Committee, Humanities and Social Sciences, of Dalhousie University for their confidence and support; to Irene Robinson, Dianne Crouse, Yvonne Landry and Verena Grünther for their valuable assistance with the preparation of typescripts and correspondence.

Michael Bishop

CONTENTS

THE LANGUAGE OF POETRY: CRISIS AND SOLUTION

INTRODUCTION

Michael Bishop

The Language of Poetry: Crisis and Solution is a book that has set itself the task of working out, in a series of independent though interrelated essays, some of the problems and tensions that have arisen in modern poetry of French expression to do with poetic language itself. More specifically, the authors of the twelve essays presented have endeavoured to show how a variety of poetic solutions have more often than not proved themselves not only marginally permissible but eminently viable, both existentially and aesthetically, via a series of personal shifts and re-orientations - private solutions to privately conceived, though also often shared crises, personal continuings, however anguished or fragile, revealing the durability and the flexibility of the language of poetry. Our concern here, then, is not just with analysis of the parameters of a dichotomy which would view crisis in terms of raw, concrete experience and solution in terms of poetry, roughly in the manner of poets such as Baudelaire or Reverdy. Of course such considerations may be highly relevant, but so many of these poets - and this is perhaps particularly so with the poets of France, from Yves Bonnefoy and Francis Ponge to Henri Michaux and Denis Roche - upon whom we focus attention in these studies, construe language itself, initially if not continuingly, as constituting its own particular obstacle, a crisis every bit as formidable as that so commonly posed by self-world experience and thereby creating a tripartite basis for crisis and solution: self-word-world. Language, then, in this optic, becomes central, pivotal. French - and indeed all francophone - poetry since Mallarmé, but perhaps especially that of the last thirty years or so, has become increasingly self-reflexive, a poetry about poetry, a discourse upon a discourse, and has even reached in some poets the point of a certain didactic or exemplary self-destruction in which codes of signifying are highlighted to the deliberate detriment of any normally construed signified. Such cases are extreme and demonstrate with critical acuteness one particular dimension of the complex problematic of modern poetic expression. As for the 'solutions', they are as numerous and varied as the poets themselves. Together, however, the poets studied here, richly mixed as their experience of language is, offer a fine overview of much that has threatened to tear francophone poetry apart at the seams, but which, by means of a series of privately eked out - or joyously heralded - solutions, has only succeded in demonstrating its immense suppleness. If the book, moreover, centres its concern initially upon the poetry of major contemporary writers in France, outside France, too, the French language of poetry has found itself caught in various webs, sociopolitical as well as aesthetic, but all betraying urgent existential concern, and this volume attempts to show something of the uniqueness - and yet at the same time the broad universality - of certain experiences and struggles in Québec, Africa, the Caribbean and Belgium.

The crisis of the ultra-modern era that affects poetry and, indeed, literature and culture as a whole, resembles no doubt in certain general characteristics crises of past eras - such as those of the Romantic and Symbolist periods or, more particularly, the explosive Dada movement - yet it is a crisis that possesses its own pressing drama and tense atmosphere, as well as its own modes of *dénouement*. The specific detail of this poetic drama will, of course, emerge in the essays to follow and this Introduction will not therefore seek redundantly to trace the intricate patterns elaborated there in accordance with the individual logics of divergent poetic theory and practice. The aim of this brief liminal exposition is, rather, to stress certain general aspects of the problem with which all the essays subsequently grapple in one way or another, explicitly or somewhat more implicitly, and, it might be noted, according to freely elected and therefore occasionally varying critical perspectives. My purpose, here, then, is simply to offer a succinct examination of some of the fundamental and recurrent factors of crisis and solution as they pertain to the logic and practice of the language of francophone poetry of recent years.

Like other creative endeavours, poetry starts with the need to release an inner, highly personal energy that has accumulated to the point of excess and now threatens to brim over. Poetry is a more or less instinctive and intuitive channelling (which is thus by no means to deny its capacity for control and order in the midst of adventure) of such energy in order to solve the initially purely existential, experiential problematic that has led to this dangerous and near-explosive accumulation. What is so often characteristic of the poet, however - and what we observe with many of the subjects of these essays - is that what we may think of as this initial classic phenomenological problematic which opposes self and world in a struggle for domination, may eventually, perhaps increasingly, incorporate the poet's very means of solution - his poetry, his language - within the original problematic, thus complicating it, vitiating it, infecting poetic language with a similar and fundamental sense of lack and inadequacy. In this way, not only may the poet experience an anguishing deterioration of his relationships with others and things, a qualitative reduction of his general being in the world, but he may also be obliged to cope with a distressingly difficult and perhaps worsening relationship between word and world, between the anticipated means of solution and the elements of his original crisis. Poetic expression, whilst perhaps still suspected of - and, hopefully, capable of - possessing some lost archaic link with reality, may thus be seen to constitute a symbol of the exile of the poet, the hiatus that separates him from the world - both its human and non-human phenomena. Worse still, poetic expression, even if continuing to offer perhaps the only chance of casting before the poet a just and adequate form of himself, may be recognized as ontologically deficient because of its inevitable otherness, the fact that the poet is always, and according to that terrifying Rimbaldian logic, other, inauthentic, divorced from himself by and in his very own poetic expression of himself. Though necessarily, compulsively espoused as a salvatory medium, the language of poetry may find itself therefore under attack, criticised and even at times mercilessly exposed by its user, who may see in it a significant factor of aggravation in his experience of and dealing with an already problematical primary mode of being in the world.

What is central to an appreciation of all the poets discussed here, however, is the simple but fundamental fact that problem, whether purely existential or rather more specifically linguistic, poetic, is simultaneously stimulus, provocation, a prodding, piercing force that, capable of utter destruction, may also goad into response. The poem may, indeed, demonstrate and even define, as Alain Jouffroy claims, 'la crise mondiale de la pensée', but its very existence, as well as its internal signification and its aesthetic quality, constitute a critical and lucid refusal of the temptation of silence. Certainly, the logic of silence and virginal whiteness has lured and anguished poets of the modern era from Rimbaud and Mallarmé to Bernard Noël and Philippe Jaccottet, but, as Reverdy was quick to perceive, the assumption of the logic of silence for anyone who has once conceived of himself as a poet, is tantamount to suicide and thus the most desperate of acts. A glance through the ranks of those associated with the Dada and Surrealist movements will nevertheless confirm that the threat of silence, if generally blunted, is frighteningly real for many poets for whom the discovery of poetry and the exploration of its many strange and wondrous caverns is by no means a panacea. No straight arrows fly from crisis to solution by means of the language of poetry. The void presses in around what is so often the exploded, fragmented body of the modern poem, with its apparently discontinuous rhythms that seem to betray the loss of some earlier possessed harmony and coherence. But the poem remains, working both *against* what presses in upon it from the outside and what threatens to erode or collapse it from the inside, and *for* the constitution and preservation of its own inner dynamism, its perhaps strange, irregular syncopations, its tattered, enigmatic structural - and ontological - wholeness. Whilst exhilaration is often difficult, even impossible, to achieve for many poets in positing and demonstrating the poem's capacity to be *for*, there is of course a long line, running from Claudel and Saint-John Perse, through Eluard and Breton, to Francis Ponge and, strangest of companions, Denis Roche, that reveals in wildly varying manners to what extent factors of jubilation and celebration persist in the language of modern francophone poetry. Even poets like Tchicaya U Tam'si and Philippe Jaccottet experience their moments of intense and uplifting poetic emotion, though with them, as with so many others - and Denis Roche again springs to mind -, jubilation can be so decisively and painfully muted by recognition of the disastrous limitations of an only intermittently or partially buoyant power of poetic language. If, then, all the poets treated here accept to some degree the imperfect, but at least potential capacity of language to repulse fear, to keep the poet from the haunting reality of death and nothingness, and, just perhaps, to push back the unknown, even if it is by the disturbing means of what Michel Deguy has termed 'les chiffres de l'indéchiffrable', we must not lose sight of the fact that the reconciliation of poetic language's impossibility or varyingly sensed inadequacy and its necessity, is fragile and vulnerable in the extreme. Yet for all its lack of definitiveness and stability - poetry involves a constant beginning again, a returning to zero, to the reality of void and nothingness in order, once more, to briefly eliminate them - the 'solutions' afforded by the language of poets from René Char to Gaston Miron are operative, viable and spiritually available. Just as the poem is what one may think of as the locus of the crisis of all solution, so is it the means of solution, however minimal, however tenuous, of such crisis, and it is the internal *justesse* of the text, of the language of a given poetic text, that allows this sometimes grim-faced victory in defeat, this celebration of life in the tightening clutches of death. The tensions and precariousness of such a situation may thus become the object of the poet's hatred or derision or may occasion profound anguish, but they are also commonly recognized to be the conditions of a possibility and their presence decrees that an at least minimal, though essential positivity attaches to an activity that can so afflict. Certainly, not every poet is able to muster the alternatively furtive and invigorated sense of an *invisible profusion* that for Michel Deguy is never absent. For others, like André Frénaud or Jacques Dupin, the quest is more dogged, the point of attainment more deeply recessed, the language of their poetry, however brilliant and illuminating, bearing witness to the barely continuing or massively difficult exploitation of a powerful but sparse energy. Perhaps most interestingly - alarmingly, if one's view is less detached - it is evident that specific poetic means, given individual linguistic techniques adopted as means of solution, do not seem to be, in themselves, determining. The criteria of poeticity, of poetic language's solution, are not stable. There is no aesthetic *sine qua non*, there are no poetic or 'scriptive' prerequisites or guidelines. On the contrary, such criteria, even were they to exist, would be felt to be impossibly restrictive, deadening. The poet is obliged, not only in a broad creative sense, to begin his quest again with each written enterprise, but also, almost as a matter of principle despite any profound influence exercised upon him by earlier poets, to handle with extreme caution and even set at nought such influence, such channelling, in order to produce a form that is more perfectly and naturally moulded to the unique contours of his own sensibility. Without this sometimes painful gesture, the language of his poetry tends to wither and atrophy, the specific means of projection of his imagination remain stunted in their growth. The parasitical voices within must thus be silenced, the poet must expose himself fully to the special language that everything, in the self and without, works to suppress.

The essays that follow will permit then, it is hoped, many penetrating and fascinating insights into the parameters of a view of modern poetic language that holds the latter to be simultaneously the locus and even the cause of distinctly appreciable and perhaps intense crisis, as of miraculous and continuing solution to such crisis. Whether the pressure upon language (that of poetry, to be sure, but also that of all literature, all free imaginative expression), pressure both from without, from the impinging forces of francophone societies and their politics, and from within itself and the individual poetic-linguistic history of a given poet - whether this pressure is capable of snuffing out those voices that presently can be heard, is purely a matter of conjecture. Certainly it is, unfortunately, by no means difficult to envisage an era either of total mufflement from without, as a result of socio-political forces, or of impotent poetic implosion whose energy will never manage to break through the walls of the individual consciousness. Such a nightmare is, despite the many blatant and disguised pressures upon the poetic activity of contemporary francophone societies, in no way a firm reality at the moment. As this year's Cambridge Poetry Festival so dramatically demonstrated - I think of the eager fascination that greeted readings by Wendy Mulford, Hélène Cixous and Glenda George, as well as the often tumultuous receptions given to poets as diverse as Edmond Jabès, Allen Ginsberg, Anne Waldman and Kenneth Koch - the language of poetry is still very much alive. Indeed, many other living poets might have been examined in the pages to follow, were it not for limitations of space, and all would have merited close attention not just for the pertinence of their work to the broad concerns of this book, but also for the inherent quality of the measure of triumph they bring to the struggle against the problems they encounter: Philippe Jaccottet, André Frénaud, Edmond Jabès, Eugène Guillevic, Jean Follain, Bernard Noël, Jacques Roubaud, Jean Daive, Emmanuel Hocquard, for example, and only to speak of France. In fact, elsewhere also, in Québec, Africa, the Caribbean, Belgium and Switzerland, the vitality of reviews and small presses, many privately financed - often on a shoe-string - and with limited audiences, testifies to the continuingly and perhaps even increasingly felt power of poetry, the capacity of its language to resolve and transcend or, at least, to offer a minimally adequate counteraction to forces, both intrinsic and extrinsic to poetry itself, that seek to stifle or destroy the delicate (though surprisingly robust) dynamism of mankind's multiple voices. It cannot be denied that poetic celebration is today infinitely more conscious than was generally the case one hundred or even fifty years ago of its own vulnerability, even absurdity in a certain sense, of the fact that the dance of its language takes place over, and in risky defiance of, a varyingly characterized yet so often thinly veiled void. Poetry, however, like art in general, is not dead. It is arguable that it is, more and more, picking at its own flesh out of nervousness and sometimes for nourishment, but, even in a poet such as Denis Roche, the flesh provides an incredible energy, permitting a form of life, even an exhilarating one, to be salvaged in the midst of menace and decay. As long as man is free to generate energy, poetry's language will spark and flash, fizzling and sputtering no doubt at times, but capable of intense illumination and fiery, searing heat. It is in a spirit of admiration for and in emotional response to such energy that this book has been written and it is back towards this same energy that, it is hoped by all those who have contributed to this collective enterprise, the reader's attention will irresistibly be drawn.

September, 1979
Halifax, Nova Scotia, Canada

THE LANGUAGE OF RENÉ CHAR

James Lawler

Il me faut la voix et l'écho.
(Chants de la Balandrane)[1]

Char's poetry from its origins is written in a language of crisis. From his first authentic verse contained in *Les Cloches sur le coeur*, he has been obsessed by disruption, held by a Mallarméan anxiety to shore up that which subsists. The former schemes have failed and what is left is a moraine of words. As he writes in a poem published shortly after the war:

> Quand s'ébranla le barrage de l'homme, aspiré par la faille géante de l'abandon du divin, des mots dans le lointain, des mots qui ne voulaient pas se perdre, tentèrent de résister à l'exorbitante poussée. Là se décida la dynastie de leur sens.[2]

It is in this properly tragic context that his efforts are pursued. The nineteenth century discovered the dark night of Baudelaire and Mallarmé - 'où gît tout ce qui nuit';[3] for Char, as for many another contemporary, the word is more acutely threatened today. Yet to make of the diverse fragments a sign and sense becomes his consuming passion.

The search has been carried out with lucid dedication. In evolving by way of surrealism Char was not tempted to view poetry as a self-sufficient activity. On the contrary, like his fellow surrealists, he took it to be central to life, and in continuous relationship with anguish and desire. To this end words have had to be used with proper regard to intrinsic ceremonies and rites. The wisdom of adages, regionalisms, etymologies, myths, varied felicities and surprises of sound: here is a festive matter as capacious as the poet's imagination. He treats words as living things, strives to handle them with full awareness. "Prends garde", he notes in an urgent summons to himself, "prends garde, quand tu peux, aux mots que tu écris'.[4] But he who achieves his goal liberates the elements, realizes the opposite of enslavement; he is the lover who gives delight: 'Donner joie à des mots'.[5] Char has come to poetry with the aim of marrying sleep and waking, reason and feeling, of celebrating a vibrant sensibility alert to its own contradictions.

No doubt the most dramatic period in his career was his discovery of nature as the fundamental resource after 1935. Surrealism had taken him into nocturnal obsession from which withdrawal was not easy, but the poetry that postdates *Le Marteau sans maître* contains the assertion of a Mediterranean warmth and of a language deliberately renewed. He delights in the multiplicity of plants, animals, landscapes, transforms the vocabulary of his poems; at the same time he is attentive to an implicit wisdom that he seeks to convey. He becomes the fervent hunter of meanings who reinvents the myth of Orion. In his most recent collection we read: 'Peu auront su regarder la terre sur laquelle ils vivaient et la tutoyer en baissant les yeux. Terre d'oubli, terre prochaine, dont on s'éprend avec effroi'.[6]

His poems allow us to gauge his artistic integrity. He composes most often with assurance as if his work came ripely to his pen; yet he is also ready to wait long months for a single word and to revise completed writings. He is meticulous in his analyses, in the elaboration of his themes. Of the many texts that might serve our study, none is more eloquent than 'Biens égaux' which has come to us in two distinct states. Begun in 1937, it first appeared the following year in the collection *Dehors la nuit est gouvernée*. From the start, however, Char considered it incomplete and designated typographically the lacunae. He described it has having been 'abandoned', only much later reworking it and publishing a second version in April 1946.[7] So we have twin documents of an unusual kind that bear witness, for the decade between Char's thirtieth and fortieth years, to his search for an adequate language.

The title denotes a change from the temper of surrealism. Breaking with masterless hammer, it gathers the paradoxes of the closing poem of *Moulin premier* of 1935. 'Commune Présence' voiced the antagonisms of poetry and life, and the need for dynamic renewal; but 'Biens égaux' carries the confrontation much further. Depression and confidence, dejection and courage, loss and gain, suffering and consolation, and - pivotally - nature and woman: a nexus of contrasting images brings tension to the point of drama, declares a fertile duality. The ultimate good supposes an equal and opposite attraction, results from an extreme encounter that is rooted in lucid desire. Nature is affirmed with a vigour not previously shown, an affection begun in childhood and felt as lasting refreshment. But at the same time nature merges with this woman who is less an individual than a paradigm of love. Out of the moral and aesthetic crisis that severed his bond with surrealism Char welds a liberating *equalness* that is his poetic ideal.

We recall that 'Commune Présence' was written in the second person singular:

> Tu es pressé d'écrire
> Comme si tu étais en retard sur la vie
> S'il en est ainsi fais cortège à tes sources
> Hâte-toi
> Hâte-toi de transmettre
> Ta part de merveilleux de rébellion de bienfaisance.[8]

The conditionals, the repeated injunctions, the duplications translate the poet's self-consciousness, the stylistic source of which is an antithetical relationship with Apollinaire's 'La Jolie Rousse'. In 'Biens égaux', on the other hand, the self is dedicated wholly to each discrete moment: 'Je suis épris', 'je me distingue', 'moi je jouis', 'je veille', 'je n'ai retenu personne', 'j'affirme', 'je soulèverai'. A second person is indeed invoked in the second paragraph; it is not the self, however, but the absent and unforgotten woman who will once more be possessed, as Rimbaud sought, 'dans une âme et un corps'.[9] Manner and mode are thus crucially transformed, so that the intertextual reference becomes the non-discursive intensity of *Une Saison en enfer*, rich with the parataxis of reason and feeling.

It is above all this richness that marks the distance from Char's earlier writings. Like other surrealists, he had made much use of the prose-poem but the texture is now transformed. Each paragraph, each sentence, rejects digression, finds its virtue in fusion. The syntax has changed from substantival to predicative; linkages have become elliptical; and short protasis and long apodosis are the characteristic inflexion of an urgent energy. Nothing in *Le Marteau sans maître* can compare with this new charge of intellectual passion. The poet quite literally puts himself on the line, enunciating phrase by phrase the drama.

The first version as it appeared in 1938 reads:

> Je suis épris de ce morceau tendre de campagne, de son accoudoir de solitude au bord duquel les orages viennent se dénouer docilement, sans prendre à parti les rôdeurs; mais je dois veiller à ce que le chef-croupier de l'autorité de qui je dépends n'en opère illicitement la substitution sous prétexte d'un fort banco à la table VALETS DE FERME. Il y a aujourd'hui de l'esprit de pain dans l'air malgré le peu d' oiseaux indigènes. Sur le champ du travail l'avarice accable l'artifice de la sieste. Tribunaux de midi, ne veille. La botanique m'intéresse en fonction de son extrême trajet. A sa poursuite la vie n'y suffit pas, même subventionnée de vieillesse. D'aussi loin que je me souvienne, je me distingue penché sur le jardin désordonné de mon père, attentif aux sèves, baisant des yeux formes et couleurs que le vent semi-nocturne irriguait mieux que la main infirme des hommes. (Je n'exclus pas la mienne).
>
> Plage en fer à mulet. Une colonie s'élance vite happée par les vagues, à l'infini ailes subalternes de l'aphone corbeau citerne. Où germerai-je, moi qui jouis du privilège de sentir tout ensemble accablement et confiance, défection et courage, et surtout, surtout la reconnaissance olographe de deux avenirs? Je n'ai retenu personne, sinon l'angle fusant d'une Rencontre.
>
> ---
>
> Sur une route de lavande et de vin, nous avons marché côte à côte dans un cadre enfantin de poussière à gosier de ronces, l'un se sachant aimé de l'autre. Ce n'est pas un homme à tête de fable que plus tard tu baisais derrière les brumes de ton lit constant. Te voici nue et entre toutes la meilleure, seulement aujourd'hui où tu franchis la sortie d'un hymne

> raboteux. L'espace pour toujours est souillé de sang, chétive volte-face. Mais disant cela, j'affirme que tu vis, le sillon s'éclaire entre ton bien et mon mal. La chaleur reviendra avec le silence comme je te soulèverai Inanimée.[10]

Eight years later, and a war apart, the revised version appeared in the review *Les Cahiers de la Pléiade* and shortly after in the collection *Le Poème pulvérisé*:

> Je suis épris de ce morceau tendre de campagne, de son accoudoir de solitude au bord duquel les orages viennent se dénouer avec docilité, au mât duquel un visage perdu, par instant s'éclaire et me regagne. De si loin que je me souvienne, je me distingue penché sur les végétaux du jardin désordonné de mon père, attentif aux sèves, baisant des yeux formes et couleurs que le vent semi-nocturne irriguait mieux que la main infirme des hommes. Prestige d'un retour qu'aucune fortune n'offusque. Tribunaux de midi, je veille. Moi qui jouis du privilège de sentir tout ensemble accablement et confiance, défection et courage, je n'ai retenu personne sinon l'angle fusant d'une Rencontre.
>
> Sur une route de lavande et de vin, nous avons marché côte à côte dans un cadre enfantin de poussière à gosier de ronces, l'un se sachant aimé de l'autre. Ce n'est pas un homme à tête de fable que plus tard tu baisais derrière les brumes de ton lit constant. Te voici nue et entre toutes la meilleure seulement aujourd'hui où tu franchis la sortie d'un hymne raboteux. L'espace pour toujours est-il cet absolu et scintillant congé, chétive volte-face? Mais prédisant cela j'affirme que tu vis; le sillon s'éclaire entre ton bien et mon mal. La chaleur reviendra avec le silence comme je te soulèverai, Inanimée.[11]

A cursory glance notes few changes between early and late versions. For the most part the articulations remain intact, and the verbal outline is unmodified. Nevertheless, on closer inspection we find highly significant revisions. Thus, for example, the 1938 text begins with the affirmation of the poet's tenderness for nature and its reciprocal tenderness for him, but an adversative introduces the imagery of the gambling room. Vigilance answers affection: this is the alert response to possible over-indulgence. There must be no romanticism that would entail an illicit evasion. The self is this croupier within us for whom and against whom we play, who must be kept from illusions of grandeur. By the second half of his sentence, then, Char interrupts lyricism in the name of measure; yet the images, with their emphasis on play, have come stylistically from surrealism, and unity of tone will only be achieved in the later text by their suppression. The poet's attention will instead be turned to an inner encounter, the illumination of remembrance, a link that already denotes - 's'éclaire', 'me regagne' - the union of nature and love.

The second sentence of the original version might stand as a separate aphorism in the way of so many of Char's reflexions.

> Il y a aujourd'hui de l'esprit de pain dans l'air malgré le peu d'oiseaux indigènes.

Rather than a surrealist image, we have now a moral appraisal couched in the ironic pattern of statement and negation that is already found in the opening lines. Char castigates the rootlessness of contemporaries such as the 'Contadouriens' of Jean Giono who preached facile regionalism. The circumflex intonation goes from warmth to bitterness, the metaphor bends to a polemical end; and these elements are still more explicit in the next sentence which, phrased once more in the manner of a judgment, subsumes a chapter of reasoning.

> Sur le champ du travail l'avarice accable l'artifice de la sieste.

Here, greed replaces spontaneity, and the siesta becomes a sham. By the force of an abstract vocabulary heaviness imposes itself, which is the poet's stern criticism of those who violate the soil. In this way he multiplies his awareness, couples attachment and concentrated anger.[12]

Yet neither of these sentences will be retained. We must suppose in the final version an anguish surmounted as Char turns to salvatory images of garden, plants, wind, light. He will also eliminate without trace two other sentences of the first paragraph, but for reasons different from those we have noted:

> La botanique m'intéresse en fonction de son extrême trajet. A sa poursuite la vie n'y suffit pas, même subventionnée de vieillesse.

Closeness to nature is asserted in terms of reasoned distance, general reflexion. Nature's vastness corresponds to men's desire, but Char's language indicates a distrust of sensuousness. The revised text will, however, turn away from austerity and have no recourse to words like 'botanique' or 'fonction'. This is similarly true of the last words of the paragraph which append self-criticism to a criticism of other men. Such irony in respect of his own feelings will be no more than implicit in the ellipses of the final version, for despite the experiences of war, strength and vivacity prevail in a measure alien to the early poem.

Thus the opening paragraph of the first text expresses harshness towards others and the self, a bitter insistence that gives vent to nervous turmoil. When the poet took up 'Biens égaux' a second time he built on these feelings but muted and transposed them by way of an encompassing sensuousness. Periods were rearranged, aphorisms removed, social criticism deleted. But the detailed reworking can be described less as semantic or stylistic or syntactic than formal, so that past pleasure and future hope are reconciled. The myth of a paradise lost yet recoverable - that of Rimbaud's *Saison* and of 'Génie - provides the rigorous rhythm and line.

In the course of his revision Char incorporated most of the second section of the original text into his first paragraph. What was lost in the process was a landscape drawn in terms of beach and waves, circumscribed space, mirrored image of undulating water and flight of birds.

> Plage en fer à mulet. Une colonie s'élance vite happée par les vagues, à l'infini ailes subalternes de l'aphone corbeau citerne.

The Rimbaldian conjunction of sky and water - 'C'est la mer mêlée/Au soleil' - looks forward to the admirable post-war image of the ideal in 'Le Requin et la Mouette'. But in the first 'Biens égaux' it serves as vehicle for the poet's self-questioning with regard to his inner germination. The second text will cut the evocation of landscape, birds, seed, in favour of the single initial scheme of reference, striking by its economy.

Indeed, the closer we look at the second version the more we realize the imperious claims of form. In progressing towards the final text Char's voice grows firmer, his vision more assured, so that goodness is now demonstrated not only in the imagery but, most clearly of all, in the binary structure. The two paragraphs are of a length, each evolving from the particular to the mythical; memory ('De si loin que je me souvienne ...') and prediction ('Mais prédisant cela ...') are symmetrical; and roundness is emphasized by the two uses of the verb 's'éclaire' which connote illumination at the beginning and end of the text. It is important to observe that the concluding paragraph was hardly modified; on the contrary, it stood as a retroactive model for the first, in which the tenderness to be revived by conscious effort determined the pith and sense of the past. The previous ternary arrangement becomes two-fold, and the brevity of the final part disciplines the relative looseness of the first.

Nevertheless we need to note that a sentence of the early text - the only one to be changed among the last lines - offers a telling vestige of crisis:

> L'espace pour toujours est souillé de sang, chétive volte-face.

The line has the resonance of an image from *Une Saison en enfer* (we remember: 'Dure nuit/ Le sang séché fume sur ma face ...'). The obverse of beauty bears a fatal stain. But Char will revise his period in keeping with his new-found confidence and will write:

> L'espace pour toujours est-il cet absolu et scintillant congé, chétive volte-face?

Between question and affirmation the syntax is ambivalent; but if there remains some hesitation (which is countered in the next sentence by the phrase 'prédisant cela') we are clear that this is no bloody event but a space and time of enduring desire. His goal, the Orion-horizon of will and imagination, is not just of the past but ahead of him and yet to be won. This it is which the force of a binary structure presents according to a first paragraph of past and present warmth and to a second one of present and future certainty.

I take 'Biens égaux' to be one of Char's most successful poems. It shows his struggle with external and internal spirits as he puts new faith in nature and love. The shadow of anguish falls across the poem, points up conflicts, stirs hostilities. He seeks to express these contrasts, to give them face and name. His first attempt was felt to be a failure, blanks indicating unrealized ambitions, the stylistic variations - from surrealistic to tragic - designating the tensions unresolved. On returning to the poem, however, he could elaborate his language of paradox. A law of equalness was realized; the poem takes as its limit the symmetry of the title, the severity of a balanced form. The second paragraph constrains the first, imparts the curve of desire. Despite the apparent congruence of the dual texts we find in them the difference between a lyric of personal commitment and this allegory of time redeemed.

Similar exigencies of form and style and sense are to be found in a poem which is contemporaneous with the second version of 'Biens égaux' and which I take to be perhaps the finest of all Char's poems in verse. Although subtitled 'Chanson pour Yvonne', 'La Sorgue' is not a spontaneous lyrical expression since - 'poésie et vérité, comme nous savons, étant synonymes' - desire here engages conscience, and conscience desire.

The earliest manuscript dated 1946 is clearly a fair copy of previous drafts. It shows the text in its definitive form.[13] A second manuscript inscribed 'Le Thor 25 sept. 1947' is written on glossy paper in black and green inks and illustrated by Yvette Thomas with small suns, flowers and other motifs; while alongside the title are figured the astrological signs of Taurus and Gemini (the latter is Char's own).[14]

All has been done with care and taste. The presentation of the poem is, however, different in that the text is no longer arranged in couplets as before. Starting with line 8 ('Rivière des apprentis ...'), each new sentence is written without a break, thus forming a series of copious periods instead of the quasi-regular syllabic groups of the definitive version. A penultimate line is also added which does not recur in published versions: 'Rivière aux majestés d'amants sur un trône de solitude'. Finally, beneath his signature, Char has written 'Chère Yvonne, la Sorgue vous appartient, et ce poème qui s'essaie à la dire'. 'La Sorgue' first appeared in the review *La Licorne* in the fall of 1948 and was included the same year in the section 'La Fontaine narrative' of *Fureur et Mystère*.

The liturgical couplets of non-syllabic verse will not be found again in Char. Plainly the intertextual reference is to Claudel who, in *La Messe là-bas* and *Feuilles de saints*, made the form distinctively his own ('Rimbaud, pourquoi t'en vas-tu, et pourquoi est-ce toi une fois de plus comme sur les images,/L'enfant qui quitte la maison vers la ligne des sapins et vers l'orage?').[15] It is not surprising that Char once named Claudel among his poetic ancestors for he could not but be sensitive to this breadth and vitality and power. But his stance is not that of a weak poet before a strong one. Even as he singled out Claudel, he called him 'irresponsable', a term by which he indicated his lack of sympathy with a writer who, he felt, had renounced his human burdens and replaced crucial tension by wilful surrender. For Char this was not the answer: he himself invokes no divine ocean of faith but rather the river whose disciplined suppleness and plurality respond to his ethical concern. His parallelisms are not addressed to God but to waters of actuality. The twenty-one *versets* are built on four rhymes, one of which occurs twelve times as a lyrical frame and melodic consonance. We find, then, phonetic continuity - an uneven flow, however, since it is restrained by end-stopped couplets and by the variations on the basis octosyllabic meter in each hemistich. Indeed, the rhythmic energy is reinforced by its very scruples, like the sharp pebbles (in

Latin 'scrupuli') which the stream carries in its beds.

A trimeter opens the sequence, sets the amplitude:

Rivière trop tôt partie, d'une traite,
sans compagnon,
Donne aux enfants de mon pays le visage
de ta passion.

There is firmness in the opening prayer to a godhead of visible presence. The importance of the initial word - the song's central sonority for it occurs thirteen times - is pointed up by the rhythm that makes a customary disyllable into a tetrasyllable: we hear an invocation without indirections, an urgent plea not for the self but for others. The image is at once the message, the adjectival phrases describing a scene whose sense is sacred. As Char writes in *Le Soleil des eaux*: 'La rivière pour nous, (...) c'est un peu comme le ciel pour les dévots ... Mais un ciel qui accorderait le pain et l'apaisement de chaque jour au lieu de promettre la vie future'.[16] The response to Claudel cannot, then, go unheard for this liturgy turns to immanence and not transcendence, immediacy and not immortality. All of us are in need of intensity, and it can be found, says the poet, in the Heraclitean river. One thinks of Rimbaud, the reflection of whose 'Génie' is here apparent ('Et nous nous le rappelons et il voyage ... Et si l'Adoration s'en va, sonne, sa promesse sonne.'). The vast precipitancy of desire will provide and replenish; solitary passion will offer its grace to the children that are its own.

Rivière où l'éclair finit et où commence
ma maison,
Qui roule aux marches d'oubli la rocaille
de la raison.

The anaphoric development, the division into rhyming couplets, the rhythms underlined by assonance at the caesura convey a measured voice. The poet speaks from his experience, declares his tributary relationship. For him the river is the locus of beginnings and endings, lightning flash and habitation ('Si nous habitons un éclair, il est le coeur de l'éternel')[17] forgetfulness and awareness, loose stones and stairs. Its vigorous divinity does not banish but embraces; it draws strength from inclusiveness; it marries reason with reason's contrary. (We remember a similar evocation of liberating opposites in Rimbaud: '... il a fait la maison ouverte à l'hiver écumeux et à la rumeur de l'été ... lui qui est le charme des lieux fuyants et le délice surhumain des stations ...')[18]. On this one and only occasion the first person singular is used whereby Char establishes that his song is founded in dependence: he identifies with the river's space, espouses its time. Richly the word pattern finds a parallel balance of sound as words echo one another ('rivière', 'éclair'), a back vowel is sensuously prolonged ('où', 'roule', 'oubli'), plosive and liquid consonants accompany a tense action whose meaning is ceaseless change.

> Rivière, en toi terre est frisson, soleil anxiété.
> Que chaque pauvre dans sa nuit fasse son pain
> de ta moisson.

The river is not quietude but ripple and tremor, restlessness and tumult. Earth and sun are shimmering things for no element or object may remain innocent when mirrored in the depths. A disturbance introduces ferment and spasm: 'Ce qui vient au monde pour ne rien troubler ne mérite ni égards ni patience'.[19] Both the sun's warmth and the earth's substance require the waters that will quicken them and that will serve ever and again to consummate the harvest. The cycle of growth reveals its sense in the loaf of bread, anxiety finds its complementary nourishment. Thus is articulated a fertile disruption which the rhythm of the first line emphasizes, like the absence of rhyme and assonance at the caesura; but 'frisson' recalls the continuity that 'moisson' recovers, and the insistent alliteration welds the couplet into a single unit.

'Rivière souvent punie, rivière à l'abandon./ A verte fontaine, fruits souvent meurtris.'[20] Abandonment and sacrilege are the river's fate, like that of every god. Laconically the poet recalls rejection and disrespect, defilement and infidelity. His expression needs no amplification, its economy indicating the common paradoxes of ecological wastage - active infliction passive neglect. We are not frequently worthy of a pure presence; the abundance the river brings is 'reviled and rejected of men'. The abrupt single line evokes contrasting attitudes in each hemistich, proposing without sentimentality the awareness of a godhead spurned.

> Rivière des apprentis à la calleuse condition,
> Il n'est vent qui ne fléchisse à la crête
> de tes sillons.

The poem now rediscovers rhythmic regularity on its four hemistichs which have new recourse to the paired diction of caesurae and end-words. A simple opposition contrasts the sores of young workmen who are inexperienced in nature's ways with the balm - gentleness, protection, modification - that the river freely offers. This is the waters' healing which is figured by the inflection of the wind touching the ripples. 'Calleuse', the first strong adjective in the poem, receives force from the preceding verbal austerity and from its pronominal position. But no pathos supervenes, just as there is none in the oblique image of the second line which formulates the resolution of pain in impersonal terms and with the syntactic brevity of a proverb.

> Rivière de l'âme vide, de la guenille et
> du soupcon,
> Du vieux malheur qui se dévide, de l'ormeau,
> de la compassion.

The ternary division of each line signifies the measure wherein pain is made tolerable, suffering assuaged. The soul can be morally and physically dispossessed - empty in a thousand ways; it can also be full of sorrow, impoverishment, distrust. It finds its familiar compeer, unhappiness, which lengthily spins a tale of self-pity. Such dolour has its accompaniment in the river that pursues a parallel course and a defiant solitude. Yet the waters also contain the reflected freshness of a young elm, a verdant growth, an exultant solace; they channel a restoring succour. The polarities of ennui and rejuvenation are thus present in the manner of a pre-Socratic image, not negating one another but proclaiming a profound sympathy between river and men.

Rivière des farfelus, des fiévreux, des
équarrisseurs,
Du soleil lâchant sa charrue pour s'acoquiner
au menteur.

After the preceding three sections that identify an idea of pain, a change of homophones at the caesura and the end-word introduces a new emphasis. The river is like common men who live, work and take their ease by its banks, be they fanciful and free in their manners as the familiar 'farfelus' suggests, or else of fevered temperament. On the other hand, there are men like the humble knackers who laboriously dissect a dead animal to make a living. The river recognizes men's diversity as its own, just as it greets the sun, both diligent and casual, which momentarily drops its prescribed task to tarry and chat with a congenial story-teller. In this way the couplet names the extremes of rural amity and earnestness, fantasy and toil - necessary if opposite attributes of the river's spaciousness.

Rivière des meilleurs que soi, rivière des
brouillards éclos,
De la lampe qui désaltère l'angoisse autour
de son chapeau.

Against egotism the river has powerful remedies. One becomes aware of his own shortcomings in frequenting those that obey the highest callings of strength, benevolence, sensitivity. The poet knew these qualities as a child who lived among the riverains: 'Je me suis tapi dans des roseaux, sous la garde d'êtres forts comme des chênes et sensibles comme des oiseaux'.[21] Around him, then as now, was the generousness of fogs unfolding like flowers, refashioning traits, combatting reason. Yet at the same time the river can be as a lamp that dispels the night: Char's image of anguish overcome has no grandiloquence but the homely warmth of 'chapeau'. (We recall the like comfort of the vigil-lamp and its oil of consolation in 'Madeleine à la veilleuse', Char's poem on a painting by Georges de la Tour.) However paradoxical, the lamp's glow and fog are both the river's own, and show the vastness of comprehension to which men can turn.

> Rivière des égards au songe, rivière qui
> rouille le fer,
> Où les étoiles ont cette ombre qu'elles
> refusent à la mer.

As in the previous couplet, the repetition of 'rivière' in the first line establishes a lyrical incantation which is reinforced by alliteration and assonance. Two further virtues of the Sorgue are sung: its complementary toughness and subtlety, its 'fureur' and 'mystère'. There is a need for perseverence, for the tenacity of water that causes iron to rust, that penetrates by affusion. The waters destroy and espouse at the same moment of action ('Enfin, si tu détruis', says the poet, 'que ce soit avec des outils nuptiaux'). But the river also initiates revery and nourishes it, permits the uniquely discreet reflection of stars that the ocean in its turbulence cannot achieve. The broad scheme of moral polarities is the river's force and sacrament as it is of love: 'Loi de rivière, loi au juste report, aux pertes compensées mais aux flancs déchirés, lorsque l'ambitieuse maison d'esprit croula, nous te reconnumes et te trouvâmes bon'.[22]

> Rivière des pouvoirs transmis et du cri
> embouquant les eaux,
> De l'ouragan qui mord la vigne et annonce
> le vin nouveau.

In this second last section Char proposes the notion of communication between elements and men, men and elements. The Sorgue turns the paddle-wheel like those used in other times for silk factories and oil-mills; the current serves, as do the nourishing waters, for beast, field and man, and the silt they bear, and the fish they carry. The river creates for us the image of transmission, the refusal to have and hold, the mutual virtues of receiving and giving. The idea is first expressed in abstract terms as in the opening hemistich of the preceding couplet, then interpreted concretely. The violent cry is channelled into usefulness: undirected pathos discovers a vehicle, a river-bed, an orientation like the shout that becomes a poem, or the emotion that becomes purposeful energy. A second illustration of such efficaciousness is the unruly forces of the hurricane whose rage allows us to look to the vigour of the wine to be. Thus past, present and future participate - like abstract powers, human voice, natural force - in order to compose the fury and the certain tenderness:

> Et qui sait voir la terre aboutir à des
> fruits,
> Point ne l'émeut l'échec quoiqu'il ait
> tout perdu.[23]

The tenth section, then, brings the interlude of four couplets (11.12-19) to a close and completes a pattern of rhymes (CDED). Now Char returns to the initial scheme of assonance at the caesura and the end-word.

> Rivière au coeur jamais détruit dans ce monde
> fou de prison,
> Garde-nous violent et ami des abeilles de l'horizon.

This phonetic return accompanies a reiteration of praise and at the same time a prayer that is said not only for some as in the first couplet, but for one and all, including the poet himself. In his eyes the river is a very personal godhead and he must speak of its heart: 'coeur' - this inadequate word ('... nous disons *le coeur* et le disons à regret ...')[24] - states nonetheless the humane values that alone justify existence in the frenzied prison of the world. He does not lose sight of men's continuing folly, their blindness to freedom, but his faith tells him that the river's meaning is immortal. However it is not enough to revere it, for men must act in its likeness - violent as tumult, unfettered yet fertile as bees. The contraries of turbulence and tenderness conjoin in a way that provides hope in the face of death and the absurd. At this point the river is seen to be the inspiriting word and force and luxuriance inseparate from love. 'Ce n'était pas', Char writes in a piece contemporaneous with 'La Sorgue',

> Ce n'était pas un torrent qui s'offrait à son destin
> mais une bête ineffable dont nous devenions la
> parole et la substance. Elle nous tenait amoureux
> sur l'arc tout-puissant de son imagination.[25]

It becomes apparent that such a poem demands close reading for its course to be traced. Only thus can we apprehend the achieved union of nature and thought, poetic object and project. In the parts as in the whole there is energetic adherence to the scene described, rigorous scrutiny, strict explanation. Obscurity does not come from any deception by the poet but rather from his uncompromising probity that proceeds by ellipsis, shifts from concrete to abstract and back again, ensures its intensity by multiple focussing. To study the text is to become aware of meaning as movement - as the sum total of the furious paradoxes of passion and grace, quickness and stability, anxiety and fulfilment, suffering and abandonment, pain and balm, solitariness and pity, relaxation and toil, anguish and comfort, mysterv and toughness, severity and promise, violence and friendship. In each couplet as in the ample development the poem models itself on the river that is indefinable by any single aspect, for it is complex, multiform, unfailingly open to contradictions. The rhetoric of antipoles is a properly moral vision which, past ideologies having been set aside, creates a compelling figure of responsible strength.

NOTES

1. 'Le dos tourné, la Balandrane ...', *Chants de la Balandrane*, Gallimard, 1977, p. 81.

2. 'Seuil', *Fureur et Mystère*, Gallimard, 1967, p. 181.

3. Stéphane Mallarmé, 'Toast funèbre'.

4. 'Le Rempart de brindilles', *Poème et Prose choisis*, Gallimard, 1957, p. 270.

5. *Faire du chemin avec ...*, Avignon, Libraire 'Le Parvis', 1976, n.p.

6. 'Ce bleu n'est pas le nôtre', *Aromates chasseurs*, Gallimard, 1975, p. 10.

7. *Les Cahiers de la Pléiade*, April 1946; then in *Le Poème Pulvérisé*, Fontaine, 1946.

8. *Le Marteau san maître*, Corti, 1953, pp. 107-108.

9. Arthur Rimbaud, 'Adieu', *Oeuvres*, Garnier, 1960, p. 241.

10. *Dehors la nuit est gouvernée*, G.L. M., 1938, n.p.

11. *Fureur et Mystère*, p. 173

12. In a comment on the poem Char has written: 'Le mal et ses aides m'exaspéraient, m'indignaient. Cent colères, des brouilles, des pugilats même avec des gens fréquentés et des inconnus ont marqué les journées de ce temps d'angoisse', *Arrière-histoire du poème pulvérisé*, Jean Hugues, 1972, p. 21.

13. The manuscript is reproduced in the catalogue of the Exposition René Char, Fondation Maeght, 1971.

14. Collection René Char - Yvonne Zervos, Bibliothèque Jacques Doucet, Paris.

15. Paul Claudel, 'Consécration', *Oeuvre poétique*, Gallimard, 1957, p. 500.

16. *Trois Coups sous les arbres*, Gallimard, 1967, p. 147.

17. *Fureur et Mystère*, p. 198.

18. 'Génie', *Oeuvres*, p. 308.

19. 'A la santé du serpent', *Fureur et Mystère*, p. 195.

20. 'Hôte et possédant', *Le Nu perdu*, Gallimard, 1972, p. 103.

21. 'Suzerain', *Fureur et Mystère*, p. 192.

22. 'La Scie rêveuse', *Le Nu perdu*, p. 69.

23. 'Redonnez-leur ...', *Fureur et Mystère*, p. 165.

24. 'Rougeur des matinaux', *Les Matinaux*, Gallimard, 1969, p. 78.

25. 'Les Premiers Instants', *Fureur et Mystère*, p. 213.

HENRI MICHAUX: IMPETUS AND INFINITY

Peter Broome

Michaux's sparse autobiographical revelations, 'Quelques renseignments sur cinquante-neuf années d'existence' given to the critic Robert Bréchon in 1958,[1] signal the first symptoms of a problem of language in the author's work and point to an awareness, from the earliest moments, of a fundamental discrepancy between experience and expression. Indeed the autobiographical notes themselves, written in the third person and in a stiff, undernourished shorthand, form an alienated biography, a sloughed skin offered somewhat dismissively, even ironically, for public consumption: language here has captured almost nothing; the vital movements roam *ailleurs*. In these notes Michaux records the young child's intuitive resistance to the pressures and encroachments of physical reality, its superficial distractions, divisions and dispersions of focus; and his attachment, as if to a nourishing source, to a unified, constant inner realm of 'Rêves, sans images, sans mots'. Just as his body flinches instinctively from smells, contacts and gross physical necessities, so his mind is set, it seems, against social communication and collective language as if it were a degraded matter and compromise with it a breaking of faith with some unnamed, perhaps unnameable fluency of apprehension. The text 'Le Portrait de A.' (PLI, 107-17)[2], a half-real, half mythical self-portrait corresponding in Michaux's work to 'Les Poètes de sept ans' in that of Rimbaud, corroborates the image of a nascent poet refusing commerce with the rigid imperatives of the external world, turned obsessively inwards on 'un univers dense et personnel et trouble où n'entrait rien, ni parents, ni affections, ni aucun objet, ni leur image', and sensing within himself the slow-moving, powerful passage of 'de grands trains d'une matière mystérieuse'. It depicts the character A. living for years, seemingly interminably, 'l'oeil sur le bassin intérieur', and conjures up a metaphor of wordless, contemplative commitment: 'De grosses lèvres de Bouddha fermées au pain et à la parole'.

A.'s relationship with words in the form of literature is revealing. Whereas he views the phenomenal world as a trivial crust, hard and immovable, books give access to a nebulous, pliable zone and propose a kind of spiritual disengagement. In fact his reading, strangely inattentive and unretentive, bypasses the words themselves and the actual thoughts in order to communicate with what moves between and beyond the words: 'Car tant que son fond restait indécis et mystérieux et peu palpable, son attention consistait à trouver dans un livre ce même univers fuyant et sans contour'. They become, as it were, a dispensable hollow through which the indeterminate impulses of his own deep space join with those of another vast space (a description which applies equally to Michaux's later art criticism where the encounter with the paintings of Klee in 'Aventures de lignes' (P, 173-80) or Magritte in *En revant à partir de peintures énigmatiques* results in the formation of a new reciprocal *nébuleuse*). As A. reads, he chases a fitful contact with some vague essence, intuitions of fluidity, promises of illumination - only to fall back again finally from the convoluted to the compartmentalized, the potential to the piecemeal, and the levitational to the lethargic:

> Dans les livres, il cherche la révélation. Il les parcourt en flèche. Tout à coup, grand bonheur, une phrase ... un incident ... un je ne sais quoi, il y a là quelque chose ... Alors il se met à léviter vers ce quelque chose avec le plus qu'il peut de lui-même [...] Il est là quelque temps dans les tourbillons et les serpentins et dans une clarté qui dit 'c'est là'. Après quelque intervalle, toutefois, par morceaux, petit à petit, le voilà qui se détache, retombe un peu, beaucoup, mais jamais si bas que là où il était précédemment.

He realizes that the extension of awareness is not simply the addition of a new idea to one's repertoire but what he calls 'un désordre ivre, une perte de sang-froid, une fusée, ensuite une ascension générale': significantly, these words prefigure Michaux's own war-time definition of the process of 'exorcism', (worked in order to 'tenir en échec les puissances environnantes du monde hostile' (EE, 7-9), to turn imprisonment into liberation and project the self airily out of a situation of incompatibility and stress), the symptoms of which are described variously as 'une exaltation', 'cet élan en flèche' and 'cette montée verticle et explosive'. One of the major revelations gleaned by A. from his bookish trajectories is that reality is not single or static but innumerable living atoms constantly in motion, swept and reswept in endless patterns: 'Mouvement infini, infiniment prolongé'.

Michaux himself marks two contacts with language as key 'events' in his hesitant evolution between the ages of twelve and fifteen. The first, his discovery of words in a state of *disponibilité*, not yet subservient to grammatical structures, congealed forms and frozen connotations but offering themselves, in all their multiplicity and virtuality, to individual creative adventures: 'Découverte du dictionnaire, des mots qui n'appartiennent pas encore à des phrases, pas encore à des phraseurs, des mots et en quantité, et dont on pourra se servir soi-même à sa facon' (RBM, 17). The author develops this thought in one of the essays of *Passages* (pp. 23-5), saying that one of his oldest joys has been to take up a dictionary and to contemplate, 'dans un état détaché' and regardless of specific meanings and definitions, all these seething, unfurling buds of human effort: 'Etincelles du monde du dehors et du dedans, j'y contemple la multitude d'*être homme*, la vie aux infinies impressions et vouloir être'. It becomes a voyage in the world of potential, movement in an area somewhere between the compartments of outer and inner space. He soon succumbs, he says, to 'ces myriades d'orbites'. Some of his own latent shadows loom up from his *espace aux ombres* and gain strength as they reach towards and imprint themselves against 'cet horizon de fuyants, de pousses, de miroirs, de fruits et d'approximations'. And then he proceeds to write:

> Bien peu m'importe le comment et le pourquoi, mais il me devient pressant de conduire à mon tour quelque équipage à travers l'infini moutonnement des possibles. Petit cortège que le mien, mais qui, sur ce fond vaste et infiniment glissant, *marche* pour moi d'un pas si étrangement accentué, d'un pas qui frappe le silence d'un accent inégalable.

(It is interesting here that the literary act ventures out experimentally with no idea of final goals and no respect for the demands of *métier* and formal perfection; that the infinity of possibility which is its domain is described in liquid terms as an ocean; that his own little thread of words, threatened constantly by space, vertigo and extinction, moves precariously through limitless unstable expanses which allow no firm foothold; and that this tenuous verbal expedition is characterized above all by its unique *rhythm* set against the void). In this process, by which he periodically loses himself (breaks the false unity and stability of a pretended personality) and finds refreshment, it is not that he is chasing these numerous elements of language in order to appropriate and claim ownership over them. On the contrary: 'J'aime ces voix nombreuses, pas à moi, leur petit son, leur petit sens pétillant un instant à la tête, pour redisparaître en lieu étranger où je ne les retrouverai plus'. Their joy is their passage, their re-departure into the alien, their irretrievability. The second linguistic event mentioned by Michaux was his learning of Latin, 'belle langue, qui le sépare des autres, le transplante: son premier départ' (RBM, 17). Already in this notation, applying to the years 1911-1914, one has a foretaste of language used, not as a communication, but as a private transubstantiation, as a system of signs facilitating a projection elsewhere. As the poet says in *Mouvements*, these are 'Signes surtout pour retirer son être du piège de la langue des autres' (FV, 20). His early contact with Latin in this respect is hardly different from his compulsive journeys to Turkey, Italy and North Africa in 1929 which he describes as 'Voyages d'expatriation', undertaken 'Pour expulser de lui sa patrie, ses attaches de toutes sortes' (RBM, 17): it represents a loosening of attachments, an escape from local linguistic imprisonment.

No writer has been more aware than Michaux of different speeds of experience (of all that, free from the regulated metronome of normality, races away from the sluggish consciousness, twirls the self from its centre of gravity or, alternatively, expands into a sea of slow-breathing rhythms or finds suspense in a contemplative immobility). Recently he has stated, in the light of a long experience of adjustments to the turbulences of reality and all the wayward forces which put a strain on human brake-power: 'la vitesse demeure à jamais *le* problème, clef sans doute de quantité d'autres' (GEE, 31). At one moment we slip with the poet into the world of *La Ralentie* ('Ralentie, on tâte le pouls des choses; on y ronfle; on a tout le temps; tranquillement, toute la vie' (PLI, 41), into the frozen serenity, purity, eternity and silence of '*Icebergs*' (the icebergs themselves being also described as 'augustes *Bouddhas* gelés sur des mers incontemplées' (NR, 93), or, through an act of wilful magic, into the anaesthetized interior of an apple (NR, 9-10). At other moments, and far more frequently, we follow him in hot pursuit of fleeting intuitions and apparitions, communications and vibrations which traverse the being in a flash and disappear, multiple forms and metamorphoses which no word or concept can hold. As early as *Qui je fus*, his first major collection, Michaux projects an image of himself as the embodiment of verbal impotence: 'J'étais une parole qui tentait d'avancer à la vitesse de la pensée' (QJF, 22) - a declaration which poses the problem of discrepancy of tempos and the need to elasticate and accelerate language beyond its normal solid habits if it is to correspond to the rapid *parcours* of mental space. It is a problem which the author's encounters with hallucinogenic drugs since 1956 have led him to explore with greater and greater acuteness. Sacrificing his own 'tempo', he has allowed himself to be pulled into the rapids of the interior where consciousness is broken into a thousand galloping grains, where thoughts proliferate, multiply and leap in innumerable directions at once, where ideas flash by and to-and-fro at lightning speed, unassimilable. In this *infini turbulent*, language is a hopeless cripple. As the writer lands to file his report periodically, his plane has taken off without him and the report is irrelevant. Michaux calls it a very real 'chute dans la verbalisation' (GEE, 28). Language drags thought down into its comfortable channels, turning infinitude into finitude, whirlwinds into straight lines, processions into segments, movement into motionless blocks. It pretends to recuperate what is in fact irreducible to social life, personal life (in the sense of subjective and self-possessed authority) and words. On another occasion Michaux reverses the image, saying: 'Tranquillement les phrases vont par-dessus des abîmes de vitesse. Ne pas en être dupe' (GEE, 33). But whether language is seen as a grateful coming to ground or as an art of equilibrium inching along a single line at its own pace high above great chasms of speed and vertigo, his point is the same: verbal expression itself (at least in its conventional forms) is an opting out, a desertion, a false salvation. It can only make links where they are already broken or never existed, poke brittle sticks into moving wheels, distort and render evasive the very thing on which it superimposes itself.

Michaux returns persistently to the theme of the untranslatability of authentic experience. 'Tout ce qui est rare perd 90% dans la traduction' (IT, 55), he writes. His essay in tribute to his friend, the Ecuadorian poet Alfredo Gangotena,[3] poses the problem besetting any original writer, that of giving an adequate account of his exceptional states of perception, strangled as he is by a language broken in by centuries of compromise and always tightening towards a common denominator of social intercourse and average experience:

> Opiomane, il assiste à de l'inoui. Il ne l'écrira pas. Il ne le peut. Ivre, il n'écrit pas. Fou? Le langage qui lui échappe va dégrader l'état qu'il aurait fallu rendre. Au-delà d'une certaine bizarrerie, les mots ne rapportent pas.
>
> En rêve, on n'écrit pas. Le mystique en transe n'écrit pas. Ravi, on n'écrit pas. Si on écrit après, après c'est tout sauf *ça*.

Similarly, a text originally entitled 'La Lettre du dessinateur'[4] tells how the artist's confrontation with the blank page instantly conjures up a play of movement and multiplicity: firstly a frightened man (the false and shamed 'first self' disappearing into infinity?) running away into the distance, then 'le rite ridicule d'hommes qui tournent en rond' (the pretentious stability of society at large turned, in a satirical ritual, into a potential state of vertigo?), and finally the endless passage of a multitude of under-nourished men (the countless possible selves within the personality aspiring to unity and global human definition?) which extends not only through space but time: 'foule non pour un tableau mais pour une époque'. But when it comes to containing them or holding them together and bringing this seething life within the compass of the page, the artist is reduced to frustration and rage. Slashing at the paper wildly, he carves out the image of a hideous grieving face - of the kind which over a period of ten years has made his reputation as a painter. But he himself is not misled by this meagre travesty nor by the efficacy of the means which produced it: 'Mais je ne suis pas dupe. Dans les pleurs et la rage, je rejette loin de moi cette maudite usurpatrice, et l'art qui se dérobe m'emplit de son souvenir décevant et amer'. It is not surprising that at the time of the mescalin experiments Michaux should feel the need for a new language not his own. He writes:

> Comment dire cela? Il aurait fallu une manière accidentée que je ne possède pas, faite de surprises, de coq-à-l'âne, d'aperçus en un instant de rebondissements et d'incidences, un style instable, tobogannant et babouin.
>
> (MM, 14)

And the epigraph to *Misérable miracle*, invoking the ideal of an infinitely elastic language which would be multiple and metamorphic, simultaneously affirmative and self-denying, apprehensible and evasive, reads:

> ... et l'on se trouve alors, pour tout dire, dans une situation telle que cinquante onomatopées différentes, simultanées, contradictoires et chaque demi-seconde changeantes, en seraient la plus fidèle expression.

The mention of a complex *carrefour* of onomatopoeia, or a language where sounds and the actual substance of words would coincide as nearly as possible with meaning (or would intimate and shape such meaning before the intervention of the conceptual), leads one to look back to the 'sound-language' of some of Michaux's earliest poems. Whether one considers it primarily to be 'lyric esperanto', an absurdist Jabberwocky, a rudimentary hygiene (the poet speaks in 'Glu et gli' (QJF, 61) of 'un homme qui n'aurait que son pet pour s'exprimer' and in 'Homme de lettres' (NR, 189) of a self-enclosed and resistant writer who '... pète par toutes les fissures/En blocs, en lames, en jets et en cristal'), or simply an act of derision and revolt, it exemplifies a poetic language shaking off the strictures of significance and moving inventively in an uncharted area somewhere between communication and non-communication. In the case of 'L'Avenir' (NR, 199-200), individual words no longer respect their watertight boundaries but spill out unimpeded, gradually swamp all idea of grammatical function, contaminate each other and form strange new compounds which could proliferate *ad infinitam:*

Quand les mah,
Quand les mah,
Les marécages,
Les malédictions,
Quand les mahahahahas,
Les mahahamaladihahas,
Les matratrimatratrihahas,
Les homdregordegarderies,
Les honcucarachoncus,
Les hordanoplopais de puru para puru,
Les immoncéphales glosées ...

The poem becomes an act of rhythmic and phonetic sorcery by which the solidity of the World is demolished and nothing is finally left in its place by "Espace! Espace non stratifié ...'. The poem 'Ra' (as if satisfying the desires of the character A. who resents the exclusiveness of the French language, 'unilatéral, et toujours coffré par la perfection' (PLI, 114), and its tendency to intercept and filter out all that is alien to its notion of formal order), twists the neck of grammatical links and syntax, leaving the various liberated parts of speech jostling around in a fluid, problematical relationship:

A tant refus secoue l'abeille manège son trou.
Avec arrêtez-là debout dans rouf-à la rouffarde;
Des plus, des sautes allégresses, des laisse-moi-assis,
Des rachète-moi-tout-cru, des libelle-donc-ça-autrement.
(NR, 196)

At other times it is a more radical reduction to non-sense in which language, ripped from all intellectual overlords, is allowed to roam as an ominous primitive force:

> Ou te bourdourra le bodogo,
> Bodogi.
>
> (NR, 192)

As for the famous 'Le grand combat', the succession of half-familiar, half-foreign verbs, sensuously and self-indulgently vicious, creates a sense of energetic action in and for itself rather than any awareness of the nature and object of that action, and invites the imagination and deep unformulated human instincts to toy with potential meanings at will:

> Il l'emparouille et l'endosque contre terre;
> Il le rague et le roupète jusqu'à son drâle;
> Il le pratèle et le libucque et lui barufle les ouillais;
> Il le tocarde et le marmine,
> Le manage rape à ri et ripe à ra.
> Enfin il l'écorcobalisse.
>
> (QJR, 74)

Words here are not the servants of comprehension but creative signs. Michaux has looked upon poetry as a 'nouvelle occasion de lâcher pied et de déserter l'odieux compartimentage du monde' (PLI, 70). One could say, equally, that in all these cases the poem is an act of revolt against 'l'odieux compartimentage du langage'. Whether the author is dealing with the words of others or with his own, his resistance to the conspiracy of the ready-made is the same:

> ... on ne se laisse plus faire, les mots dans les phrases, les phrases dans la page, on les bouscule, on les retourne, on les retire, on les échange, on les recompose, non pour refaire le livre mais pour le défaire, pour les faire sauter et se dévergonder ailleurs, pour le plaisir pur de la non-obéissance, de la non-soumission.
>
> (FEFE, 203-4)

He is no less resistant to the adopted role of writer. The Bréchon notes tell how his first French composition written at the age of fifteen caused a shock: a shock at the discovery of so much surprising matter swarming in his imagination. But, despite the encouragement of teachers and several school friends, he could not reconcile himself to the pursuit of literature: 'il se débarrasse de la tentation d'écrire, qui pourrait le détourner de l'essentiel' (RBM, 17). Even the crucial revelation of Lautréamont some eight years later, triggering off his own first texts with the realization that one could actually write and publish all that is most extraordinary in the hidden field of force of the personality, and then the sympathetic recognition granted him by Franz Hellens, director of *Le Disque vert*, and Jean Paulhan, editor of *La Nouvelle Revue Française*, were not enough to win his commitment:

> Toujours réticent. Il n'aimerait pas 'devoir' écrire. Ça empêche de rêver. Ça le fait sortir. Il préfère rester lové.
>
> (RBM, 19)

Just as A. appointed to a teaching post can only feel the discrepancy and inanity of his new-found title and function, saying 'A. est nommé professeur! Sottise! L'Océan est au-dessous; se cache, se défend par les armes propres à l'Océan, qui sont couche sur couche et enveloppements' (PLI, 117) (an image which reminds one of his access to 'les tourbillons et les serpentins' swirling at a level beyond the crust of the words he reads), so Michaux cannot find a pseudonym which might encompass his whole sprawling self, its tendencies and its virtualities. His signed name 'Henri Michaux', like the literary function itself, is only a meagre, derisory materialization over a sea of possibilities and latent voices. Perhaps a silent contemplative communion would be the ultimate response. But as the poet says in his quasi-philosophical maxims, *Tranches de savoir*: 'Qui cache son fou, meurt sans voix' (FV, 65). And in the meantime he can only struggle to force words to commit a lesser infidelity.

Few contemporary works have dramatized more colourfully the aspirations and impotence of language. There is the passage 'Fils de morne' from *Qui je fus* (pp. 80-90) where the King (often a symbol of unimpeachable authority in Michaux's image-patterns, in the face of whom the poet feels degradation, guilt, frustration and the imperfection of his means) goes round his Kingdom to find in astonishment that the people are suffering from a strange malady: 'C'est l'expression qui s'est décollée, décollée de l'homme'. Naturally, among the first to feel the pinch are the professional writers, dependent as they are on the exchange of significances; but the clowns, those comic, ungainly outcasts with whom Michaux identifies himself in a poem such as 'Clown', make the most of the modern disaster with their contortionist's language of gesture, sign, mime and movement.

> Des hommes sont directement frappés dans leur métier, tant mieux, je parle pour les écrivains, plus crissants que la craie, enfin disparus. Mais pauvres clowns. Enfin ils ne sont pas à un métier près, et tout le monde sait que le plus infime des clowns possède une occupation objective, si l'on peut dire, et des qualités acrobatiques qui ont leur utilité.
>
> (ED, 249-50)

It is no doubt the same crisis of expression or linguistic fall from grace which leads to the discrepancy, felt in the author's South American travelogue *Ecuador*, between poetry in its traditional form and *voyage*. 'Je n'ai écrit que ce peu qui précède', he writes, 'et déjà je tue ce voyage' (E, 11). As words turn the virtual into fact, promise into achievement (what is *achevé*), the ideal into reality, and reality into nothing but its shed skin, they become an immediate death-process. They reduce an expansive and inexplicit state of mind to the pigmy proportions of a state of language: 'Il y a quelques minutes j'étais large. Mais écrire, écrire: tuer, quoi' (E, 16). As the traveller consigns his broken laconic notations to the log-book, his mind plays with the prospect of a different kind of journey: 'plastic cinema' or animated sculptures along a railway track which the movement of the train would bring to life and fuse into an indivisible racing sequence ('Elles se superposeraient à la vue, ébaucheraient des mouvements, agiraient. Trains sans ârret animés d'une vitesse constante' (E, 19)); or roller-skating on the Atlantic, swayed by its rhythms, speeding down its dizzy slopes, suddenly discovering vast horizons then losing them again in a single motion. A significant essay by Michaux entitled 'Les poètes voyagent' (P, 61-6) suggests that the language and form of poetry have never really been fused with travel in a single authentic experience. The only exception he makes is Blaise Cendrars, whose major poems 'se lisent comme un rapide vous prend, comme un hydravion amerrit dans un golfe des Tropiques'. Otherwise, there have only been artistic *invitations au voyage*, where the voyage itself has been lost in the love of contemplation, anticipation and in the riches of style; and Surrealist journeys beyond the confines of the real, which have in the end, despite their unimpeded metamorphoses and transubstantiations, become predictable and boring. 'Tous les élements du voyage étaient là. Mais pas de parcours', he concludes, 'C'est pourquoi on l'attend encore, on l'attend à nouveau, le poème du vrai voyage ... et les poèmes de l'appel au voyage demeurent'. The ideal language would not set itself against the grain but would be totally at one with the life of movement, transition, multiplicity and dimension.

It is the discrepancy between the word and the act which leads Michaux to pursue poetry as a form of magic. One reads in 'Portrait d'homme':[5]

> Il serait bien écrivain, car il a de continuelles inventions mais il voudrait les voir, non écrites, mais réalisées, et que nos conditions d'existence changent du tout au tout, suivant elles. Il se gargarise peu de ses inventions, au rebours de l'écrivain, il veut voir l'impossible miracle, c'est-à-dire leur passage dans la vie. (C'est donc plutôt à la magie qu'il aspire.)

Already in India he has been attracted by the traditions of magical thought, by the *mantras* or magic prayers ('Celui qui prie bien fait tomber des pierres, parfume les eaux' (BA, 26), by verbal formulae which press the trigger of essential forces and of which the *Khandogya-Upanishad* says: 'Ces paroles seraient dites à un vieux bâton, il se couvrirait de fleurs et de feuilles et reprendrait racine' (BA, 21). He writes of the Southern Hindus, 'C'étaient des gens qui aimaient entre autres la magie des mots' (BA, 116), adding in a footnote '*Magie* dans le sens fort du mot'. He quotes the example of Tulsi Das, the poet of the *Ramayana*, who by an *act* of poetic meditation conjured up an army of monkeys and liberated himself from prison, an achievement which prompts the following challenge: 'Bien, maintenant ouvrons un concours: Quel est le poète européen qui en puisse faire autant?' And yet one senses in Michaux's own journey through the *Pays de la Magie* (1941) - seemingly one of the poet's most effective acts of magical transpositions and a text in which he creates a strange new language at the same time finite and infinite (on the one hand measured, logical, lucid, familiar and reassuring; on the other hand lurching into great gaps of the enigmatic, the irrational and the ambiguous) - deep underlying doubts which weave into the texture of the work a tracery of images denoting impossible expression. There are the magic costumes designed for the pronunciation of certain key sounds such as 'Vstts' or 'Khng', without which communication with the mysterious super-reality of the 'Mages' is impeded and people can only stammer as these 'psychic' words speed by. (This is an image reinforced by a piece entitled 'Le Manteau qui fend l'espace' (VP, 106) where the narrator, in an atmosphere of mystery and reverence, is regretfully given the cloak in question but does not know how to draw on its penetrating powers nor, apparently, how to don it and thus envelop his own inadequate *persona*: 'Cependant, une loque à la main je m'en allai'). There is the violent 'nipping of the cord' which, by some occult intervention causes speech to seize up: 'Quelqu'un parle. Tout à coup le voilà pris d'un éternuement irrépressible, éclatant, que rien ne laissait prévoir' (A, 170). There are the voices of silence stronger than his own which, in a completely empty arena put the victim on trial, question him and reduce him to nothing with wavelike, echoing repercussions of non-existent (unvoiced) sound. There are urgent telepathic messages which the traveller cannot decode and reply to in time. There are phrases used, like the reference to an 'horizon retiré', which he thinks are just a figure of speech, 'une sorte d'expression verbale, de plaisanterie uniquement dans la langue' (A, 209), only to find that there is no such safe division in this realm between the verbal and the actual. There are zones where he dare not speak for fear of upsetting a crucial balance, interfering with a play of forces or bringing a catastrophe on himself as an importunate foreign body.

Few poets have held literature, the role of the writer and the potentialities of words in such suspicion and contempt, a suspicion and contempt which have led Michaux to elaborate a poetics of the imperfect. The epigraph presiding over the essays of *Passages*, a title which itself suggests impermanencies, instabilities and unfinished transitions, reads:

> Koyu, le religieux, dit: seule une personne de compréhension réduite désire arranger les choses en séries complètes.
>
> C'est l'incomplétude qui est désirable. En tout, mauvaise est la régularité.
>
> Dans les palais d'autrefois, on laissait toujours un bâtiment inachevé, obligatoirement.

It implies the ideal of a structure which fights for its life against the finite, the regular, the harmonious, and seeks to leave a void, an unfinished dimension, an *ailleurs* (just as the imaginery countries of *Ailleurs* itself were born of 'la soif de transformer, de refaire, de dépasser ...' (A, Préface)). It is remarkable how many times Michaux clarifies his poetics in architectural terms, thus showing his responsiveness to structures in space. In almost every case the theme is the same: the need to avoid the living death of false order and the final version. Speaking of the facility with which the art of music moulds itself to the complex, variable continuum of *la vie intérieure*, he draws this comparison:

> Ici sont exposés ses tâtonnements, ses hésitations, ses brusqueries, ses accentuations, ses brouillons, ses reprises, ses retours en arrière que les autres arts tiennent soigneusement cachés (comme ce serait émouvant, pourtant, de trouver tout autour d'une cathédrale, les beaux restes en pierre de tentatives avortées, les ébauches à demi terminées, d'autres menées plus loin mais tout de même arrêtées avant la fin, tous ces commencements de cathédrales se pressant autour de la grande ...).
>
> (P, 183)

And just as, in spatial terms, the Japanese palace did not imprison the mind within an inalterable harmony and forbid it all initiative, so he imagines an art, perhaps more destructive than constructive, which could eschew eternal form and seek to live authentically in time with all its erasures and resurrections:

> Mais si un architecte construit un château, en le détruisant aussitôt après, même avec des gradations très savantes et originales dans la destruction et la ruine; personne n'appréciera. De même dans un tableau on a coutume, pauvrement, de se contenter de l'état final.
>
> Aussi des artistes de génie existent peut-être, qu'on ne découvrira que par le cinéma, dans un nouveau genre d' architecture uniquement à filmer, artistes capables de monuments et d'oeuvres inouis 'dans le temps', défaits à mesure en de magnifiques 'retombées'. Des bâtisseurs viendront, de villes fantastiques, bientôt croulantes et retournées au néant, mais dont les passages resteront dans toutes les mémoires.
>
> (P, 150-1)

Michaux's break with Classical aesthetics is absolute. Describing a 'low period', Egyptian temple at Dandara, multi-structured and seething with signs and figures, he enthuses:

> Venant après les temples grecs qui décidément ne sont pas pour moi, ce monument ptolémaique aux larges bandes horizontales de personnages et d'hiéroglyphes, me présentait, malgré ses défauts, grâce à ces figurations énigmatiques, quantité de choses à déchiffrer sur plusieurs plans.
>
> (FEFE, 27-8)

And in the turbulent magnetic field of his own poetic processes, where everything is broken and redistributed according to the new 'infernal rhythms' (or, more recently, the beatific rhythms) of a revolutionary art, this is what happens to the stiffness of Classical statues:

> J'y mets aussi des statues. Intéressant. Quoique je sois allergique aux statues, surtout aux grecques et aux romaines, j'en mets ici, pièces de choix qui n'ont jamais été à pareil enfer. Eh bien, dans ces moments, sur mon plateau magnétique, on les dirait - c'est extraordinaire - on les dirait émues, elles, ces grandes poseuses immobiles depuis des millénaires, quelque chose passe en elles, presque la vie, quelque chose comme un sentiment secret, comme dix, vingt sentiments secrets se précipitant dessus, ou plutôt dessous, bouleversement que je ne puis voir moi-même sans bouleversement.
>
> (FEFE, 222)

At the same time one could say that Michaux's art has moved progressively towards a language of 'inexistences' rather than existences, a tendency already seen in germ in *Un Barbare en Asie*. He admires in Chinese graphic arts, theatre and writing their 'génie du signe'. Their landscape paintings have a quality of the essentialized, the evasive and the disengaged: 'Le mouvement des choses est indiqué, non leur épaisseur et leur poids, mais leur linéarité si l'on peut dire' (BA, 158). Unlike its European counterpart, which laboriously reconstructs on the stage all that it needs to project its pretence of reality, Chinese theatre uses fast-moving signs enabling 'scene' changes every few minutes: 'Son théâtre est extrêmement rapide, du cinéma' (BA, 183). When a woman on stage needs to knit an article of clothing, she proceeds to do so without any props (a language foreshadowing the strange play of absence and presence in *Au Pays de la Magie*, a work which, one might say, is stitched with air):

> L'air pur seul erre entre ses doigts, néanmoins, tout le monde éprouve la sensation de la couture, de l'aiguille (car qui coudrait de l'air pur?) qui entre, qui sort péniblement de l'autre côté, et même on en a plus la sensation que dans la réalité, on sent le froid, et tout. Pourquoi? Parce que l'acteur se représente la chose. Une sorte de magnétisme apparaît chez lui, fait du désir de sentir l'absente.
> (BA, 184)

Similarly, the mime of a love-drama, performed without words and without contact, seems not only freed from obsession and vulgarity but more spontaneous, more imperious and, paradoxically, more tangible: 'Elle n'était pas *en chair*, mais à l'état *de tracé*, comme certaines figures vues en rêve' (BA, 185). For the same reasons Michaux is attracted by the *Wayang Koelit* or shadow-theatre of Bali (and again one thinks of his title *L'Espace aux ombres*), where an oscillating light throws the shadows of pliable leather marionettes on to a screen, investing their disembodied movements and gestures with 'une étrange vie palpitante, trépidante et électrique' and creating the effect of 'une surréalité tranchée au couteau et retirée du ciel' (BA, 232-3). Even when certain figures have finished their actions and retire into the distance (a kind of *lointain intérieur*), the actor's hand continues to shake them and they remain 'floues et vibrantes', lurking ominously and with an obscure influence in the background. As for Chinese poetry, 'elle ne rencontre jamais une idée (au sens européen du mot)' (BA, 160): it evades the sterilizing grip of Western rationalism and brushes on things so delicate that it cannot be translated. There can be no doubt that Chinese art has brought many new prospects to Michaux's own, perhaps even more so in recent years. He writes:

> Mais c'est la peinture chinoise qui entre en moi en profondeur, me convertit. Dès que je la vois, je suis acquis définitivement au monde des signes et des lignes.
>
> Les lointains préférés au proche, la poésie de l'incomplétude préférée au compte rendu, à la copie.
>
> Les traits lancés, voltigeants, comme saisis par le mouvement d'une inspiration soudaine et non pas tracés prosaiquement, laborieusement, exhaustivement façon fonctionnaires, voilà qui me parlait, me prenait, m'emportait. (ER, 16)

Indeed, it is his persistent chafing against the limitations of literature that has propelled Michaux into the language of painting and drawing. He speaks of all that shifts below the surface of words like a fugitive submarine life: 'véritables bancs d'idées, nombreux à en avoir la respiration coupée, mais d'un délicat, d'un flou, d'un tel en deçà des mots-pensées!' (P, 31); and referring elsewhere to these multiple organic life-forms drifting in invisible oceanic currents as his secret 'plankton', he shows disgust for the verbal realm which, pretending to give account of them, is their inevitable betrayer: 'Mots, mots qui viennent expliquer, commenter, ravaler, rendre plausible raisonnable, réel, mots, prose comme le chacal' (P, 132). (The image of the jackal implies a coarse, wasteland creature battening on dead flesh). A 1938 essay entitled 'Peindre' (P, 83-5) celebrates painting as a switch to another network of lines of distribution and a creative rebirth. It extols the value of 'l'opération déplacement' (ER, 74), of dislodging oneself from fixed positions and venturing into a new sphere of reference:

> Le déplacement des activités créatrices est un des plus étranges voyages en soi qu'on puisse faire.
>
> Etrange décongestion, mise en sommeil d'une partie de la tête, la parlante, l'écrivante (partie, non, système de connexion, plutôt). On change de gare de triage quand on se met à peindre.
>
> La fabrique à mots (mots-pensées, mots-images, mots-émotions, mots-motricité) disparaît, se noie vertigineusement et si simplement. Elle n'y est plus.

An unselfconscious, immediate language, painting corresponds to an ideal which, obtainable or not, has never ceased to haunt the writer: 'Le désir, l'appel et le mirage d'une vraie langue directe subsistent en moi malgré tout' (FEFE, 39). It is not concerned with being its own analyst or investigator: as Michaux writes of one of his early 'Dessins commentés' (NR, 40), 'un dessin ne s'ausculte pas'. It represents a rediscovery of spontaneity, all the more effective in that the participant himself is comparatively unskilled and unschooled. It is in this medium that he finds himself most liberated from 'ce que j'ai hai le plus, le statique, le figé, le quotidien, le "prévu", le fatal, le satisfait' (ER, 43). The laborious 'word-factory', with all its processes of selection and premeditation, is brought to a halt, and he is plunged into an expansive, disordered *laisser aller* where, like Gide's Lafcadio, he abandons himself to creative change and affords himself no 'droit de retouche'. The original inspiration and final form hardly matter, but simply the unleashed energy and speed of what takes place in between and acts as a kind of transport. The value is not in the after-effects or end-product, but in the motive act itself: 'Noyau d'énergie (...) il est l'obstacle et le tremplin magique qui va me donner ma vitesse de libération' (ER, 64). A painting, for Michaux, is an *oeuvre ouverte*: not so much a process of doing as of undoing, and its aim not so much to resolve as to release. In a crisis of feeling, he snatches up a blank sheet, falsely virginal and removed from reality, and proceeds to disfigure it, spoliate it, turn it into an open wound:

> L'humeur sombre, je commence, en ayant attrapé une, à fourrer dessus quelques obscures couleurs, à y projeter au hasard, en boudant, de l'eau, par giclées, non pour faire quelque chose de spécial, ni surtout pas un tableau. Je n'ai rien à faire, je n'ai qu'à défaire. D'un monde de choses confuses, contradictoires, j'ai à me défaire.
>
> (ER, 35-6)

For Michaux the paper is a place of clash, encroachment, metamorphosis and destruction where nothing is left intact, identities are negated and definitions dissolved. No painting, moreover, has any final or ultimate value. Each is part of the disposable matter of the creator's inner dynamics; each is swallowed in a whirlwind of appearance and disappearance, creation and destruction, discovery and loss. Michaux repeatedly stresses the values of painting as speed and movement, peculiarly appropriate to turning a status quo into a revolution, a prison into an horizon, and a blockage into a release. 'Je suis de ceux', he writes, 'qui aiment le mouvement, le mouvement qui rompt l'inertie, qui embrouille les lignes, qui défait les alignements, me débarrasse des constructions. Mouvement, comme désobéissance, comme remaniement' (ER, 65). It is the poetic act in which he becomes most easily sheer *élan*. It allows him to switch, without artifice or impediment, into his most vibrant inner tempos. It yields to the rhythms of the universal continuum and espouses the sinuous, fluctuating contours of authentic reality. It is for this reason that the poet turns to the graphic arts in order to 'dessiner l'écoulement du temps', saying:

> Au lieu d'une vision à l'exclusion des autres, j'eusse voulu dessiner les moments qui bout à bout font la vie, donner à voir la phrase intérieure, la phrase sans mots, corde qui indéfiniment se déroule sinueuse et, dans l'intime, accompagne tout ce qui se présente du dehors comme du dedans.
>
> (P, 197)

and that in a dream he opens, not a book, but a folder of the most expansive gouaches and exclaims: 'Enfin je voyais, non plus l' esquisse fuyante, mais le monde comme je le conçois dans son étalement prolifique' (P, 104). Not only does painting, free from the restrictive practices of words, rejoin the primitive and the primordial but it opens itself to a totality of experience. This is as true for the creator as for the spectator:

> Les livres sont ennuyeux à lire. Pas de libre circulation. On est invité à suivre. Le chemin est tracé, unique.
>
> Tout différent le tableau: immédiat, total. A gauche, aussi, à droite, en profondeur, à volonté.
>
> Pas de trajet, mille trajets, et les pauses ne sont pas indiquées. Dès qu'on le désire, le tableau à nouveau, entier. Dans un instant, tout est là.
> (P, 115)

One should turn finally to Michaux's desire, felt especially in his recent adoption of the form of the long verse-poem, to infuse into poetry the virtues of the language of music: a language of waves, vibrations and continuity appropriate to the 'déroulement du film psychique, du ruban émotionnel, du chant perpétuel; and to 'la vie intérieure' in its fluid, endless yet ever-switching succession, 'l'étonnante vie intérieure qui procède et par coulées et par déclics' (P, 183). It is an art which, dissolving the solid state of the world, its mass and its structures, becomes an 'opération du devenir' and enjoys a kind of divinity: 'Art des désirs, non des réalisations. Art des générosités, non des engagements. Art des horizons et de l'expansion, non des enclos. (...) *Art de l'élan* ' (P, 185). It is an art, not of rupture, but of constant harmonic reunification: it has nothing in common with 'la pensée *parlée*' which immediately breaks the world into contradiction and duality, into halts and stuttering starts. It is closer than painting to perpetual motion and the miracle of self-renewal. It is an art of 'aerial' composition, a kind of space travel, incorporating infinite invisible movements of ascent and descent in the abstract ('Le seul voyage intelligent" l'abstrait' (P, 193), says Michaux). It is an interaction of vertical and horizontal expansions - the pitch of sounds played against the elastication of tempo and rhythm - which takes one beyond the limits of the *pensable*. It is an adventure of displacement, a publication of *trajets intérieurs* - not to be conceived or imagined,

also diff to Surrealists because
(1) more scared of the subconscious
(2) often more of search for fixed & stable
See Bowie

but to be traversed in a metaphysical realm. Michaux has always been more than ordinarily sensitive to the infinity and 'redemptive power' of music. He tells how he returns, after the ragged frustrations of journeys, to his piano: 'je m'allonge par-dessus les touches d'où émane le nappe sonore, je m'y trempe, je m'y masse, je m'y dénoue et m'y noie' (P, 129). He succumbs longingly to this ideal: 'être litanie, litanie comme la vie, être longtemps avant de finir' (P, 133-4). One might see the following words as a condensation of his poetics: 'Ce que je voudrais (pas encore ce que je fais) c'est musique pour questionner, pour ausculter, pour approcher le problème d'être' (P, 134). And the tormented spirit of *L'Espace aux ombres* , sucked violently between incompatible forces and nameless zones, aspires ultimately to become 'musicienne de la Vérité' (FV, 189). It is only in the most recent period, however, that Michaux has responded fully, in the actual forms of his poems, to 'la musique silencieuse qui m'habite, non moins vibrante, non moins symphonique et beaucoup plus surprenante que sa soeur sonore' (IT, 144); and that he has fulfilled in artistic terms an earlier intuition:

> Dans ma musique, il y a beaucoup de silence.
> Il y a surtout du silence.
> Il y a du silence avant tout qui doit prendre place.
> Le silence est ma voix, non ombre, ma clef ... signe sans
> m'épuiser, qui puise en moi.
>
> (P, 118-9)

For the words 'musicienne de la Vérité' one could substitute Mallarmé's 'Musicienne du silence'[6] and see Michaux's ideal of music as a *poésie sans les mots*.

NOTES

1. See Robert Bréchon, *Michaux*, Coll. La Bibliothèque idéale, Paris: Gallimard, 1959, pp. 15-23. Subsequently referred to as RBM.

2. Reference is made to the following editions and the following abbreviations are used throughout: PLI: *Plume, précédé de Lointain intérieur*, Paris: Gallimard, 1938; P: *Passages*,

Coll. Le Point du jour, Paris: Gallimard, 1963; ERAPPE: *En rêvant à partir de peintures énigmatiques*, Montpellier: Fata Morgana, 1972; EE: *Epreuves, exorcismes*, Paris: Gallimard, 1945; FV: *Face aux verrous*, Paris: Gallimard, 1954; GEE: *Les Grandes Epreuves de l'esprit*, Coll. Le Point du Jour, Paris: Gallimard, 1966; NR: *La Nuit remue*, Paris: Gallimard, 1935; QJF: *Qui je fus*, Coll. Une oeuvre, un portrait, Paris: Gallimard, 1927; IT: *L'Infini turbulent*, Paris: Mercure de France, 1964; MM: *Misérable Miracle*, Coll. Le Point du jour, Paris: Gallimard, 1972; FEFE: *Façons d'endormi, Façons d'éveillé*, Coll. Le Point du jour, Paris: Gallimard, 1969; ED: *L'Espace du dedans*, Paris: Gallimard, 1966; E: *Ecuador*, Paris: Gallimard, 1929; BA: *Un Barbare en Asie*, Paris: Gallimard, 1945; VP: *La Vie dans les plis*, Paris: Gallimard, 1949; A: *Ailleurs*, Paris: Gallimard, 1948; ER: *Emergences, résurgences*, Coll. Les Sentiers de la Création, Geneva: Skira, 1972.

3. Reprinted in *Cahiers de l'Herne*, 8 (1966), pp. 340-2.

4. *Ibid*

5. *Ibid.*, pp. 334-9

6. See the poem 'Sainte'.

FRANCIS PONGE

Ian Higgins

Ponge is popularly, and rightly, known as the creator of exhilaratingly vivid renderings of humble objects. But he has called language itself a 'monde, aussi concret ... aussi sensible pour moi que ... les *choses* du monde dit physique' (EPS, 47)[1]. The linguistic and non-linguistic worlds are distinct, together constituting the perceptual world. In this essay I am going to look at some consequences both of this fact and of another one - that the linguistic world is also an active human creation. The linguistic and non-linguistic worlds imply one another, and Ponge's practice of language is a way of coming to terms with the world around him, and therefore with himself.

Ponge's presentation of objects is characterized by dynamic tensions, both between phenomena and between the terms in which a single phenomenon is isolated. The contemplation of a single undifferentiated mass is hypnotic, a threat to the mind and therefore the self:

> *la variété des choses est en réalité ce qui me construit ...*
> *si je n'en considère qu'une,* je disparais: elle m'annihile.
> Et ... s'il faut donc que j'existe, à partir d'elle, ce ne
> sera que par une certaine création de ma part à son propos ...
> *Le texte* (GRM, 12-13; cf. TP, 64).

A result of this is that analogy is all-important in Ponge's work, in that it is seen to be negation: to see that two things are alike is to see that they are not one. Both comparison and contrast, analogy guarantees the individuality and integrity of the mind because the mind is seen to be capable of negating the world by imaginatively questioning it and introducing into it ordered discontinuity: 'Les analogies, c'est intéressant, mais moins que les différences. Il faut, à travers les analogies, saisir la qualité différentielle ... Nommer la qualité différentielle ... voilà le but, le progrès' (GRM, 41-2).

So, for example, Ponge's dislike of amorphous homogeneity leads him to prefer the skin of an orange to a sponge, the crust of a loaf to the crumb, the subtly contradictory qualities of the dried fig to the 'forme ... simpliste' and the 'mollesse ... ignoble' of the fresh one (TP, 47-7, 51, Fig, 87). If he considers water, an amorphous element, it is as a glassful, or at the seashore, where it contrasts with the land, or as rain falling, dripping, running and splashing in the back yard (GRM, 113-67, TP, 64, 35-6); he apprehends fire by introducing and juxtaposing conflicting qualities: 'il marche à la fois comme une amibe et comme une girafe, bondit du col, rampe du pied' (TP, 52). The phrase *à la fois* is very common in Ponge's work, typifying the dialectical tension, found in all his texts, between the terms of conjunctions, oppositions, contradictions, paradoxes and oxymorons - all different forms of analogy as negation.

Such, very generally, are the characteristics and existential importance of the non-linguistic world for Ponge. He uses the referential aspect of language - what he calls, as we shall see, the abstract, exterior aspect of its 'épaisseur sémantique' or semantic density - to indicate these features. I have looked at them more fully elsewhere[2]. But there is another aspect of this semantic density: the concrete, interior one, the substance of language - the sounds of a spoken utterance and even the shapes of a written one. The two aspects imply one another. Whereas in my earlier essay I look at the expressive relation between them mostly in terms of the non-linguistic world, I want in this one to look first at the existential importance of language for Ponge, and then at the concrete aspect and its expressive relation to the abstract one mostly in terms of the linguistic world.

Ponge's earliest published text shows his fascination with language as a phenomenon among others in the outside world. After referring to the relative uncertainty of meaning, when set against the certainty of the sounds or the letters of a word, he thinks of cherishing words simply

à *refuser* tout ce qui n'est pas ce que nous attendons, et que nous *reconnaîtrons* , à n'en pas douter, quand il se présentera' (Mal, 247).

The waiting is an act. What Ponge 'has to say' is a negation of the given which takes the form of a questioning, the cognition or 'discovery' of objects being realized as 'une attention redoublée à leur nom' (Fab, 22): not a passive waiting for something to happen, but an active, patient consideration and refusal of a host of possibilities thrown up largely by exploration of the resources of the language (Mal, 247). This is achieved supremely through analogy: 'par comparaison, par éliminations successives: 'Ce n'est pas ceci, ce n'est pas cela' (TP, 405; cf. Fig, 16). 'La rage de l'expression' is of so great an existential importance that it is never allowed to be an indiscriminate outpouring of emotion or analogy: it is a 'cold' rage (TP, 233). A great characteristic of much of Ponge's work is hesitation, repetition, correction, trial runs, 'variants', apparent digressions, reflections on intention and on what has been achieved so far: the final formulation, one long, complex, interrogative negation, *includes* the refusals.

Will, resistance, emotion, individuality: existence *is* language for Ponge. Of course, there is in his work, not surprising in someone so aware of the absurd as language, a strong sense of separation between writer and text (Mal, 208). In conversation with Sollers, Ponge speaks of 'la mort de l'auteur' and is willing to use *Tel Quel*'s formula of *scripteur* (EPS, 171, 145). Such an attitude is implied by the insistence on a text as something that functions above all, and is accompanied by an acceptance that the interpretation of a text is entirely the reader's, independent of what the writer may have intended (GRM, 221). There are often no explicit references to the speaker's emotions in Ponge's texts. Many are reflections on language, most are 'renderings' of humble objects. Yet even where Ponge the man, as someone with a biography, is not referred to, there is always urgently manifest an intention, a subjectivity.

This is, of course, implied in the 'absurd' dialectic of self and world. It is misleading to speak of the 'death of the author' in Ponge's case, inasmuch as it implies a simple dualism and a reification of language.[4] What the reader encounters in 'L'Orange', for example, is not so much an orange or the orange as the struggle of a mind to create a linguistic reality *adéquate* or equivalent to any orange outside language. This project is the real theme of the text, and in Ponge's work there is an increasing tendency for it to be the subject-matter as well. It is revealed partly in the idiosyncrasies of subject-matter, but more in those of the language used.

The abstract, exterior aspect of semantic density is investigated through comparison, paradox, negation, and so on. It could hardly be otherwise. What concerns us most in this essay is the concrete, interior aspect. It is made apparent in many ways. Some - the use of words in an etymological sense, assonance and alliteration, and imitative sounds and rhythms - function more as interrogative negation of the non-linguistic world, and I have analysed them in this capacity in the essay already mentioned. Others function more as a scrutiny of the linguistic world, and these are the ones I shall look at here - the search in Littré for suitable words, the appeal to etymology to 'confirm' the choice of a word intuitively felt to be apt, the coinages, and the puns and formal associations. In these last, which approach assonance, alliteration and onomatopoeia, the mutual implication of word and referent, as of abstract and concrete, is clear; and indeed we shall see, in looking at examples of Ponge's linguistic play, that his interest in the concrete aspect is itself an interrogative negation of the substance of language, implying and implied by that of the non-linguistic world.

The attention to the name of an object is founded on the intuition that this may reveal something about man: 'Il suffit peut-être de *nommer* quoi que ce soit - d'une certaine manière - pour *exprimer* tout de l'homme ' (GRM, 255; cf. Fig, 118). Mental growth is possible through a 'contemplation attentive (et active, c'est-à-dire nominative)' (TP, 566). The wish is to name things in a way as powerful as their original naming:

> Point d'imposture, nous préférons l'explication à la poésie. La prétérition à l'imposture. Il n'y avait point d'imposture dans la nomination originelle. Voilà ce qu'il nous faut retrouver (Fab, 255).

But this is no dispassionate designation of an object:

> Il s'agit ici, plus que de nomination, de louange; mais de louange réduite à la nomination. Toutes les harmoniques du *mot* doivent être lâchées (comme un lâcher de pigeons) et réduites (Fab, 249).

The insistence on language as active and on the 'reduction' - that is, the control and exploitation to an end of enthusiastic expression - of the associations of a word, suggests clearly how serious the 'redoubled attention to the name' of an object really is. It is not a surrender to the dictionary or to gratuitous association, but the concrete, interior aspect of the refinement of expression 'par éliminations successives'. It is the element of active search and refusal included in the patient wait for the right expression.

The 'imposture' absent from the original naming of things is the imposture, the 'confusion scandaleuse', of the kind of poetry which seeks to efface in some talismanic way the distinction between word and object (Fab, 254-5, Fig, 116). Now, an avowed interest in vocabulary rather than syntax (Mal, 201), an ideal of realizing all the meanings of a word in a single text (EPS, 170; cf. GRP, 156), a fascination with the substance of words - all these, in another writer, might imply an old-fashioned concern with the word at the expense of context, an almost occultist notion of some absolute metaphysical significance of verbal sounds, the survival of some Adamic language. But Ponge's interest in the roots of words as a primitive 'onomatopoeia' is different:

> (Nous avons à nous arranger avec nos mots, du moins avec nos syllabes, nos racines, racines sans significations.) Onomatopées originelles: comment en sortir? Impossible! Donc, il faut y rentrer .... Leurs variations, leurs

> développements, diversifications, ramifications, feuillaisons, floraisons, fructifications, réensemencements suffisent à dire la complexité de la vie et du monde .... Encore faut-il les prononcer .... Liaisons opérées au niveau des racines, où se confondent les choses et les formulations (Fab, 239-40; cf. GRM 198, Fig, 93).

There are two essential points here. First, the roots in themselves, like things in themselves, are meaningless. The primitive naming is something notional: poetry is an imposture if it claims to realize some *identité originelle* of thing and word. In Ponge's texts such an identity is always seen, and often said, to be impossible: the meaning of the links made is *la signification même* - precisely the fact that they are not there for the taking, but have to be made; such meaning as they have is given them in an individual act of language. The second point is that, since the meaning of a word is not absolute, but depends on utterance in a situation, it is perpetually changing. This is the force of the metaphor of development and growth in the quotation. The 'complexity' of the world is its contingency and dynamism. The reference to Littré's etymologies, far from fixing the language somewhere in the past, on the contrary draw attention to its own contingency and dynamism, being in themselves a new context in which it grows still further. The functioning of the text, as dense as that of the world it refers to, draws attention to the dynamic complexity of language, analogous to that of the world it refers to. The recourse to Littré, the play on etymologies, the coinages, the puns, the associations, even the naming of things only to reject them (the 'prétérition' of Fab, 255) - all are instances of the truth that the only way of circumscribing a phenomenon is to say what it is very like, but is not: the closer the similarity, the more obvious the difference, the specific individuality, both of phenomena and of words - and therefore of the speaker, who draws attention to their specificity through his individual manipulation of the meaningless roots.

Now it is time to look at some examples of Ponge's playful investigation of the concrete aspect of semantic density, and to see how it is a 'résolution de notre projet existentiel' (Mal, 203).

In 'Notes prises pour un oiseau', Ponge looks up *bomber*, a word used nowhere else in the text, and notes:

> BOMBER: 1. V. actif. Rendre convexe à la facon d'une bombe, c'est-à-dire de manière à présenter un segment sphérique ou à peu près. 2. V. n. Bomber: être convexe. Ce mur bombe.
>
> Rebomber ou rebombir n'existent pas, mais rebondir. rebondi (arrondi par embonpoint) (TP, 282).

After earlier references to the roundness and plumpness of birds, the 'perfection de formes dans l'oiseau replié', and the notation of *bréchet* which immediately precedes that of *bomber*, the simple definition of *bomber* itself adds to these evocations of roundness. To coin *rebomber*, with the prefex *re-*, one of whose regular functions is the expression of completeness or completion through a turning over or round, is then to reinforce the *bombé*-ness of the bird. *Rebombir* does the same, partly through suggesting the possibility of a near-synonym of *bomber*, and partly through the force of *re-*. In each case, mentioning the word in order to say that it does not exist of course confers existence of it; and in the context, it reinforces the words which do exist in the dictionary - *bomber*, and especially *rebondi*. This reinforcement is thanks, notably, to the creation of *bombé*-ness in the -*bon*- element of *embonpoint*, and to the association of *arrondi* with *bomber* through the rich rhyme with *rebondi* and this word's phonetic near-identity with *rebombi*. The result of this mutual reinforcement of coinages and dictionary words is an almost palpable amplification of the earlier evocations of the bird's shape.

As regards etymology, there are typical examples in the 'Carnet du bois de pins'. Ponge evokes the starkness of the pine-trunk: 'Rongées de lichens les basses branches sont déchues. Et point d' encombre à mi-hauteur. Point de serpentement de lianes ni de cordes' (TP, 343). Later, he looks up *encombre* and notes: '*Encombre*:

accident qui empêche, mais vient de *incombrum*: amas de *bois abattu* (voilà une confirmation magnifique); (TP, 345). Magnificent indeed, but only because it enables Ponge to make his evocation in yet another different way. This 'confirmation' should not lead us to imagine that Ponge accepts the dictionary's decision as final: elsewhere in the 'Carnet', he hits on these lines:

> Des épingles à cheveux odoriférantes
> Secouées là par tant de cimes négligentes (TP, 348),

which then recur a number of times. Yet before they ever appear, there is a list of words looked up in Littré, including *négligent*: 'de *nec legere*, ne pas prendre, ne pas cueillir. Convient mal' (TP, 346). Now this was actually looked up *after* writing the couplet, as Ponge takes the trouble to point out, but it figures in the text *before* it occurs in the couplet. The reader's predisposition against the word then contrasts with and heightens the pleasure of discovering its marvellous aptness in its context: the relevance of the etymology is in its irrelevance.

The function of pun and phonetic association is the same. In this example from 'La Chèvre', the play on *chèvre* and *cheval* is not gratuitous, but as apt in its context as 'négligentes':

> Par une inflexion toute naturelle, psalmodiant dès lors quelque peu - et tirant nous aussi un peu trop sur la corde, peut-être, pour saisir l'occasion verbale par les cheveux - donnons, le menton haut, à entendre que chèvre, non loin de chèval, mais féminine à l'accent grave, n'en est qu'une modification modulée, qui ne cavale ni ne dévale mais grimpe plutôt, par sa dernière syllabe, ces roches abruptes, jusqu'à l'aire d'envol, au nid en suspension de la muette (GRP, 210).

This is a typically dense, ironic and humorous passage. There is only space to point out a few features. The statement that the word *chèvre* does not *cavaler* or *dévaler* phonetically, but has a higher vocalic pitch with *che*val, emphasizes - analogically - both the tendency of goats to climb rocks and their bleat, more sustained than the descending whinny of a horse. This is of course led up to by the speaker's reference to his own 'inflexion toute naturelle, psalmodiant dès lors [that is, it is 'natural' in speaking of the goat, because it imitates what the goat does] quelque peu', and by the 'donnons, le menton haut [like a goat] à entendre que', which draws attention to the cry of goat and horse through emphasizing his own utterance as a vocalic act. But the analogies are only analogies, and imply differences; Ponge shows that to suggest that saying something about the sound of a word is necessarily saying something about the referent is an exaggeration - what it does say, it says contingently, through comparison, suggestion, 'tirant nous aussi un peu trop sur la corde, peut-être, pour saisir l' occasion verbale'. (*Tirer sur la corde* figuratively means 'to go too far', 'to tax someone's patience'). This of course draws attention to the exaggeration through yet another one, the comparison of self to goat, both straining - the goat at her tether of rope, the writer at the tether of language, which holds him back forever from fusing word and referent in an absolute expression. The exaggeration is further, and typically, underlined by the suggestion of the very pertinent expression *tiré par les cheveux* ('far-fetched'), through the juxtaposition of 'tirant trop sur la corde' and 'saisir par les cheveux'). Ponge is not ashamed of his play, it is very serious, and he reveals his truths about the functioning of language with head held high, 'le menton haut'.[5]

These examples are typical. It is typical, too (though not essential), that the syntax should convey doubt or negation: note the sentences (very common indeed in Ponge) built of a negative + *mais*; the words that do not exist; the 'convient mal'; the 'peut-être'. In every case, relations of conflict are set up between the elements of the text, permanently unresolved, permanently suggestive. The text functions through the violence done to everyday language: the concrete aspect of semantic density, like the abstract, implies discontinuity, a negation of the amorphous mass of accepted usage. Things have to be named, but 'd'une certaine manière'.

An obvious danger here is that the qualities of the word may draw attention to themselves at the expense of those of the object. Ponge therefore considers the possibility of not naming the object by name at all, but describing it so well that the reader realizes at the end what it is (GRM, 35; cf. 126-8, TP, 311). The problem is formulated most fully in 'Le Verre d'eau'. This text, about fifty pages long, is a set of notes, dictionary definitions, and successive drafts of a work whose repeatedly declared aim is to give the reader an experience as refreshing in language as a glass of water is outside language. Typically, that work never materializes, and the text we have, with its repetitions, hesitations, apparent digressions, and declarations of intent - that is, its constant projection towards absolute expression ('ce livre soit un verre d'eau', GRM, 143) - is an extraordinarily vivid evocation of the sight, taste and feel of a glass of water.[6] One of the features of the text is the struggle with the problem of naming:

> Tout le reste du monde étant supposé connu, mais le verre d'eau ne l'étant pas, comment l'évoquerez-vous? Tel sera aujourd'hui mon problème.
>
> Ou en d'autres termes:
>
> Le verre d'eau n'existant pas, créez-le aujourd'hui en paroles sur cette page.
>
> Ou en d'autres termes:
>
> Tout verre d'eau ayant à jamais disparu du monde, remplacez-le: son apparence, ses bienfaits, par la page que vous écrirez aujourd'hui.
>
> Ce qui revient à dire:
>
> Supposez que vous vous adressiez à des hommes qui n'ont jamais connu un verre d'eau. Donnez-leur-en l'idée.
>
> Ou encore:

> Vous êtes au Paradis, enchanté d'y être. Mais il y manque quelque chose dont vous vous souvenez soudain avec attendrissement: cette erreur, cette imperfection, le verre d'eau. Accomplissez ce péché de l'évoquer pour vous-même, le plus précisément possible, en paroles (GRM, 138).

There are four points of particular relevance here. (1) It is a question of conveying in language something absent. This brings out the distinction between word and referent implied in the words *évoquer*, *créer en paroles*, *remplacer*, *donner l'idée*. (2) Although Ponge posits the non-existence of the glass of water, he uses the words *verre d'eau* each time he does so! The text is addressed to people who do have experience of glasses of water and do know what *verre d'eau* denotes. (3) The terms used arouse a new awareness of the qualities of a glass of water. The very references to its absence and to the urgency of evoking it suggest the preciousness of this mundane thing. The enormity of its absence is emphasized by the '*Tout* verre d'eau ayant à jamais disparu'. Further value is conferred on it by the reference to its 'bienfaits', which in turn, of course, evokes the sensations of thirst and drinking; and this value is enhanced still more when the glass of water attains the status of a forbidden fruit, the very evocation of it being a sin. (4) The rest of the world is known, but not the glass of water. That Ponge goes out of his way to say this, instead of just saying that there is no such thing as a glass of water, brings out clearly that to 'render' it, reference to other things is necessary: any expression must in some way be dynamic, comparative, negatory. This is why he uses *paroles* instead of *mots*, even though he adds 'sur cette page' - the contrast helps to convey the temporality and contingency of his expression. It is also why he formulates the problem in five alternative ways, typically linked with 'ou en d'autres termes'. And it is why he calls the glass of water a mistake or imperfection: it is *not* in Paradise, it exists, it is contingent.

In the real world, objects are circumscribed, and defined by what circumscribes them. This is why Ponge takes the glass of water, and not just the glass or just water: glass, water and surrounding world throw each other into relief, indeed, they exist in terms of one another (GRM, 162-3). It is also why, throughout his work, the reader encounters limits, intersection, contradictions - conjunction of every kind, as much in juxtaposed objects and juxtaposed qualities of objects as in the language. In 'Le Verre d'eau', the whole problem is neatly put in one simple, unanswerable question:

> Si les diamants sont dits d'une belle eau, de quelle eau donc dire l'eau de mon verre? Comment qualifier cette fleur sans pareille?
>
> - Potable? (GRM, 123).

Simply naming an object by its name is for Ponge a 'tautology', simply a *re*naming of the world we know (GRM, 144). To say something new about the object is to qualify it (as opposed to categorizing it), and this can only be through analogy - for example, the water of a diamond. But the diamond-like quality of water is different from the water-like quality of a diamond. Analogy depends on the order of the terms, they are not reversible.[7] And what would it convey, to speak of the water of water? Neither is it any answer to his question to call the water drinkable, for that is a 'tautology', denoting a ready-made category, and does little to convey the qualities he experiences in the glass of water. But of course he has not simply categorized this water as drinkable - what is drinkable is 'cette fleur sans pareille'. A matchless, drinkable flower - the preciousness of something that is actually drinkable is brought out by the comparison to a flower; and the precious fragility of this metaphorical flower (and so also of the metaphor) is brought out by the brutal fact that it can be swallowed up at any time. It is emblematic of all Ponge's work that the comparisons to diamond and flower are also syntactically interrogative. The second question is itself a partial answer to the first, and the three questions together are enough to make the analogies, and so to force an awareness of some qualities of the glass of water. The original question is unanswerable, which is tantamount to saying, for one who accepts the absurd and sees nothing tragic in it, that while it has to be asked, it does not need an answer; or rather, that the only possible answers are themselves questions or affirmations that are negations. The whole text, like all Ponge's renderings of objects, is such a question. The paradox, fundamental to Ponge's work, is that the text does name the glass of water, because it is written in a world where glasses of water exist; indeed, the title names it by name at the outset.

In each of the examples I have considered, the reader's experience is of a vivid, persuasive affirmation of the qualities of an object through constant interrogation - a questioning and negation through comparison of the object to and with other objects and comparison of the words which denote it and its qualities to and with other words.

The progress ' par approximations successives' is then a perpetual tending towards an impossible absolute expression. All the drafts, hesitations, apparent digressions and word play affirm that the object does exist, that things and words are not one, that absolute expression is impossible - the destruction of ordinary usage brings out both the specificity of language and that of the non-linguistic world, thus guaranteeing the individuality of speaker and listener, perpetually threatened by the amorphousness of perceptual and linguistic cliché. It is this difference of word, object and individual that gives the sense of potential which Ponge's reader feels.

To draw the threads together, let us take a final look at *La Fabrique du pré*. There, the dialectical tension between word, object and self is expressed especially fully and powerfully. Ponge speaks repeatedly, within a few pages (22-6), of the urge to make word and object overlap completely so that there is no apparent difference - the urge itself, of course, constantly confirming their distinction. There is an exultant joy, for Ponge, in uttering this distinction: 'Quelle joie *d'avoir à dire* cette différence' (Fab, 24). But as well as giving joy, such utterance has supreme moral value:

> la nomination est la clé de tout - et ... si *nous nous intéressons* à cette différence des mots et des choses, c'est qu'en vérité *nous y sommes* au plus haut point *intéressés*, que c'est *nous* que cette différence (que le problème de cette différence) concerne, qu'il ne s'agit là, en somme, que de *nous* - et de notre propre existence, de notre propre liberté, de notre propre justification, de notre propre *devoir*... (Fab, 26).

Our only way of being is to feel the gap between ourselves and the outside world - and so, our individuality, imperfection, finiteness - but to feel it by realizing it in language in the existential project to close the gap and become one, God-like, with the world:

> La parole n'est qu'une façon ... d'avouer quelque faiblesse; de remplacer quelque vertu, pouvoir, perfection, quelque organe absent; d'exprimer sa damnation, de la compenser (GRM, 171-2, cf. Fab, 250).

Language, the mode of man's individuality, is both part of him and separate from him, the absurd, never-ending projection into the world of a project to become the world.

The self is, then, always provisional, constantly created in the act of language. Ponge often refers to himself in the first person plural, to convey the 'phases et positions successives du *je*' (GRP, 153; cf. Mal, 214). And this fluidity is dialectical:

> Il ne fait, pour mon expérience, aucun doute que l'amour des mots ... soit le chemin à la création (je veux dire, par l'expression sans tricherie d'une sensibilité individuelle, non seulement la fabrication d'objets de satisfaction, de jouissance pour le gôut commun des usagers de la langue, mais l'autocréation de l'individu lui-même dans sa ressemblance et sa différence à ceux qu'on appelle ses semblables) (Fab, 18).

So the expression of difference between objects itself realizes difference between speaker and others, as well as between speaker and objects (cf. GRM, 12-13).

Ponge is not a linguist. His interest is not in language as an internally coherent system of signs. Nor, on the other hand, is he interested in the qualities of things 'in themselves' or 'for their own sake' - 'Il y a toujours du rapport à l'homme' (TP, 189). Ponge's central interest in investigating language is man. A recurring wish in his work is to escape from the 'infime manège [dans lequel] depuis des siècles tournent les paroles, l'esprit, enfin la réalité de l' homme', and thereby to permit the progress of the human mind (TP, 196, 258; GRM, 254, 256-7, 295; cf. Fig, 119). The experience of language is the emotional experience of individuality; and if language is used creatively, the limitations of individuality are experienced as a liberation, because there is an infinity of phenomena to which the individual can pay interrogative attention, realizing his freedom from the stultifying cliché of the *manège*. Expression 'equivalent to' an object cannot be logical, but only analogical or metalogical, for in what terms could the equivalence be proved? The relative success of expression is a matter of intuitive assessment; hence the use of phrases like *faire passer comme une évidence* or *sans tricherie*, or the synthesis of *charme* and *conviction*(GRM, 188-92). In other words, Ponge is not concerned with the fact that signifier, signified and referent imply one another, (these are not terms that he uses), but, we may say, with the texture of the experience of that implication in a particular utterance in a particular language at a particular time - the emotional experience of language as Meaning, of self *as* the relationship between signifier, signified and referent, an exhilarating, never-ending play of negations.

NOTES

1. The following abbreviations are used: TP: *Tome premier* (Paris, Gallimard, 1965); GRP: *Le Grand Recueil, pièces*, GRM: *Le Grand Recueil, méthodes* (both Paris, Gallimard, 1961); Mal: *Pour un Malherbe* (Paris, Gallimard, 1965); NR: *Nouveau Recueil* (Paris, Gallimard, 1967); EPS: *Entretiens de Francis Ponge avec Philippe Sollers* (Paris, Gallimard/Seuil, 1970); Fab: *La Fabrique du pré* (Geneva, Skira, 1971); Fig: *Comment une Figue de paroles et pourquoi* (Paris, Flammarion, 1977).

2. See "Francis Ponge' in R. Cardinal (ed.), *Sensibility and Creation* (London, Croom Helm, 1977), pp. 183-203.

3. Note that Ponge invokes 'tous les sens du mot *refaire*': to do again; to do over again, differently; to restore or repair; and (not least) to catch out, to dupe.

4. As it does in Barthes' article, 'La Mort de l'auteur', in *Manteia*, No. 5, 1968, pp. 12-17. For example: 'dès qu'un fait est *raconté* à des fins intransitives, et non plus pour agir directement sur le réel, c'est-à-dire finalement hors de toute fonction autre que l'exercice même du symbole, ce décrochage se produit, la voix perd son origine, l'auteur entre dans sa propre mort, l'écriture commence' (p. 12). The 'finalement' introduces a dualism which also immediately brings back the concept of author as intention: Barthes simply suppresses the dialectic of writing as an act directed, whatever the degree and the mode of the writer's intention, at the world. In his preface to M. Spada's *A la Fête rouquine* (Paris, Bourgois, 1969), Ponge speaks ironically, but seriously, of 'le *topos* de la mort de l'auteur, récemment mis en évidence par l'un des plus brillants représentants de la re-scolastique qui nous menace' (p. 15): his deep-seated non-conformism is enough to make him see danger in Barthes' a-dialectical dogmatism.

5. Note also the 'muette', which means a hunting-lodge, but is here surely a conflation of the feminine of *muet* and *mouette*, a seagull which nests on rocky ledges! There is a very interesting study of 'La Chèvre' by B.M. Douthat, in *Yale French Studies*, No. 21, pp. 172-81.

6. Similarly, in *Comment une Figue de paroles et pourquoi*, Ponge says that his aim is to 'sortir la figue du monde des paroles' (p. 98) - that is, to affirm, through the failure of expression ('Il me faut me tromper de paroles', p. 99), the irreducibility of fig to mind: 'Nous aboutissons par négation (négativité) au mystère de l'objet, à la preuve de l'existence indescriptible, à la qualité différentielle de l'objet ...' (p. 16).

7. Cf. GRM, 66: 'Pendant un court instant ce soir, cette ... lucarne fut comme un citron vert, entièrement éclairé. Chaque citron vert est-il donc comme une fenêtre?'

EVOKING THE 'OBJET PROFOND':[1] THE POETRY OF YVES BONNEFOY

Graham Dunstan Martin

'La poésie française n'a pas de Mercutio.'
(RFM, 125)

Poets have often seen the supreme difficulty of their calling as the need to use the words of ordinary language. For some, 'the language of the tribe' has to be purified of reference, or raised to a higher degree of ambiguity, or given the harmonic qualities of music. For none however does the problem seem more intractable, more fundamental, than it does to Yves Bonnefoy. For him, poetry is threatened by meaning itself, by the very process through which we normally understand what others write or say.

What precisely is this threat? How does Bonnefoy seek to counter it in his poetry, and what distinguishes his poetic language from the language of ordinary discourse?[2]

What happens in normal discourse, he asks, when we speak of a 'horse'? We *refer* to an actual horse in the outside world; we use the *word* 'horse' of it' and by so doing we assimilate the particular horse we see to the *concept* 'horse'. The concept for Bonnefoy is thus not to be identified simply as one of the three terms in the semiotic triangle, namely 'word', 'concept' and 'referent', where (it will be recalled) the referent is the object referred to in the outside world, and the concept (or *signifié*) is the 'idea' or 'notion' we have of it, the mental event that accompanies the word.[3] In Bonnefoy's terminology, the concept is not simply whatever notion we may have of any external object to which we may be referring, but our classification of it as a *type* of object, as *a* horse, *a* tree or *a* meadow. When the language of ordinary discourse refers to particular objects in the external world, it assimilates these objects to concepts, that is *categories*. The particularity of the external object disappears: it becomes a mere instance of the category *horse*. As Bonnefoy says, 'Pour tous les linguistes ... le mot *cheval*... a pour contenu une quiddité, rien d'autre, et ainsi n'est-il nullement dans sa fatalité d'évoquer, comme peut le faire un nom propre quand on le crie, l'existence effective, ici, devant moi, du "cheval". Et cela semble évident. Que serait-ce que "le cheval", sinon un concept? *Un* cheval, oui, devant moi, et "le cheval" comme sa notion, quelle que soit la façon dont cette notion se détermine' (RFM, 94).

We can already guess from these remarks of Bonnefoy's, that he will seek in poetry to 'évoquer l'existence effective, ici, devant moi,' of the object (of the referent). The concepts of ordinary discourse are unable to perform this task, because they are classificatory. But they have another failing: they depend upon an implicit analysis of the referent into certain of its constituent parts. In the essay from which I have just quoted, Bonnefoy goes on to describe his entering a ruined house and catching sight of a salamander on the wall. 'Elle a été surprise, elle s'est effrayée et s'immobilise.' Looking at the salamander, 'plusieurs chemins se sont ouverts devant moi. Je puis analyser ce que m'apporte ma perception, et ainsi, profitant de l'expérience des autres hommes, séparer en esprit cette petite vie des autres données du monde, et la classer, comme ferait le mot de la prose, et me dire: "*Une* salamandre', puis poursuivre ma promenade, toujours distrait, demeuré comme à la surface de la rencontre' (RFM, 95-6). This is the process I have just described. The mind *separates* the salamander from its surroundings, and *classifies* it. And Bonnefoy writes '*Une* salamandre' to indicate that the little lizard is an *instance* of the category 'salamander'. However, this process of categorization depends upon the mind's recognizing certain of the lizard's distinctive traits (or criterial attributes), those of its features which enable one to classify it. And Bonnefoy has just described the first stage in his encounter with the salamander as follows: 'Je regarde la salamandre, je reconnais ses traits distinctifs, comme l'on dit, - je vois aussi ce cou étroit, cette face grise, ce coeur qui bat doucement (*ibid*). In short, not only does the concept involve separating the object from its surroundings and classifying it; it also involves an analysis of the object into certain of its constituent parts. When Bonnefoy expresses his hostility to 'le concept, qui divise pour signifier' (RFM, 98), he has all these processes in mind.

However, 'd'autres mouvements, plus en profondeur, sont possibles. Car, par exemple, je puis garder les yeux sur la salamandre, m'attacher aux détails qui m'avaient suffi pour la reconnaître, croire continuer l'analyse qui en fait de plus en plus *une* salamandre, c'est-à-dire un objet de science, une réalité structurée par ma raison et pénétrée de langage[4] - mais tout cela, soudain, pour ne plus rien percevoir, dans ces aspects brusquement comme dissociés l'un de l'autre, dans ce contour d'une patte absolu, irréfutable, désert, qu'un faisceau effrayant d'énigmes. Ces choses ont un nom, mais se sont faites soudain comme étrangères au nom. Et ces concepts, ces éléments, ces aspects, tout cela ne m'est plus qu'une cohérence vide, sans réponse à nulle question ... Mais je viens en somme de découvrir l'angoissante tautologie de la parole commune, et je n'ai plus devant moi, en moi, qu'un gouffre, au fond duquel résonne la chute inutile du temps. J'appellerai *mauvaise présence* ce soudain mutisme du monde' (*ibid*). In other words, if we struggle to deepen the conceptual process, to reason ourselves (as it were) into the nature of an object, we are brought face to face with the terrifying inability of this process to grasp or comprehend reality: we are confronted with a sense of nothingness.

At this point in his meditations, Bonnefoy is brought face to face with the thought of death. As if this were the key to the problem, his sense of *mauvaise présence* turns suddenly into its opposite: that mysterious *présence* which is the object of the poet's researches. 'Car voici la troisième voie: et que, par un acte toujours soudain, ce réel qui se dissociait, s'extériorisait, se *rassemble*, et cette fois dans une surabondance où je suis pris et sauvé. C'est comme si j'avais accepté, *vécu*, cette salamandre, et désormais, loin d'avoir à être expliquée par d'autres aspects du réel, c'est elle, présente ici comme le coeur doucement battant de la terre, qui se fait l'origine de ce qui est. Disons - bien que cette expérience soit peu dicible - qu'elle s'est dévoilée, devenue ou redevenue la salamandre - ainsi dit-on *la* fée - dans un acte pur d'exister où son "essence" est comprise' (RFM, 97).

What is this mysterious sense of *présence*? 'Bien que cette expérience soit peu dicible', let me tentatively point to some of its features. (1) It is a sense of the indivisible reality of the object between and beyond any of its aspects: 'Ce n'est pas un nouvel aspect qui va se découvrir sous d'autres insuffisants: c'est plutôt que tous les aspects, coagulations du visible, se dont dissous en tant que figures particulières, sont tombés comme les écailles d'une mue dans la connaissance, *ont dégagé le corps de l'indissociable*' (*ibid*). (2) It is a sense of inextricable unity of the object with its surroundings: 'disons ... que son essence est répandue dans l'essence des autres êtres ... Le mur est justifié, et l'âtre, et l'olivier dehors et la terre' (*ibid*). (3) It is a sense of the poet's own contact and unity with the object: 'devant moi, en moi, elle n'a plus qu'un *visage*... Elle est *l'ange*, à la place des innombrables démons, et l'ange qui est unique, car c'est l'Un la grande révélation de cet instant éternel, où tout se donne à moi pour que je comprenne et je lie.' (RFM, 98). And (4), as this last quotation also shows, it is a first step towards a sense of mystic Oneness with What is: '"Mien le soleil", écrit saint Jean de la Croix, parlant si loin en avant sur ce chemin qui s'ébauche, "miennes la lune et les étoiles, mienne la mère de Dieu"' (*ibid*).

It will now be sufficiently clear why Bonnefoy rejects the concept. For what he seeks to evoke in poetry is '*la* salamandre présente au coeur des autres présences. L'idée d'un être, sur ce plan ... implique son existence, et cela détruit le concept, qui divise pour signifier' (*ibid*). The processes of ordinary language classify and divide: classification locks the reader out from a sense of solid reality, directly apprehended;

and division of the object *into* aspects and *from* the rest of reality, blocks the reader from a sense of mystic unity. The 'meanings' of ordinary language must therefore be eschewed by the poet: 'Dans l' espérance de la venue, on ne signifie pas, on laisse une lumière se désenchevêtrer des significations qui l'occultent.

Mais ce n'est pas pour autant se détourner du langage' (RFM, 98-9). Poetry has to be written in words, and it is through words that one has to seek to evoke *présence*. Poetry must seek, 'miroitement d'unité, non plus de résorber la réalité dans le sens, mais au contraire le sens dans ma participation au réel' (RFM, 99). Through meaning we must seek not to interpret reality away, but to see reality more immediately. How is the poet to achieve this miracle?

One of Bonnefoy's most wishful notions is that the French language may, by its nature, be somehow specially suited for this task. He points to the differences between French and English poetry (differences which he himself, as a fine translator of Shakespeare, has felt acutely). As is often observed, English poetry has a remarkable capacity for evoking, as it were, the physical presence of objects[5]. This may be connected with the great disparity in size of vocabulary between the two languages and indicates the concern of English for the detail of concrete reality: '[En anglais] un mot appelant la précision ou l' enrichissement d'autres mots (plus de 21 000 mots chez Shakespeare, remarque Jespersen) et [en français] un lexique aussi réduit que possible pour protéger une unique et essentielle expérience ... D'une part le *miroir* et, dans la poésie française, la *sphère*' (H, 239). French gives the impression of being a language of 'essences', i.e. it seems to evoke a realm of almost Platonic Idea, a realm of universals revealed behind the purely aspectual surfaces of the objects it refers to: 'ce qui semble évident de notre langue, c'est que ses mots connotent pour la plupart, non des aspects empiriquement définis, mais des entités qui ont l'air d'exister en soi, comme supports d'attributs ...' (RFM, 109). Thus reality and reason seem to be identified in French; and this phenomenon Bonnefoy calls the 'principe d'identité' (RFM, 110). It follows that even 'les institutions sont appréhendées par le français comme des substances' (RFM, 111).

What are the justifications for Bonnefoy's remarks on French and English?[6] It is true that there is a striking contrast between the very concrete and physical imagery of such poets as Keats, Hopkins, Hughes and Lowell, and the less tangible evocativeness of such poets as Eluard, Jouve, Guillevic, Dupin and Bonnefoy himself. However, this is not to say that English poetry is limited to describing the outer surfaces of reality, and is incapable of grasping or projecting universal truths. 'Qui a jamais douté qu'il y a une poésie anglaise?' (RFM, 109). 'Je reviens aux paroles de Cléopâtre, entre toutes sublimes, moment absolu de la poésie:

> I have
> Immortal longings in me.

D'une part l'anglais peut saisir le plus concret, le plus immédiat, le plus instinctif de l'acte d'être: de l'autre, il garde la ressource - par *immortal*, par ce mot qui est pure idée - de découvrir au coeur même de cet élan l'intemporel et l'universel qui sont nos plus pures aspirations' (H, 237). And the apparent evocation of essences by French is ultimately an illusion: 'essences' have no reality, there is no metaphysical guarantor, no 'higher realm' for them to subsist in.[7] They are mental figments. How, even, is the *illusion* of an essence to be produced? Even if French more readily produces that illusion than other languages, this fact itself constitutes a danger: '... s'il y a dans les mots que nous employons cette virtualité de présence, ce grand espoir, - il en découlera qu'on parlera sous ce signe, comme enivrés, sans avoir critiqué, comme il se doit, notre pratique des choses' (RFM, 124). The French poet runs the risk of trusting his language to do all his work for him, and ending up with the empty automatic gestures of a conventional rhetoric (cf. *ibid*). In short, we are still left with the problems of how to effect the miracle: how to evoke *présence*.

The answer to this question must of course be a linguistic and psychological one: if the miracle *does* occur, it must be thanks to the linguistic techniques Bonnefoy adopts, and to the effect of these techniques upon our minds. About these factors Bonnefoy has almost nothing to say, but it is not surprising that the poet himself should shy away from self-analysis: we cannot expect him to place his verse upon an operating table, or to take a scalpel to his own mind. I shall seek here, however, to dispel some of the mystery.

Let us look first, briefly, at two or three of the suggestive hints which Bonnefoy drops in his theoretical writings (for though he does not analyse himself, he suggests to us some of the tools for doing so). For instance in *L'Arrière-pays* he relates his project for a story on 'Un Sentiment inconnu' (AP, 133-149). I have not the space to discuss this here in depth, but it will be recalled that, visiting an exhibition of the works of a minor Italian artist and his school, Bonnefoy found himself fascinated by the expression on a face in one of the paintings. It represented, he thought to himself, an unknown feeling, 'un mode d'être aussi important que la foi, l'espérance, et qui pourtant nous échappe ..., en vérité nous transcende ...' (AP, 135). In a fever of excitement, he begins to write a story in which a historian posits the theory that there used in prehistoric Italy to be a name for such a feeling, but that the word and its significance have since been lost. A linguist brings him supporting evidence ... but in the end demurs: 'Un sentiment inconnu? Vous avez peut-être raison. Mais ce qui me frappe le plus, depuis que je l'interroge, c'est qu'elle est, en somme, quelconque ... En fait j'ai pensé souvent, depuis que j'ai lu votre article, que tout visage en peinture pourrait passer pour marquer un sentiment inconnu ...' (AP, 144). At this the historian feels an extraordinary joy. And a few lines later Bonnefoy is deciding not to write his story after all and asserting joyfully that 'La terre *est*, le mot *présence* a un sens' (AP, 149).

What are we to make of this? The experience showed Bonnefoy that *présence* could be communicated, but not defined. But it has also a bearing on the communicability but indefinability of the simplest and most ordinary human feelings: they are *all* ineffable. And let us leave it at that for the moment.

Secondly, Bonnefoy speaks, in 'Transposer ou traduire "Hamlet" ', of the conscious and unconscious elements in poetic meaning, and emphasizes the importance of those elements which lie too deep for rational analysis. 'Expliciter le "sens" ..., n'est-ce pas surtout le trahir, puisque c'est méconnaître la dualité, au plus intime de la parole, du formulé et du retenu ou, d'une autre façon, du conscient et de l'inconscient? ... On ne peut pas plus accoucher une parole de son sens que l'on ne peut dans le concept transporter la densité du symbole, dans le discours le tragique de l'immédiat, dans le nivellement d'une formule ces étagements indistincts par lesquels des dits ou sous-entendus du sens manifeste rejoignent les mystères de ce qui demeure inconscient' (H, 248).

Finally, I recall the words of the Sibyl in Bonnefoy's dream, 'J'efface ce que j'écris, tu le vois, c'est parce qu'il faut que tu lises' (AP, 84), and wonder if they may not suggest to us the importance of that obscurity in a work of art which forces us to an *effort to interpret it*. For what is 'easy to understand' is so because we can easily categorize it and reduce it to rational statement. And may its power not then be lost, so that it ceases to touch us, move us or involve us? We conceptualize, Bonnefoy suggests, to protect ourselves against the deepest and most disturbing feelings. 'Y a-t-il un concept d'un pas venant dans la nuit, d'un cri, de l'éboulement d'une pierre dans les broussailles? De l'impression que fait une maison vide? Mais non, rien n'a été gardé du réel que ce qui convient à notre repos' (I, 13).

These hints of Bonnefoy's suggest to me that one might well apply to his poetry the following ideas[8]: (1) that poetry (particularly modern poetry) is normally so constructed that the categorizing tendency of ordinary language is prevented. To achieve this the poet has many techniques at his disposal, but they can all be seen as devices which make poetry 'odd' in various ways. (2) We have therefore to interpret poetry in a different way from ordinary discourse. Poetry's odd use of language forces on our attention unexpected connotations of the words. (3) These connotations however *are not purely verbal*, and cannot be interpreted as such except at the most superficial level. Of course, when explicating a text, we are inevitably thrown back on words, but we should always be aware that these are but useful approximations. It is clear that with an easy or obvious metaphor in ordinary speech, for instance, the connotations will be so evident as to be easily verbalized, categorized, and taken for granted. Let us imagine someone calling the front of an aeroplane its 'nose' for the first time. One cannot imagine how the term 'nose' could be understood by the hearer, unless he sees, say, the *position* and the *shape* of the aeroplane's prow as constituting the link between it and the term 'nose'. But these connotations (the particular position and shape) are easily verbalized, understood and accepted by the rational mind.

The situation in poetry, however, is more complex. When Robert Lowell writes of 'yellow dinosaur steamshovels', we are required to visualize the two objects in question, and to adjust the one to the other, seeing the steamshovels, through the lens of the dinosaurs. We can say of course that it is the gnashing action of the steamshovel's jaws, the dipping movement of its 'neck', and so forth, that are suggested. But to say this is merely to give an inexact verbal approximation of what we 'see' when, reading the image, we understand it by drawing on memories of sense data, pictures or models of dinosaurs, recollections of steamshovels at work, and so on. It is impossible to reduce such visual memories to a purely verbal formula without leaving out the exact shape and form of the visual memories.

With imagery of a still less tangible nature, such as Shakespeare's 'dark backward and abysm of time', the image's effect is still less easy to reduce to conceptual categories, and we may be drawing (in part) on feelings and tendencies deeply embedded in our unconscious minds.

I should argue, then, that when seeking to understand unusual turns of phrase, metaphors, etc., we are obliged to refer to fragments of our past experience, and that many of these fragments of experience are not parts of the semantic structure of our language so much as parts of our past sensory and emotional experience of the world and of ourselves.[9] And if this is so, we have found an answer to the problem of *ut pictura poesis*: poetry may seem to 'depict' reality, because it is only via our memories of reality that we can understand the poetry.

We can make rough distinctions between different levels of connotations: (a) verbal, (b) sensory, (c) emotional, and (d) profound (belonging to the deepest levels of the conscious and unconscious mind). Poetry seeks above all to arouse connotations on the last three levels, for here recalled experience is directly brought in. Thus meaning itself is not merely 'conceptual' (to use Bonnefoy's terminology); there are levels of meaning which, though words may evoke them, run too deep for words to define. And I should therefore reinterpret Bonnefoy's distinction between language which conceptualizes and language which evokes *présence*, as a distinction between language which arouses merely superficial and easily reclassifiable connotations, and language which evokes fragments of experience, both remembered and unconscious. The latter type of language gives a sense of 'wholeness', for the experience it evokes is not reducible to verbal formulae. And Bonnefoy himself sometimes distinguishes between 'les significations' and 'le sens', rejecting the former, but accepting the latter (PJJ, 61). But a word of caution must be inserted at this point. It may well be that he regrets this, but Bonnefoy does not suppose that *présence* can be in any way 'realized' by the poem, but merely evoked. Poetry is not the mystic Logos.[10]

All this sheds considerable light on the difference that Bonnefoy sees between French and English as poetic languages. Both languages can of course suggest connotations on all of the last three levels, sensory, emotional and profound. But it may be that English poetry more commonly suggests connotations on all three; whereas Bonnefoy's view can be explained by saying that French poetry's preferred levels are the emotional and the profound, bypassing the more directly concrete and sensory level.

If true at all, this is only true of certain types of French poetry - or is at most a matter of degree. Despite what Bonnefoy says of Rimbaud, for instance, one feels that there are often strongly sensory connotations evoked by his verse.[11] However, the distinction may be found to be largely true of Bonnefoy's own work.

Poetry can thus function as a means of bringing the reader into touch with aspects of experience that are not normally, or perhaps cannot be, categorized in language. We can understand how poetry can suggest 'unknown feelings' or a sense of living reality, can bring us face to face with basic impulses and intuitions, and with elements of the unconscious where logical contradiction is no longer felt to be contradiction. We can also see how Bonnefoy's requirement that reality should be the purpose of meaning, not meaning of reality,[12] can be complied with:

> Ici,
> Un grand espoir fut peintre. Oh, qui est plus réel
> Du chagrin désirant ou de l'image peinte?
> Le désir déchira le voile de l'image,
> L'image donna vie à l'exsangue désir.
>
> (PE, 79)

As Jean-Claude Renard puts it, '... le propos de la poésie n'est pas de se transformer en silence, mais de parler sans cesse assez profondément pour nous rapprocher le plus possible du point où la parole devient inutile parce qu'elle cède la place à l'être'.[13]

We have now, therefore, discovered a mental and linguistic mechanism for the evocation of *présence*. But it still remains to see what means Bonnefoy uses to cause this mechanism to operate. What is it that confers the strength and force of a possible *présence* on the poet's words?

As for the technical means used, Bonnefoy has no fully expounded theory to give us. But again, we can find suggestive hints in his theoretical works: (1) Some subjects are perhaps beyond the power of the concept to reduce to a neat and protective classification. Among such things, I shall quote again 'Y a-t-il un concept d'un pas venant dans la nuit, d'un cri, de l'éboulement d'une pierre dans les broussailles? De l'impression que fait une maison vide?' (I, 13). (2) Some words have, for the poet, the force of archetypes, e.g. stone, fire, blood, a light in darkness, trees, foam, the sea, a sword, etc. When Bonnefoy turns from discussing the concept *horse* to discussing the poetic use of words, he immediately takes a new example: 'Que je dise "le feu" (oui, je change d'exemple, et cela déjà signifie) ...' (RFM, 94). Later in the same essay he speaks of 'les mots profonds - ils varient certes avec chacun de nous - [qui] portent la promesse de l'être, donnent l'idée d'un verbe ...' (RFM, 102). These words tend to correspond, of course, to the most basic of those non-aspectual words that he praises as approaching most nearly to 'essences' (RFM, 104-5).[14] (3) It follows therefore that Bonnefoy tends to use relatively few unusual or aspectual words in his poems; and this entails a corresponding reduction in breadth of vocabulary. His first three collections are written in a rigorously limited vocabulary. Of French poetry's normal tendency (he means first and foremost the French poetry that he personally prefers) he writes: 'Dire, ce n'est plus commencer de décrire ce qui est, mais s'enfermer avec certaines choses élues dans un monde plus simple et clos' (H, 237). (4) It is clear that at least some of these archetypal words (and Bonnefoy speaks of stone as an archetype in *L'Improbable*, p. 18) may imply a union of opposites, beyond rationality. 'Voici avec la tombe et dans cet éclatement de la mort qu'un même geste dit l'absence et y maintient une vie. Il dit que la présence est indestructible, éternelle ... Voici la vie qui ne s'effraie pas de la mort ... Il faut pour les comprendre un autre langage que le concept, une autre foi. Le concept se tait devant elles comme la raison dans l'espoir' (I, 34). Let us guess that the use of words to arouse connotations that are contradictory may force the reader's mind to operate at a pre-rational level. (5) Bonnefoy has an interesting remark to make about his early fascination with the density and compression of Latin syntax: 'avec les cas, les déclinaisons, on pouvait se passer de prépositions pour les relations entre vocables. Avec des ablatifs absolus, les prépositions infinitives, les participes futurs, on pouvait contracter dans un mot, ou une structure dense, second degré de l'esprit, ce que le français n'eût exprimé qu'en le dénouant. Loin de les affaiblir, ce resserrement me semblait aller plus intimement aux relations signifiantes: et découvrir ainsi, bien que de façon voilée, quelque chose d'une intériorité inimaginée (d'une substance) du fait verbal' (AP, 107-8). We might well seek for a similar effort towards compression in his own work. Not that there is anything surprising here: it is of the very nature of modern poetry to seek compression and density. (6) We may expect an inner structure of analogy in his poems, from remarks such as this: 'Disons ... que [l'essence de la salamandre] s'est répandue dans l'essence des autres êtres, *comme le flux d'une analogie*, par laquelle je perçois tout dans la continuité et la suffisance d'un lieu, et dans la transparence de l'*unité*' (RFM, 97). Again, there is nothing surprising or unusual in this. (7) Analogy spreads also into the *form* of a poem: form and meaning are connected; and he writes of these connexions in alarmingly confident tones: 'On ne s'étonne pas de voir apparaître dans la [*Chanson de Roland*] ce vers décasyllabe si "objectif", lui dont les quatre pieds initiaux engagent si fermement la conscience dans la stabilité d'un savoir, cependant que sa deuxième partie, dans son rythme ternaire infus, consent au temps humain par un acte de sympathie qui revient se fondre dans l'éternel' (RFM, 113). We are perilously close to nonsense here. Elsewhere, however, Bonnefoy's remarks about poetic metres are perhaps a little more acceptable. The Shakespearian pentameter or the Racinian alexandrine seem to him to stand for a supreme myth of Order imposed upon our minds. Any disturbance to the metre signifies a disturbance in this Order: reality breaks in and refutes the myth: 'Que "le pentamètre boite", et [c'est] parce que l'homme lui-même ne peut plus ou ne veut tenir [son rôle], faire confiance à un mythe, échapper au doute ou au désarroi. Il arrive ainsi que le mot refuse vraiment la forme - le réel réfutant l'idée. Le mot fait obstacle au rythme et le rompt ...' (H, 251; cf. CTS, 349-50). We shall not therefore be surprised to find in many of Bonnefoy's own poems a tendency to approach the regular rhythms of the traditional alexandrine, yet equally a tendency to disrupt these rhythms. This practice is close to that of T. S. Eliot,[15] and harmonizes with a persistent theme in Bonnefoy's poetry. 'L'imperfection est la cime', he writes (HRD, 35). And it may well be that there are similar reasons both for his disrupting the perfect form, and for his avoiding the conceptual process: the experience must not be pigeon-holed: intractabe reality must be allowed to break in. (8) Finally, though it is only a small point, we cannot but be struck by Bonnefoy's use of the definite article in some of the passages I have quoted, or in this one for instance: 'Tout [dans la *Chanson de Roland*] est simple, précis - abstrait? Mais non, car l'universel y respire. Vergers qui sont *le* verger' (SCR, 55: Bonnefoy's italics). We should certainly pay attention to the types of article used in a Bonnefoy poem: there may be an attempt to use them as a factor in conveying the universal.

I shall now seek to illustrate these techniques from one of the poems in *Pierre écrite:*

L'écume, le récif

Solitude à ne pas gravir, que de chemins!
Robe rouge, que d'heures proches sous les arbres!
Mais adieu, dans cette aube froide, mon eau pure,
Adieu malgré le cri, l'épaule, le sommeil.

Ecoute, il ne faut plus ces mains qui se reprennent
Comme éternellement l'écume et le rocher,
Et même plus ces yeux qui se tournent vers l'ombre,
Aimant mieux le sommeil encore partagé.

Il ne faut plus tenter d'unir voix et prière,
Espoir et nuit, désirs de l'abîme et du port.
Vois, ce n'est pas Mozart qui lutte dans ton âme,
Mais le gong contre l'arme informe de la mort.

Adieu, visage en mai.
Le bleu du ciel est morne aujourd'hui, ici.
Le glaive de l'indifférence de l'étoile
Blesse une fois de plus la terre du dormeur.

This is a love poem, or rather a poem of farewell to love. Death, either literal or psychological, intervenes to separate the lovers.

There are almost no 'aspectual words' in the poem (though 'gong' is certainly an exception, and 'récif' might be taken to be another: I shall return to these words). Almost every word belongs to the vocabulary of 'essences', though most are concrete, and could almost stand for a vital (or mortal) principle. Similarly, nothing is *seen* closely, and it is not at all clear that even those concrete terms which seem dimly to place the poem in a physical context ('robe rouge', 'sous les arbres', 'dans cette aube froide', 'le sommeil', 'ces mains', 'ces yeux', or even 'Le bleu du ciel est morne aujourd'hui, ici') necessarily do so. Certainly even these dimly glimpsed physical details are more suggestive of emotion and situation than any actual physical context. Is the sky blue, though it seems gloomy? Or is it gloomy, though it should be blue? The image's force is emotional. The sky is blue for joy, but, though clearly seen, is out of reach. And joy that is unattainable and about to end is joy's opposite. Similarly the dawn may well be literally cold; but the effect of the image is to remind us of death, of the end of passion, and to echo the poet's 'Adieu'. Again, the trees in line 2 may perhaps be literal; but they are also so general that we must take them to be images of life, its continuity, its eternity, flawed because cyclical. Again, the red dress is glimpsed as something more essential than in its mere appearance: it stands for, and is, the woman; and it stands for life, vigour and joy. But because it is also the colour of blood, we are reminded of death's restriction upon life. Yet the colour, in this otherwise sober context of blacks and whites (until perhaps line 14), has such vividness that we may be reminded of 'l'étrange joie qui s'éveille souvent ... au plus près de l'objet mortel'[16] (I, 163-4). It will be seen that none of the connotations I have discussed is sensory; they are all emotional or profound. It is at these levels that the poetry functions.[17]

Nor does it matter if we classify the *récif* of the title as 'aspectual'. The reef does not function 'aspectually' in the poem, for we must interpret it as the hard contrast to foam, into which it breaks the sea, so causing the foam to appear. It is at once the cause of the foam's appearance, and of its disappearance. It is a creator and destroyer, an active element in the tangled mystery of life and death. And it is also, here, more specifically the death of love. Rock and foam are mingled even more inextricably in line 6, where the eternal rock meets and causes the ephemeral foam, and where this meeting of life and death is seen also as the meeting between two human lovers' hands. The eternal movement of love is linked with its temporality, it is eternal though temporal, temporal though eternal; and it links again mysteriously with the secret of life and death. The foam is an image, perfect in its aptness, for what Bonnefoy calls 'l'éphémère': 'L'éphémère est ce qui demeure, dès lors que sa figure *visible* est sans cesse réeffacée; (NPE).

Similarly Mozart and the gong in lines 11 and 12 stand for feelings or mental processes: Mozart, it is true, is also the musician of the pathetic G-minor symphony, and of the opening movement of the D-minor piano concerto; but joy, energy, and an ultimate repose in the perfection of form, are perhaps his most constant attributes. By contrast, the gong destroys the perfections of a classical music, protests and warns like a tocsin, and (being a tocsin) contains in its sound the hopelessness of its own protest against death. Again, though this image has a sensory basis, it can only be understood through its emotional overtones.

We can characterize the vocabulary of this poem, then, as (in the main) concrete, but as if archetypal; for it arouses basic emotional associations, some of them at a profound level. And it demands such an interpretation in part through its persistent use of definite articles: 'les arbres', 'le sommeil', 'l'ombre', 'l'abîme', 'l'étoile'. But the demonstrative 'ce/cette' is also common in the poem. This is perhaps Bonnefoy's attempt to link universal with particular, the archetypal experience of lovers' parting with this particular experience of parting.

A further point to note is the number of images which crystallize a logical contradiction. The red dress, the reef and the gong are three we have noted already. Let me mention two or three more. The 'paths' in line 1 suggest ways up the unscaleable mountain of solitude. As we have seen, *présence* seems unattainable, yet in especially precious moments, it can be grasped. The real sense of communication with another human being is similarly difficult, but possible. Yet there are *many* paths: the struggle has always to be started again. And yet again, the line may suggest that, many though the paths may be, the mountain peak is still out of reach. The hours in line 2 come close, 'the hours are nigh', but the poet does not assert their presence.

Even the little word 'encore' in line 8 has a similarly ambivalent effect: it signifies continuation, but also an imminent threat of non-continuation. And the star in line 15 stands for hope, for heaven, for a supernatural point of reference. Yet it is indifferent, out of reach. Yet it reaches *us*, by giving us 'immortal longings', and by disappointing them. This disappointment, this wound, is the guarantee of human truth. It is Bonnefoy's purpose to communicate emotions which function on the further side of reason.

One must also note his use of compression. The suppression of articles in lines 9 and 10, though it has nothing unusual about it, nonetheless links 'voix et prière/Espoir et nuit' more tightly, and hence emphasizes the contradiction implicit between the speaking voice and the silent prayer, the bright hope and the dark night. The exclamation 'que de chemins' in line 1 has a similar fortunate effect. Statement is compressed into exclamation, and thus ceases to be statement, but an expression of emotion; moreover, it may thereby more easily express ambivalence, for we may be less tempted by an exclamation to seek a single, rational sense.

It will also be clear by now that there is an inner structure of analogy working in Bonnefoy's poem. The principles of life and death are interwoven into many of its images: 'robe rouge', 'arbres', 'aube froide', 'l'écume et le rocher', 'espoir et nuit', 'abîme/port', 'le gong', 'L'étoile'; and even the phrase 'Adieu, visage en mai', since spring is not the time for farewells. Each of these images contains the contrary pull of a positive and of a negative force; each image stands for both, and hence echoes and supports the other images. As the foam is both brought to life and broken by the reef (which is the paradox of human existence), so May and the cold dawn are symbols of joy - but a joy which passes and involves its own farewell; so also the blue sky symbolizes joy, which is now about to cease, sought to unite these irreconcilable opposites; and that the time for such uniting has now gone. But, ironically, they are more united at this moment, in this poem, since life is evoked more distinctly when it is under threat, joy's meaning is felt more distinctly when its end is present. Thus 'espoir et nuit', 'abîme et port' echo, too, this turning point where joy and grief are evoked together. The unity of being which it was love's struggle to achieve, is evoked again, though in its tragic mode, at love's ending.

Finally, we might consider the treatment of metre. All the lines except two are twelve-syllable lines, and a number of these are orthodox alexandrines. This sort of procedure is typical enough of Bonnefoy's work, and we may feel perhaps that the poem seeks the mood and pattern of high seriousness (for this is conventionally the metre of the highest seriousness in French verse) in order to *touch* that repose and order which would signify the grasping of *présence*. But 'la poésie moderne est loin de sa demeure possible. La grande salle aux quatre fenêtres lui est toujours refusée. Le repos de la forme dans le poème n'est pas honnêtement acceptable' (I, 185). Poetry may touch this perfection, but does not rest within it. Reality must interrupt the dream, and does so most strikingly in lines 13 and 14.

> Adieu, visage en mai.
> Le bleu du ciel est morne aujourd'hui, ici.

Line 13 is the first half of an alexandrine: the movement of the verse is cut short: loss is expressed by the pause, and perhaps the finality of that loss. As for line 14, the hiatus makes it limp; there is an imperfection in the sky. At line 15,[18]

> Le glaive de l'indifférence de l'étoile,

a long, caesura-less line announces the return of the poem's basic rhythmic movement; announces it too by the use of the 'poetic' word 'glaive'. And we end with

> Blesse une fois de plus la terre du dormeur,

a perfect classical alexandrine. Is perfection, then, re-established out of imperfection? Such a movement is perhaps suggested by the rhythm. But we must remember the absence of rhyme, echoing a similar absence in the first stanza, and contrasting with the partial, but regularly placed, rhymes of the two middle stanzas. It should be noted too that the two middle stanzas contain a higher proportion of classically placed caesuras. The balance of the inner stanzas as against the two outer ones, corresponds perhaps to a contrast in themes. For the inner stanzas declare the end of the experience, the approach of death. They are both constructed about the fatalistic 'il ne faut plus'. The outer stanzas utter the actual farewell, and speak with a sharper accent of regret and pain. If the poem's last line shows some sort of acceptance, it comes only after the broken rhythms of lines 13-14, and cannot rise to the smooth finality of a terminal rhyme. Bonnefoy's verse technique is a matter of subtle approaches to, and withdrawals from, the serenity of classical form. And indeed this process itself mirrors the Janus-like character of his subject-matter: both poles of the contradiction must be present for both to be subsumed. Hence also his effective use of non-classical syncopations within the alexandrine itself. The rhythms of lines 1 and 2 mirror each other perfectly:

line 1: 8
3 + 5 + 4

line 2: 8
4 + 5 + 3

But reality is not subordinated to the pattern: for the natural rhythm of these phrases syncopates across the alexandrine's fundamental rhythm. Here is yet another variety of that departure from classical form which symbolizes for Bonnefoy the irruption of reality.

It would seem, therefore, that we can explain Bonnefoy's metrical techniques as follows: a note of high seriousness must be struck; the possibility of a supreme order must be hinted at. These techniques are the launching pad: they *prepare* the reader, as it were, for a movement out of mere perfection into a less rationally comprehensible state, one where the tragedy of reality (of the mortal material world), which is the flaw of an ideal perfection, comes to be part of a higher and more complete reality. So the tragic intransigence of reality must be symbolized:

> Aimer la perfection parce qu'elle est le seuil,
> Mais la nier sitôt connue, l'oublier morte,
> L'imperfection est la cime.
>
> (HRD, 35)

This discussion of the poem may have seemed rather general. This is in fact quite deliberate: the same, or similar, points could doubtless be made in discussing many of Bonnefoy's poems; and the purpose here has been to attempt to descry some of the nuts, bolts and pistons in Bonnefoy's poetic machine.[19] Perhaps to enumerate them may seem a pity; perhaps on the contrary it may assist the reader in making the machine work. But it must not be forgotten that the machine functions only within the reader's mind; that he alone is the judge of its functioning; and that its action is intended to extend to a level beyond the grasp of reason or perhaps even beyond the power of consciousness to pierce. Thus, despite my earlier promise to dispel some of the mystery, it cannot be dispelled: it can only be driven back to some still darker recess of the mind. The problem is connected with the remark, in the first paragraph of this essay, that Bonnefoy feels poetry to be threatened by meaning. It is not so much threatened by meaning ('le sens') as threatened by a narrow and analytic conception of meaning ('les significations'). But unfortunately one can discuss a poem only by analyzing it. It must always be borne in mind that analysis is merely an approximation, an abstraction from the poem's reality. To pretend to pin the poem down on the page and totally explain it would be to kill the poem. My analysis consequently amounts to no more than a series of pointers or signposts. I have labelled some of the connotations; but the way they actually operate within the mind is a different matter, active and not schematic, evoking not abstract thought but fragments of felt experience, the more so since this experience cannot be defined by reason or reduced to analysis. '[Le poème] ne prétend, en effet, qu'à intérioriser le réel. Il recherche les liens qui unissent *en moi* les choses' (RFM, 100).

NOTES

1. The term is taken from H, 244, where it appears to signify the real inner *présence* of objects, on which level the universality of Shakespeare and of French poetry can meet.

   Key to references (works are by Yves Bonnefoy unless otherwise stated): AP: *L'Arrière-pays*, Skira 197; BCR: 'Baudelaire contre Rubens', *L'Ephémère* 9, Spring 1969, pp. 72-112; CTS: 'Comment traduire Shakespeare', *Etudes Anglaises*, Vol. 17, 1964, pp. 341-351; H: *Hamlet* (traduction de Shakespeare), Mercure de France, 1962; HRD: *Hier régnant désert*, Mercure de France, 1958; I: *L'Improbable*, Mercure de France, 1959; LTP: Graham D. Martin, *Language, Truth and Poetry*, Edinburgh University Press, 1975; NP: Jean-Claude Renard, *Notes sur la poésie*, Seuil, 1970; NPE: Notice publicitaire pour *L'Ephémère* (1966) sans nom d'auteur; PE: *Pierre écrite*, Mercure de France, 1965; 'Pierre Jean Jouve', *L'Herne: Pierre Jean Jouve*, Paris 1972 (ed. Kopp and de Roux); RFM: *Un Rêve fait à Mantoue*, Mercure de France, 1967; SCR: 'Sur la Chanson de Roland', *L'Ephémère* 4, Sep. 1967, pp. 55-65; YBTP: Graham D. Martin, 'Yves Bonnefoy and the Temptation of Plato', *Forum for Modern Language Studies*, Vol. 10 no. 2, April 1974, pp. 95-108.

2. See my earlier remarks in YBTP. There, I confined myself largely to discussing 'La Poésie française et le principe d'identité' (RFM, 91-125), for this is the essay in which Bonnefoy looks most closely at language and its functioning in prose and in poetry. Here, I try to cast the net a little wider, though I avoid all reference to Bonnefoy's most recent poetic work, *Dans le leurre du seuil*.

3. The semiotic triangle looks as follows:

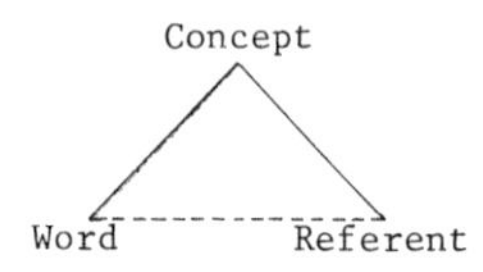

Thus, the word 'means' the referent (or object in the outside world) through the mediation of the concept (or mental process in the speaker's and listener's minds). See the diagram and discussion in John Lyon's *Introduction to Theoretical Linguistics*, Cambridge 1968, p. 404. See also my own LTP, particularly chapters 1, 2 and 3.

4. Because it is language, the rational mind and science which classify the salamander's traits, and which 'build' the class *salamander* out of them.

5. 'En anglais ... une nuée d'expressions permettent de saisir avec autant de precision que de promptitude la façon dont l'événement - tout devient événement - se propose à la conscience immédiate ... Les mots ... se pressent l'un contre l'autre en continuité opaque, comme les cristallisations d'une superbe matière - en fait, comme des éclats d'intelligibilité arrachés d'un réel délibérément abordé d'une manière empirique' (RFM, 106-7).

6. See also YBTP.

7. 'Il est aisé d'être poète parmi les dieux. Mais nous autres venons après les dieux. Nous n'avons pas le recours d'un ciel pour garantir la transmutation poétique ...' (I, 151).

8. Cf. LTP.

9. See LTP, Chapters 5 and 16(a). There is considerable controversy among linguists as to how much of our knowledge of the world can legitimately be claimed to be a part of our knowledge of the language. Whenever an actual sensation (a colour, a feeling, a sound) is actually called to mind by language, however, it is clear that experience is being called on, and not merely verbal categories. Whether we still call this part of language or not, is perhaps a matter of definition. But, whatever we call it, the important point is the necessary link *between* language and experience; and, most importantly, that unusual (e.g. poetic) language can force us to refer to our experience to understand it.

10. For instance, in *L'Improbable* we find him writing: 'La parole peut bien, comme je le fais maintenant, célébrer la présence, chanter son acte, nous préparer en esprit à sa rencontre, mais non pas nous permettre de l'accomplir'. How, then, he asks, can poetry hope to achieve this impossibility? He answers: 'Je crois qu'il faut plutôt reconnaître ses limites et ... la prendre seulement pour le moyen d'une approche ...' (I, 175-6). Almost the same formula can be found again in 1966, in NPE: 'L'EPHEMERE a pour origine le sentiment qu'il existe une approche du réel dont l' oeuvre poétique est seulement le moyen'.

11. See RFM, 105.

12. Cf. *supra*.

13. NP, 50, note. Cf. ., p. 46.

14. See YBTP, pp. 100-101.

15. It will be recalled that Eliot writes: 'The ghost of some simple metre should lurk behind the arras in even the "freest" verse; to advance menacingly as we doze, and withdraw as we rouse'. (*To Criticize the Critic*, London, 1965, pp. 183-9) Bonnefoy mentions Eliot's *Waste Land* as 'le vrai mythe de la culture moderne' (I, 170).

16. Bonnefoy's words refer to Baudelaire; but it is equally clear from his remarks that he is speaking of his own feelings.

17. To be more precise: the splash of red is an exception here, since the sober context may well, by contrast, evoke its sensory image. It is partly *via* this evocation that the emotional and profound connotations come.

18. We may perhaps count line 14 as containing 11 syllables. Bonnefoy writes 'Le vers qui me paraît le plus proche du pentamètre élizabéthain n'a pas de nom et guère d'histoire, c'est le mètre de onze pieds. Quand on le coupe après le sixième, il commence comme une indication de l'idéal, mais c'est pour s'achever, avec les cinq syllabes qui ramassent et laïcisent, comme un fait ouvert à l'avenir, d'autres faits. Ainsi réel et sacré, par son office, se dialectisent ...' (CTS, 350). And indeed the irruption of time and ordinary reality could not be made clearer than by the words 'aujourd'hui, ici'.

19. Needless to say, he would not care for the way I put this.

JACQUES DUPIN

Brian Gill

Born in Privas, a small provincial town in the *massif central*, in 1927, Jacques Dupin has published, over the last thirty years, a number of small collections of poetry, books of art criticism on Miró and Giacometti, as well as numerous articles in contemporary art journals. Since 1963, his poetry has been published almost exclusively by Gallimard, the largest and most prestigious French publishing house, and in 1971 a collected edition containing most of his poetic output appeared in the popular paperback series 'Poésie Gallimard'. His more recent works are *Dehors* (1975), *Ballast* (1976), and *L'Eboulement* (1977). A critical study of the man and his work appeared in Seghers' well-known series 'Poètes d'aujourd'hui' in 1974. If the appearance of this latter monograph, and more especially the publication of his work in the 'Poésie' series can be seen as a manner of consecration for a French poet, the sign that this work is recognized to be of a quality and importance which command its being put before the general reading public, Dupin nevertheless remains little known in France, outside of a relatively narrow circle of writers, critics and students of poetry.

The principal reason for this is not hard to find: Dupin is a difficult poet to read. He is often in fact one of the most uncompromisingly impenetrable poets among a generation which itself is not noted for its easy readability. The following poem, often reproduced in anthologies or critical works as an example of Dupin's poetry, will no doubt serve to illustrate this.

L'Egyptienne

Où tu sombres, la profondeur n'est plus.
Il a suffi que j'emporte ton souffle dans un roseau
Pour qu'une graine au désert éclatât sous mon talon.

Tout est venu d'un coup dont il ne reste rien.
Rien que la marque sur ma porte
Des mains brûlées de l'embaumeur.

(G, 17)[1]

The only immediately intelligible units in a poem such as this are the images. Here, as often, they are strikingly beautiful: 'j'emporte ton souffle dans un roseau', 'qu'une graine au désert éclatât sous mon talon'. What is far less clear is the structure in which these images are set, their relationships one to the other. To begin with, one may, for example, have difficulty following the logic of

Il a suffi que j'emporte ton souffle dans un roseau
Pour qu'une graine au désert éclatât sous mon talon.

On reflection, of course, it will seem quite natural that the life-giving qualities of breath should bring about the sudden sprouting of a seed in the desert, and that the poet should carry this life-breath in his flute. However, the link between these images and the last verse of the poem is still far from clear, and may resist the reader's probing for a considerable length of time. Going beyond this, the overall context within which the poem and its set of images fits is left unspecified: we do not know to whom the 'tu' and the 'ton' refer (again, on reflection, we may surmise that the poet is speaking about poetry), nor do we know what occurrence is referred to by the 'Tout' of the fourth line. Since the meaning of any complex whole comes partly from the relationships among its various parts, partly from the reference those parts have to a domain outside it, and since here neither those relationships nor that reference are immediately apparent, we have difficulty in attributing a meaning to the poem; and unless we happen to be a critic or student of his work, or are irresistibly attracted by the beauty of the images themselves, we may well be tempted to give up.

The obscurity here is not gratuitous, of course, nor is it the result of muddled thinking, or of a desire to write for the happy few who can follow. In Dupin's work, obscurity is one of the unavoidable consequences of a reappraisal of the role language plays in our perception and representation of reality, a reappraisal which is itself part of a larger crisis in values in the modern world. I shall return to the particular role of language in a moment, but first I would like to consider the larger question, which informs much of Dupin's work. The crisis in values, which the modern world is still undergoing, is not a recent phenomenon. Indeed, one of the difficulties faced by a writer like Dupin, as he began his work in the early fifties, was the extent to which previous writers had successfully dealt with the crisis and incorporated it into their work - success being measured here in literary and artistic terms of course. Where others may have felt that they could take advantage of this tradition, either by building on its achievements or by revolting violently against it, Dupin found the success of his predecessors rather an obstacle to be overcome. He would have liked to be able to revolt against them, and build anew, but writers like Rimbaud and Kafka, who saw the world in the same bleak negative terms as himself, had found artistic forms to express their despair which were complete in themselves and could not be built on, except by followers and epigones:

> Nous n'avions pas la ressource d'une prise de position contre ceux en qui nous retrouvions nos traits .... On ne peut édifier que sur des ruines. Réduits à n'être que des prolongements, des simulacres ou des redites, le meilleur parti était le silence.
>
> (C, 93)

Rather than slavishly follow in the footsteps of those who had gone before, Dupin is very severely tempted to say nothing at all, not to write, not to publish. This temptation of silence was overcome of course, by him and by many of his fellow poets who underwent a similar 'crise de l'expression' (P, 159), but that he should have even considered abandoning poetry is a measure of the seriousness of the crisis and the force of his conviction that new artistic forms, and with them a new language, must be found.

In the article 'Comment dire' from which we have quoted above, Dupin claimed as his spiritual brothers Rimbaud and Kafka, linking himself with them in what he terms an 'obsession du noir'. Like them, he finds no order he can believe in, no values he can affirm, he feels alone against a hostile, uncomprehending and essentially alien world in which no place has been provided for him. His is the typically modern anguish of a man for whom God and all the absolutes have shown themselves to be false, and who cannot, and knows he cannot, replace them. As deep-felt expressions of this despair, the poems are built of hard, hostile elements. Rocks, crevasses, lava, slag, ashes, rubble, toads, snakes, birds of prey, bees and beetles share this forsaken land with cactus and poison ivy, while epidemics, explosions, dismemberments, human sacrifices, splitting, burning, bleeding go on around them.

> Nous marchons avec discernement la bouche ensanglantée
>
> c'est le flou de l'auvent qui déjà nous blesse, le feu
> qui nous chasse
>
> si haute est la nuit que nous sommes dans l'ignorance
>
> l'émerveillement comme à la frontière d'un territoire
> excessif
>
> après l'incorporation de la marche à l'étendue
>
> d'un feu désaltérant de souches la cendre est blanche
> à nos pieds
>
> à peine la clarté que laisse la mer en se retirant
>
> (G, 197)

The possibility that love, a woman's touch, might provide solace and some measure of escape from this anguished state is never suggested, although physical desire and union are frequent themes. Woman here is as hard and cold as the world around, she is a thing to be attacked, and split open.

> Même si je m'enfonçais / comme un coin / dans
> l'hostilité de ton ventre / (E, 74)

> Ta nuque, plus bas que la pierre
> Ton corps plus nu
> Que cette table de granit
> [...]
> Amours anfractueuses, revenez,
> Déchirez le corps clairvoyant. (G, 72)

> Ah, qu'il jaillisse et retombe,
> Ton sang cyclopéen,
> Sur nos labours harassés,
> Et nos lèvres mortes! (G, 77)

It may appear from the examples given thus far that Dupin overcame the temptation not to write, only to fill his pages with cries of unrelieved gloom. A very cursory reading of some of his books might also give this impression. There appears indeed to be little hope, little to look forward to, 'à peine la clarté que laisse la mer en se retirant'. In his article 'Comment dire', Dupin compares his own despair with that of the previous generation of poets. They, he says, had lived through the 'Belle époque' at the beginning of the century, when Paris was the gleaming and prosperous centre of the progress-happy civilized world. Their anguish, forced on them by two world wars and the collapse of everything they believed in, was coloured by memories of this period and the inevitable hope of its return:

> Fait de trous et de bosses, ... le *désespoir* de nos aînés n'exprime qu'une oscillation désordonnée entre deux âges d'or également vains. (C, 94)

Dupin's generation, having known no golden age, is attracted by no such hopes, no illusions:

> Notre désespoir [...] est ironique et tranquille, sûr de soi, parce que conscient de reposer sur la base vivifiante et vraie du vide. (C, 94)

Dupin's anguish is more complete and more permanent than that of his predecessors: his tunnel has no light at the other end because it has no end; the tunnel is our lot, and we must live in it. However, if this explains the darker tone of this poetry, the gloom referred to earlier, it will not preclude glimmers of hope, nor a certain, if severely limited success in making the despair livable, finding cracks in its surface, scents of summer on a steep mountainside. Almost every poem contains some positive striving and achievement, some affirmation of a dearly won joy, a joy which may appear pale and wan at first, especially compared to the often buoyant, even exultant celebrations of poets such as Eluard or Perse, Ponge or Char, but which, placed in its setting of general hostility and despair, shines out as a genuine victory over anguish and pain:

> Cette chose nue, introuvable et paralysante, sa mort ne m'a rien coûté. De son bannissement, de son agonie perpétuée, je tire un bonheur faillible, des lèvres durcies au feu, et la chance d'un plus haut voyage. (G, 32)

> Ici, un lieu habitable à cet instant à cause d'une imperceptible fracture, de l'infime intervalle qui mesure ma liberté de mouvement et de don (G, 133)

One of the most perfectly realised examples of Dupin's capacity to 'élire domicile au coeur de l'entr'acte' (G, 28), to build a whole existence on the slightest hint of a break in the hostile surface of things, is this splendid poem entitled 'Le prisonnier':

> Terre mal étreinte, terre aride,
> Je partage avec toi l'eau glacée de la jarre,
> L'air de la grille et le grabat.
> Seul le chant insurgé
> S'alourdit encore de tes gerbes,
> Le chant qui est à soi-même sa faux.
>
> Par une brèche dans le mur,
> La rosée d'une seule branche
> Nous rendra tout l'espace vivant,
>
> Etoiles,
> Si vous tirez à l'autre bout. (G, 48)

This sort of mitigated, yet magnificent victory over despair is matched by the victories Dupin achieves over the failings of language itself. Just as he wrests value out of the ruin of all values, so he succeeds in infusing new meaning into the dead wood of language. And here, as there, the victory is tiny, splendid, precarious. Language is the most subtle and powerful instrument at our disposal for filtering and fixing our perceptions of reality. It is, however, an inadequate, finite instrument; it proceeds by abstraction, classification and analysis and it necessarily dessicates and impoverishes, reducing what we perceive to a mere shadow of its real being. Language is not, as was often supposed, a simple calque of reality, such that the representation of that reality by the poet would simply be a matter of choosing the right words and combining them in the right way. Language is much poorer than the reality it seeks to represent; besides, it has a structure of its own which does not by any means necessarily mirror the structures of the world and can therefore only present us with a distorted or arbitrary image. What this means, of course, is that man is irremediably divorced from the world of objects, separated from them by his language filter, unable to see them as they really are. The poet, like any artist, seeks to go beyond the filter, to reach 'absolute reality' in a way which Dupin has most perceptively discussed in his essay on Giacometti:

> Giacometti doit immédiatement saisir et exprimer le tout de l'objet qu'il représente .... Giacometti ne peut nous proposer que l'ébauche d'une entreprise inaccomplie, infinie. Un reflet, une approximation du réel - de ce réel absolu qui le hante - et qu'il poursuit avec une sorte de fureur amoureuse ou homicide. (R, 112-113)

And, Dupin adds, the pursuit of this absolute reality is not a dream:

> Il le poursuit et il s'en approche. Que le terme soit inaccessible n'exclut pas en effet la possibilité d'un progrès. (R, 113)

If, then, the impossibility of the poet's task leads Dupin to the crumbling brink of a temptation to abandon it and be reduced to silence, the possibility of making progress is what allows him, indeed forces him, to continue, however small the victory he foresees, however faint the hope, however frequent the disappointments. Like Giacometti, Dupin seeks to reach a deeper, recessed and, it would seem at times, continually receding reality. And like him, the best he can hope for is to catch a glimpse of it, make a furtive approach and scurry away with a brand of burning wood:

> J'ai cru rejoindre par instants une réalité plus profonde comme un fleuve la mer, occuper un lieu, du moins y accéder de manière furtive, y laisser une empreinte, y voler un tison, un lieu où l'opacité du monde semblait s'ouvrir au ruissellement confondu de la parole, de la lumière et du sang. J'ai cru traverser vivant, les yeux ouverts, le noeud dont je naissais. Une souffrance morne et tolérable, un confort étouffant se trouvaient d'un coup abolis, et justifiés, par l'illumination fixe de quelques mots inespérément accordés. (G, 134)

Occasionally, therefore, words will come together, perhaps hesitantly but more usually in a violent, jarring movement, but in such a way that some deeper meaning is released, reality is somehow split open, its substance penetrated, its inner core of light briefly attained. But, let us make no mistake, for Dupin such occurrences are rare, 'inespérés', and cannot be controlled or made to happen at will. Any attempt to make permanent contact, to systematize our perceptions in verbal constructs is illusory: in Dupin's poetic optic 'le réel absolu' is only accessible in flashes of insight.

Systematization, construction, even the joining together of simple elements become, then, in this context, negative concepts - concepts which take us further and further away from the reality we yearn to penetrate:

> l'unité de chaque séquence est la dent pourrie
> de la mort en chaque bouche,
>
> dont on aurait le nerf, infecté,
> et la douleur, anachronique, insomniaque,
>
> pour qu'il hurle, dehors, de l'autre côté
> du mur, sur l'autre versant, clair, de la nuit
>
> [...]
>
> tout agencement de mots est politique,
> est vacant, glacé,
> appelle une lecture politique, est vacant

> ou prisonnier de la contradiction qu'il enferme,
> lié aux catégories, transits, pivots, [...]
> (B, 9-10)

The poet's task thus becomes for Dupin the paradoxical one of setting individual words into solid ground, like posts, each firm and good, but without building any sort of fence, without indicating occupation, property, fixity.

> Ficher en terre ferme un pieu, un second pieu, à l'infini le même pieu, sans que se dresse la moindre palissade - à quoi se réduit et par quoi recommence toute entreprise d'édifier.
> (G, 144)

The only sure way to advance, to approach reality, to 'capture energy', is through fragmented perceptions, through brilliant flashes of a flickering vision, through a poetic practice indeed somewhat reminiscent of Char's own *poétique de l'éclair:*

> l'énergie que je peux capter, produire, jaillit, au contraire, de la fragmentation, de la teneur de rapports fragmentaires, (D, 110)

> Il n'y a pas d'autre recours sur terre que la parole en éclats ... (E, 116)

Since the breakthrough can only be achieved through fragmentation, the individual word, in its pristine, uncombined form, outside the text, becomes a free, positive, lifegiving element of poetic construction:

> à bout de forces une parole nue (G, 118)

> En leur lieu, leur vacance ... et précédant la tumultueuse insertion dans le texte, la migration artérielle des signes. (D, 29)

> nous sommes le non-lieu et le non-objet d'une gravitation de signes insensés. (D, 27)

Correspondingly, the finished poem, the text, the book, are felt to be too fixed, too structured, incapable of holding out any hope of a breakthrough. They are thus seen as dead things, traps, fossils:

l'horizon fossilisé d'un livre (D, 14)

la chiennerie du papier (B, 3)

Tu ne m'échapperas pas, dit le livre ... tu es condamné
à errer entre les lignes, à ne respirer que ta propre
odeur, labyrinthique. (G, 140)

This feeling that a book is a dead thing, closed, fossilized, asleep, imprisoning, may well account for Dupin's tendency to adopt progressively a series of measures whose effect is to open up the book and liberate the poems from their closed, perfect forms. There is, already in *L'Embrasure*, the abandonment of individual titles which consecrate the status of finished object, and there is the widespread use of *points de suspension*, a characteristic way of leaving a sentence, or rather its meaning, open, of suggesting an unspecified further development or comment:

A la place du coeur
Tu ne heurteras, mon amour, que le luisant d'un soc
Et la nuit grandissante ... (G, 46)

There is, in addition, the abandonment of punctuation, from *L'Onglée* on, apart from the occasional comma, and including, of course, the final period, with its disproportionate power of closing the poem in on itself. And there are techniques involving the 'airing' of texts by leaving parts of lines blank:

mais la table sur laquelle ton corps   se casse
est de pierre, est immense   est torride
     est battue   par un vent qui ne faiblit pas
(D, 57):

The creation, without separation into individual poems, of a continuous linguistic flux, as in *Ballast* or whole sections of *Dehors*; and the use of virgules to break up speech into smaller units which acquire thereby a sort of added freedom, as in 'Malévitch' and, most extensively so far, in *L'Eboulement:*

> Garde-toi de lui montrer qui tu es / l'inconnue
> que tu es devenue pour lui / cette oscillation
> entre fleur et fruit / ce trait de rosée entre
> l'une et l'autre ... (E, 17)

By all such means, Dupin gnaws away at the book's solid resistance and closure, freeing, aerating, opening up the poems. Perhaps a book will always be, in the final analysis, that closed dead object he abhors, but as with Giacometti, knowing this does not prevent Dupin from working towards a change, from exploring language's potential for 'progress'.

The poet's hope, then, is to attain some fleeting glimpse of 'absolute reality', beyond the banality of conventional perceptions and configurations which necessarily deform it. Any such glimpse remains, however, just a glimpse. It cannot be fixed, it is not the simple product of carefully composed sequences of words, it does not last the whole poem through, it is a sudden, inexplicable flash of illumination which the poem secretes:

> Entre la diane du poème et son tarissement
>
> par une brèche ouverte
> dans le flanc tigré de la montagne
>
> elle jaillit, l'amande du feu (G, 129)

But, if this is so, how, then, does the poet, conscious of the impossibility of his task, set about his search for illumination, for the 'amande du feu'?

Well, to begin with, Dupin does not write in an initial act of will, of individual volition, and with a specific goal in mind. He writes in response to an 'arachnéenne sollicitation' (G, 83), to an 'injonction silencieuse' (G, 133); he is 'condemned' (G, 150) to write. So far from having a particular message to bring, he does not even know why, or for whom he writes:

> Arachnéenne sollicitation qui menez de ténèbre en ténèbre
> ma faux jusqu'à l'orée du cri, ce noeud qui vante la récolte,
> dites-moi pour qui brilleront ma sueur et mes larmes, toute
> une nuit, sur cette gerbe hostile, près de la lampe refroidie.
> (G, 83)

Pushed on by external forces, he will discover what he seeks only by advancing, by writing. Insight for Dupin comes from his interaction with language, it cannot precede it:

> Il m'est interdit de m'arrêter pour voir. Comme si j'étais condamné à voir en marchant. En parlant. A voir ce dont je parle et à parler justement parce que je ne vois pas. Donc à donner à voir ce que je ne vois pas, ce qu'il m'est interdit de voir. Et que le langage en se déployant heurte et découvre. (G, 139)

The recognition of the importance of language in determining the shape and even the content of literary constructs, and especially poems, is not of course entirely new. That it had some influence has always been apparent, at least to poets. The surrealists, ever attentive to what was outside their own rational conscious control, have, of course, been largely responsible for drawing attention to the creative power of words, a power much greater than had previously been imagined or allowed. Unlike the surrealists, however, Dupin does not abandon himself to words, to chance and automaticity: he maintains on the contrary very careful control. This does not prevent him, however, from acknowledging and using that independent creative power of language which the surrealists set free and legitimized. For language has predetermined structures and laws over which the poet has little or no control. Words set next to each other, combined in certain ways, will suddenly produce, in ways which defy rational explanation, new and unexpectedly beautiful images and insights which the poet, though he can cultivate them, cannot entirely predict or control. Indeed, as Dupin is fully aware, the poet may set out with one idea, and find his language taking over, imposing something quite different:

> En effet, tous les mots nous abusent. Mais il arrive que la chaîne discontinue de ce qu'ils projettent et de ce qu'il retiennent laisse surgir le corps ruisselant et le visage éclairé d'une réalité tout autre que celle qu'on avait poursuivie et piégée dans la nuit. (G, 165)

That the insights contained in the poems should be so heavily determined by language itself should come as no surprise to readers familiar with the work of Wittgenstein, Whorff or Chomsky on the way our language determines the ways in which we think, and conceive of reality. Indeed, in describing the poet's work, Dupin is in fact describing processes that occur in every one of us when we begin to think or express ourselves, once conventional figures of language and expression are left behind.

The form of the poem, like the content, is worked out as the poet advances. There is no preconceived notion of how it should be constructed, either metrically, or as to the overall shape, the number of lines, verses, the relationships among the various parts: all this too is determined in the act of writing itself:

> De cet édifice hors de vue, et inimaginable, j'élimine les matériaux incompatibles avec sa nature, avec son dessin. Incapable d'en esquisser les lignes ou d'en supputer la hauteur, j'arpente le sol de sa base, j'attends de l'écriture seule qu'elle en indique l'orientation et le tracé, je pèse et j'interroge de la main les pierres avancées, je saisis et je rejette avec l'obscur instinct de la bête avertie des nourritures qui lui sont néfastes. (G, 144)

As this text makes clear, the whole process is one of inspecting the various possibilities, words and their combinations, rejecting those which instinct tells him will not do, and accepting the others. It is a negative way of building, but perhaps it is the only one we have left: 'je n'étais peut-être pas sûr de ce qui m'intéressait réellement', says Camus' Outsider, 'mais j'étais tout à fait sûr de ce qui ne m' intéressait pas'.

If the way in which I have chosen to discuss Dupin's reaction to the 'crise de l'expression' shows something of a structuralist bias, I would certainly not intend to project this bias on to Dupin himself, or suggest that his poetry can be reduced to a rather simplistic if richly textured exposition of current linguistic and epistemological research. As will already have become apparent from the poems I have quoted, the insights which poetry may be shaped to provide are not primarily intellectual in nature. They are rather flashes of almost mystical illumination, 'l'illumination fixe de quelques mots inespérément accordés'. Often, as here, the illumination seems to be a direct result of the poet's work on language, so that he will speak of 'la parole irradiante' (G, 147) and of the 'rayonnement d'énergie silencieuse' (D, 32) of the poem, or see words as a means to achieve and maintain a precarious level of heightened existence:

> Ouverte en peu de mots,
> comme par un remous, dans quelque mur,
> une embrasure, pas même une fenêtre
>
> pour maintenir à bout de bras
> cette contrée de nuit où le chemin se perd,
>
> à bout de forces une parole nue (G, 118)

Often, too, this process seems reversed, and it is the reality itself which seeks expression through words:

> Entendre, ou sentir ... ce qui gronde dans le sous-sol,
> sous la feuille déchirée, sous nos pas. Et voudrait
> s'élever - s'écrire. Et attire l'écriture, lui injecte
> son intensité, son incohérence ... (D, 26)

By whatever means and processes make themselves available, the poet seeks, in effect, to attain to a special visionary state, a mode of perception or being which is not simply a cognitive experience but one in which his whole being participates, and which takes him to a deeper level of reality:

> j'attendais ici, par calcul, fourberie ou désir, que s'ouvre
> dans le réel un espace irréductible, une jouissance équilibrée,
> plus haute que la pleine mer, dont l'irruption, la fraîcheur ...
> (D, 110)

> ... un lieu où l'opacité du monde semblait s'ouvrir au
> ruissellement confondu de la parole, de la lumière et du
> sang. (G, 134)

The price for this intermittent privileged access is high, however. For the poetic metamorphosis involves, for Dupin, not only creation, but destruction, not only the attainment of a new vision, but the complete ruin of the old. In order for the poet to reach the absolute, he must first destroy himself, and he advances fully conscious of this sacrifice: 'le poète marche à sa perte entière, d'un pied sûr' (G, 135). Everything, in fact, must be consumed, not just the poet, but all his materials, all that he has been given:

> Tout nous est donné, mais pour être forcé, pour être entamé, en quelque façon pour être détruit, - et nous détruire. (G, 146)

Moreover, in Dupin's poetic equation, poetry itself cannot escape:

> Expérience sans mesure, excédante, inexpiable, la poésie ne comble pas mais au contraire approfondit toujours davantage le manque et le tourment qui la suscitent. Et ce n'est pas pour qu'elle triomphe, mais pour qu'elle s'abîme avec lui, avant de consommer un divorce fécond, que le poète marche à sa perte entière, d'un pied sûr. (G, 135)

The violence and destruction characterizing Dupin's poetry are not, therefore, simply expressions of deep despair resulting from man's feeling of alienation from the world around him. They are also intimately linked to the poetic process itself, which is nothing but a succession of violent acts:

> L'acte d'écrire comme rupture, et engagement cruel de l'esprit, et du corps, dans une succession nécessaire de ruptures, de dérives, d'embrasements. (G, 146)

For Jacques Dupin poetry is a constant struggle, where no victories can be permanent, no place secure, where the only hope can be and must be to continue, and to advance, and to leave behind but a trace.

> Tout est venu d'un coup dont il ne reste rien.
> Rien que la marque sur ma porte
> Des mains brûlées de l'embaumeur
>
> (G, 17)

NOTES

1. The following abbreviations are used: C: 'Comment dire?' *Empédocle*, 2 (1949), 93-95; P: Review of 'Francis Ponge: *L'Araignée*, Aubier, éditeur', Cahiers d'Art (1953), 159-160; G: *L'Embrasure*, précédé de *Gravir*, Paris: Gallimard, 1971; R: 'Alberto Giacometti, textes pour une approche', Georges Raillard, *Jacques Dupin*, Paris, Seghers, 1974, 108-114; D: *Dehors*, Paris: Gallimard, 1975; B: *Ballast*, Paris: Le Collet de Buffle, 1976; E: *L'Eboulement*, Paris: Editions Galilée, 1977; *Ballast* is not paginated; my page numbers begin with the title page. *L' Eboulement* is a play, albeit an extremely poetic one. Little has been written on Dupin's poetry, apart from Georges Raillard's essay, 'L'injonction maîtresse de Jacques Dupin', included in the volume quoted above (R), pp. 5-83, and the following articles: Jean-Pierre Richard, 'Jacques Dupin', *Onze études sur la poésie moderne*, Paris: Seuil, 1964, pp. 277-295; P. Chappuis, 'Jaillissement et mensonge du poème', *Critique*, XXVII, No. 289 (June, 1971), 520-531; R.W. Greene, 'André du Bouchet and Jacques Dupin, Poets of *L'Ephémère'*, *French Forum*, I, 1 (Jan. 1976), 49-67; Roger Cardinal, 'Jacques Dupin', *Sensibility and Creation, Studies in Twentieth Century French Poetry*, London: Croom Helm, 1977, pp. 220-240.

MUSING: MICHEL DEGUY'S LANGUAGE AS MASK AND MATRIX

Mary Ann Caws

It need scarcely be emphasized here that in the contemporary scheme of things, the concerns of poetry merge with what used to be more strictly the concerns of theory - that poetic language as such not only depends, in its present state, on the theoretical attitude of the poet and reader but can actually be said in a few cases to constitute them. We have taken the point of view that, since the problems posed by and the solutions yielded by poetic experiment in the most continuous if loosest sense are usually visible - sometimes audible, if you will - in the *theory* and always at least implicit in it, the best and most honest starting point is the one at which the two sorts of conerns are quite *plainly* inextricable one from the other.

But we would not overlook chronology in this particular case, quite particular indeed - thus the hybrid nature of the discussion, ranging from technique to theme, from the problematics of and the nostalgia for language as muse, to the cracking of the linguistic mask. Not for nothing does Deguy so carefully present himself in his exact relation to the surrealist endeavour as he sees it in retrospect (see the interview in *La Quinzaine littéraire* of a few years ago). For instance, the technique of obvious apposition and the celebration of the linguistic joining of elements sometimes finds itself in opposition to that of the revealed coincidence of objects: the marvelling at the linguistic tool brings up questions of dialectics as well as those of poetics.

In short, the continuity of Michel Deguy's own concern for poetic *Actes* - speech acts of the first order - is our primary concern. Such a decentering of the initial question posed may help us locate the truest centre.

> Comment être *ensemble*. Ecrire est difficile - et rare. Parler est difficile - et rare ... Notre époque, de quoi a-t-elle besoin? De quelle ouverture?
> (F, 198)[1]

Amid the recent discussions of whether or not the poem alludes to anything outside itself, what it represents or whether it represents only itself ('the poem of the poem', as Deguy phrases it), Michel Deguy is responsible for one of the major contemporary investigations in the fields of poetics, linguistics, and philosophy. He is particularly interesting, in the context of a study of what we might call the contemporary crisis in poetry, for his own evolution from the poet of the haunting landscape (*Poèmes de la presqu'île*) to texts of greater and greater fragmentation and - I think it plain - of greater unrest.

What interests me here, though, is not so much Deguy's exterior evolution, as a sort of interior haunting not easily definable, but which appears as one of the clearest manifestations of this *inquiétude poétique*, taken in the largest sense. As often happens with poets and critics, my final conclusion will most likely not be his - I have arranged the first part of the discussion in the general order of his writing, but my second part returns to earlier volumes, to offer one of the many possible forms of inner resolution. Now the critic is presumably forgiven much, even his misinterpretations: may it be so.

The critic or in fact any reader might indeed be bothered or, more properly, intrigued, by what seems to be an increasingly glittering cover spread across Deguy's texts, and the proliferation of exterior forms, simultaneous with and not always hiding an intense lyricism. Take, for example, some of the parts of his *Tombeau de Du Bellay*, where affection and ostentation, the playful, the philosophic and the profound mingle in a sort of intellectual dance. Might this cover be called a mask? From Deguy's own point of view, the mask - related to the *masque* - reveals the thought as one might develop a picture in a dark room.

> Les textes sont des 'compositions'; donc des 'masques'; soit; un masque est jeté sur le non-visible pour le faire apparaître, le configurer. Distinguons le masque qui camoufle (par exemple: *la cigarette*, qui est le dernier masque occidental), et le masque-temple qui laisse paraître.[2]

For while the time seems excessively complex ('Rien ne fut net dans nos jours ... Nulle assise ...' (OD, 55)), the poet has obviously chosen language as his way of self-discovering, of entering into the dance: 'Je me fraye passage à coup de mots' (F, 93).

The signals of what matters, matter - whether the object is beyond or within the text. But it is a question of recognition:

> Comment appellerons-nous ce qui donne le ton? La poésie comme l'amour risque tout sur des signes.
> (OD, 38)

How to tell one tone from the next, one sign from another - is this to be what matters in poetry, of wider concern than poetics, and touching the whole of language: the play of the mask and the *masque* may miss the essential? I think not: in fact this may be one of the more privileged places for observing the poet's march and his *démarche*, through the text as it unrolls, and its landscape of signs and customs, costume and form.

I. Fields and Signals

We might well open this passage with the question posed already by the poet: 'Quels signes?' (FC, 7). When the plural form is changed into the singular, the signs into the sign, then the closure is made inside and even against the progress of the poet on his walk about his own peninsula, the tone and the traces of these interrogations remaining - and heavily stressed - throughout all the texts:

> Quel signe nous fait le champ, la chose bien close?
> (FC, 34)

And in the fields, this pursuit of the object seeming to signal itself, from far or from nearby, urges us to the limits of our own comprehension and our judgement. Could there be false signs? The question will return, but now, silence falls in the centre of being itself, as if one were to await some special advent:

> L'idée tremble très loin au bord extrême de la conscience, insaisissable. Alors tout se tait ... Est-ce le vrai qui s'annonce dans les ramures?
> ...
> Le guetteur assourdi se tient au bord de soi.
>
> (FC, 49)

But the poet has the habit of remaining 'muet devant l'augure des envols' (FC, 32), whether the flight be annunciatory or not, and will not have words for each question. This lack of speech is, paradoxically, often the source for the greatest depth of feeling. Here the question by which this volume closes bears witness to the abundance buried within. 'Promenades en vue de quoi?' - why indeed these walks, and why watch the walker? But the paths are really 'de soi-même, vers soi-même, en soi-même ...'

The sower at noontime, bringing the future already in seed, sows only fragments. The interruptions by which Deguy's work is marked are themselves productive, by their inequalities - the scansion of a breath, but also of a cultivation destined to bear:

> Il
> Aux sillons gelés des villes
> Va
> Sans semence à semer que les yeux
> Il
> Aux jachères d'asphalte
> S'émiette
>
> (FC, 90)

From the earth as from the angle, the poet brings forth possible perspectives, even if by this process of self-fragmentation. From each site, he extracts 'the temple it contains' (FC, 111), believing in depth as he does in suffering: for him, as for Heidegger, 'Pain is the gift of depth reigning in each presence', and the temple is our only, and only architectural, remnant of soul. So while it is 'le jour infiniment sur la grand-place' (FC, 57), it is also toward the interior that the poet will move, and by his depth that his progress and his early withdrawal will be judged. From an initial satisfaction - 'C'est bien ainsi' - the movement is in the direction of a doubt: 'Non, ça n'a pas été très bien; jamais assez recueillis' (FC, 146).

II. Self-Discovery and Haunting

La poésie se joue là où
le désir de l'intervalle,
du disposer, se fait
entendre ...
(TDB, 144)

Now the exchange between out and in, between mask and matter, is itself the haunting place of poetry. Deguy's work on the threshold, on the *lisière* and *charnière,* is essential to our concern here.

In accordance with the kind of vocabulary we must use in speaking of Deguy's work, I would like to present his poems and essays as situated on the boundary of a boundary, *in the place of difference.*

Un poème nous hante qui soit l'hôte des différences
(PP, 81)

The poem bridges and yet holds apart: a 'poésie passerelle'. The poet looks in order to distinguish by means of his 'yeux séparateurs' (PP, 112). In the same he finds what is other, beneath its surface; this difference opens the way to the poem, he says: 'cet écart ouvre le chant' (PP, 121).

Deguy would have us begin with the whole, available in its improbable and extreme multiplicity: 'L'invraisemblable, l'excessive averse des signes' (PP, 114). He would have us find our value in the separate and singular instant, as it shows up, dissimilar, against all the elements on which it borders. Successive instants, neighbouring fields of perception, are distinct from each other, as distinct as the train from the landscape through which it rushes, another 'lisière'. And one might say that poetry thus becomes the ceaseless acknowledging of the different in the near.

Compare, in Deguy's important essay, 'Une Pratique de la poésie', his discussion of the absence never absent, of the lack not lacking, of the temptation toward 'cette vacation', or the space receding, whose concealment haunts all 'boundaries, thresholds; dividing lines; cracks; pleats ...'

Difference takes precedence over the identical, as in linguistics, but similarly, as in most contemporary French poetry, the accident and the irregular dominate the regular. Whereas consolation was formerly given by the endless patience of the same (now that the centre does not hold, the same also disappears), now difference and accident carry the weight of self-discovery: 'Laisse-moi. Je me rassemble dans la fuite, trouve mon lieu dans l'accident ...' (PP, 97). We are continually torn between interior and exterior or then stretched beyond our normal categorical limitations:

> De pierre et de velours, la maison donnait
> d'habiter le dehors, imminent espace du dedans
>
> ...
>
> Croissance
> Le jardin devenait natal.
>
> (PP, 78)

And, on the other hand, on the subject of exits, that is, what one would ordinarily think of as outside, it haunts Deguy also, but as if it had been transferred to the inside:

> il n'y a de *sortie* que dans le livre ... qui parle de 'sorties', que le lecteur lit comme fiction *et* réalistement, en tant que sorties réelles relatées; comme si le dehors devait passer au dedans, mais un dedans non psychique, qui est celui de l'espace de fiction ou conte livresque, pour pouvoir être projeté et intenté comme dehors ... La différence entre le livre et la

> vie passe par le livre, s'instruit dans le livre, s'y élabore, et repasse à la vie: jeu de Quichotte.[3]

Now of course Deguy, in speaking of Cervantes, is not speaking of him only, or of that book above all others. Like the remarks, previously quoted about the mask, this question of the 'interior landscape'[4] may be seen as omnipresent in the concerns of a number of contemporary poets.

'J'écris de ce lieu-ci' (PP, 115). Above all the threshold is chosen as this place,[5] as the place for the passage of the poem. And as for the space between - of course we think of Hölderlin's *entredeux* as the French translation phrases it, of that time between day and night, of the infinitely extensible and contractile space in such an image as the communicating vessels - its conception is responsible for a good part of the poetics of Deguy, responsible for that fascination with the *lisière* and *charnière*.[6] That is, it seems to me that the feeling comes before the theory, and replaces in some sense the early peninsular landscape of Brittany by its own more ambiguous realm. This conception haunts Deguy also, or so it seems: in the word 'haunting' itself, the basic psychoanalytic fascination breaks the surface, and is - as will be obvious - closely related to the concept of the *between*:

> 'd'un côté' la zone de la langue en ébullition, le 'dictionnaire' mobilisable d'une diction, le vivier frémissant de syntagmes ou phrases en état de fusion et d'inchoation, imaginairement 'dans la tête'; et de l'autre: la profuse confusion du visible, en réserve, d'où montent pour (ap)paraître les figurants réels et fugaces, la frise des choses incontestables éphémères, gnomons muets, ombres ensoleillées, bientôt disparaissant: et à leurs confins, à leur zone irréelle de contact, comme la surface où leur indivision se reconstitue, se commémore, le 'sujet' où se prononce, se contracte leur alliance, se scelle en mots, parfois c'est tout un 'poème', leur convention: choses en leurs mots, (mots qui ne sont pas plus à elles qu'à d'autres) é-mot-ionnées, et mots en (leurs) choses, coalescence coincidence labile *et* pérenne, qui trouve lieu à la faveur de 'moi' l' interposé lieu de transit et de traduction ...[7]

If I have quoted at such length, it is because it seems to me essential to show the way in which the conceptions mix and recur, in the place of transit and of difference, which is to say, the poem. If we read Deguy for any length of time, it is impossible not to perceive the returning to places and their betweens as a chosen, paradoxical alterity and alteration of tone challenging the obsession of the same. For Michel Deguy will never be a singer of the same: style and subject change, and he remains the host - and also the guest - of differences, in a different place, perceiving differently and often alone:

> J'ai attendu, comme un amant aux champs prend rendez-vous sous le pommier rigide ... mon mal, mon mal, transcendance qui irrompt ...
>
> (PP, 40)

and the plaint continues, page after page here, in a litanic sadness which will not reappear so openly in the later and 'harder' works:

> Je ne sais plus le nom des arbres
> ...
> Je ne sais plus le nom des arbres
> ...
> Je: noeud le plus douloureux d'être
>
> (PP, 42-3)

and then the farewell, keeping open a page to itself: only 'Adieu' (PP, 45) before the tired poem of waiting, the windowpane here devoid - or so it would seem in this reading - of any symbolic sense.

> Poème au bruit de main lasse sur la vitre obstinée.
> ...
> Poème au bruit de main lasse sur la vitre obstinée.
> ...
> Poème au bruit de main lasse sur la vitre obstinée.
>
> (PP, 46-51)

So that the text in all its presence is still made of this persisting tissue of absence, and that 'writing is writing in spite of everything': 'Ecrire, c'est écrire malgré tout' (PP, 135).

Nor is the difference so clearly felt always a disjunction: if poetry seizes the tempo of the world, the plenitude of signs, this heart of things in this universe still 'harboring depth', bears its own witness. The question is again posed to the poet as to the reader: 'Que faites-vous de ces témoignages erratiques, absolus ...' (PP, 35).

And how might we answer? the interrogative tone so frequent in these first poems places on one level that meditation on meaning and the crescence of things, which in its brusqueness, leads to more questions:

> Détournement des choses, pour où?
>
> (PP, 50)
>
> La feuille s'oriente-t-elle dans la mêlée? Est-ce
> que quelque chose grandit?
>
> (PP, 66)

Near anguish, this interrogative grill places itself upon the text, as if this framing were to correspond to the obstinate pane of glass. And the absence of which we become aware there, leaves in spite of everything a gap in the whole of the collection, at its very centre, in spite of all the accumulation of signs and of landscapes against which the essential voice of the poet develops itself, but besides, also, the daily perception of the most mundane details, pictured now in their understatement: 'l'ensemble resplendit; tout l'accroissement, c'était pour que parût le val' (PP, 8).

And this might well be the centre: 'Un poème nous hante ... O poème à la contenance de ce qui couve et s'effeuille ... Poème de l' inénarrable patience du poète très pauvre avec son monde inépuisable ...' (PP, 81-2). And the elementary exchanges between actions - going forward and remaining, touching or seeing, like the exchanges of landscapes: earth and sky, inside and out - make up the secret vision and the sufficient place:

> Place au secret enfin
> Pour accueillir les prémices de l'échange
>
> (PP, 198)

Writing of the land he loves is, says Deguy, the act of birth.

III. Muse and Reader

The volume *Biefs* is, as the poet states at the beginning of another collection, turned 'vers un autre versant' (PP, 8). The new space invented here, this depth in itself, as it is called, and this path of theatre (stated in capital letters) and of song, both lead to the sure place of poetry: much wind has tried the place, but it suffices, this place from which the poet speaks:

> Pourtant me suffit ce lieu.
>
> (B, 31)

Now the poet's profile gains in conviction and in distinction:

> Et lui aussi se levant tôt ... lui aussi s'engageait
> dans la journée vaste comme l'Empire ... homme dur comme
> une bille de lichen ou comme un fromage; et dans le coeur
> pourtant la parole le fend
>
> (B, 91, 99)

Here the walking takes on a different pace, and the poetry a different tone.

But in this new space calling into account the *scienza nuova*, will the mask persist as a sign? Or will it join with an earlier muse:

> J'appelle *muse* la bascule du ciel, le vent transbordeur à
> son gré de nos vues ...
> J'appelle *muse* la jonglerie de lune et de soleil ...
> *Muse* le voyage moral où les rêves sont de jour et le courage
> croissant dans le dos, l'exactitude poétique de la terre qui
> passe par la tête ...
> *Muse* que la montée soit montée dans le corps et la descente
> descente dans le corps, *muse* derechef l'âme étrange et les
> conditions ...
> J'appelle *muse* la liberté soucieuse de l'espace libre.
>
> (A, 121)

This brief essay can be taken as a manifesto in favour of that sort of muse: the depth found within the self at the limit of the threshold, where muse and mask can finally be seen as not so different, the latter revealing - as Deguy himself points out - what lay beneath it.

> C'est le temps du monde fini pour la consience: il lui faut inventer un nouvel espace, se frayer profondeur au-dedans d'elle-même.
>
> (B, 80)

IV. Question in Lieu of Resolution

> *... le bouleversement a déjà eu lieu*
> *n'a jamais eu lieu lent très lent*
> *et au-dehors le vent ruisselle le*
> *temps même* (B, 18)

But of course the question remains as to the viability of our one reading and as to the nature of Deguy's own poetics. The poet is seen from the side, only, by his own choice, we must suppose:

> Le poète de profil
> Le poète à l'équerre de corps et d'ombre sur les seuils
> ...
> Quand il revient parmi nous dans la transparence
> d'hiver où les choses sont des lignes
>
> (OD, 11-12)

The poet has left the signs too, open, and gaping, in all the transparency of his poetics, which never quite match the practice, never quite explain the alternations from one tone to the other ... The reader, needed though he be, risks sliding on the surface. The question of mask and muse returns to haunt him, as it does Deguy himself, and perhaps many other poets of the post-structuralist generation. In all the self-portraits found in the poetry of Deguy, contraries clash and the surface itself is troubled.

Within the major texts, or rather our re-reading of their evolution, the oppositions king/ruin, loneliness/love are more and more keenly felt, until a sort of interior friendship - like the interior horizon Deguy speaks of - becomes or seems to become manifest, concerning as it does people and things, 'vieillards devenus poètes au soleil' (OD, 27) and the sea, a wall, some wine, and a few rocks. Finally the face of the poet is evident behind the mask of the words, a mask which, as we now know, is meant also to reveal:

> Qui sont-ils ce masque ce moulage d'homme
> Dont le poème soupçonne la genèse sur son silence
> Paraître fut mourir ...
>
> (OD, 82)

Here again, 'il est besoin d'un lecteur ...' for the mask to drop and the exposure to cure. The poet on watch is vulnerable:

> Je veille, vous me trouvez silencieux ... Vous me trouvez taciturne, j'attends comme un serviteur d'accueillir ces lignes que vous négligez ... il me faut veiller sur la lampe à l'huile pour l'attendre tard et qu'il me trouve prêt malgré tout à remarquer le signe rapide dont il m'honore; vous êtes sombres parce que vous n'avez pas su ...
>
> (A, 24)

This very responsibility felt and accepted, creates a distance between poet and other, poet and reader, who has not known - perhaps - how to read the fable or the figures which the poem is. If the poet spends his time 'formant la fable qui est en même temps la fable du poème' (F, 99), his song is akin to that of Orpheus, and separates as it would save. All three volumes: *Biefs*, *Oui dire*, and *Figurations* answer in some sense those walks around the *Presqu'île*, those *Fragments* of a former work, and lead to the *Tombeau* which is called that of Du Bellay, but is in fact that of a number of hopes of unity. The brilliant collage of word and work brings the poet back to his boundary, near the *lisière* with which he began, and where our reading took its point of departure.

In résumé, then, the case of Deguy is interesting precisely for its ambivalence - the speed of thought and the underlying disquiet, the surface charm and the uncertainty of the muse. What of the mask, and deception: would the latter be his or ours? And were there, after all, false signs? Did the departure from the early land of poetry lead in another sense, one other than that we have taken? Does the contemporary crisis of poetry bring us back in fact to the wall of a tomb linking past and future, poets dead to poets present, and no more?

> vous êtes sombres parce que vous n'avez pas su ...

What could we have known other than this, or are the words addressed only to the poet's companion? It is the privilege of all readers to take the words of the poet for their own; and in fact, we have not known how to reconcile our own anguished interrogation of signs and the poet's summons, our own awkward words and their nuanced appeal to things visible and sensed. One of Deguy's deepest characteristics is his sudden lack of speech at the gravest of moments or a sudden facility which belies his and our profound discomfort in the face of the *champ poétique* he cultivates, but as it were in passing, as if toward somewhere else. This poetic gesture, unfinished yet, bears rather questions than answers, and is, so far, more concerned with the passing than with its own presence. In its very irresolution, it is of our time, and its discomfort is finally our own.

NOTES

1. The following abbreviations are used throughout: FC: *Fragment du cadastre* (1960); PP: *Poèmes de la presqu'île* (1962); B: *Biefs* (1964); OD: *Oui Dire* (1966); A: *Actes* (1966); F: *Figurations* (1969); P: *Poèmes*, Coll. Poésie (1972); TDB: *Tombeau de Du Bellay* (1972). All works published by Gallimard, Paris. The conclusion drawn in this essay is not quite the same as that in an early one in *Sub-Stance* (1972).

2. Interview with the author of this essay, published in French in *L'Atelier* and in English by *L'Esprit Créateur*. My thanks go to the editors of those journals for permission to reprint the passages concerned here.

3. *Ibid.*

4. My question which prompted these remarks had to do with the notion of an interior landscape, a *paysage intérieur*, which I believed constant in Deguy's early poetry, and for which there was, I thought, some nostalgia in the later work.

5. See my essays on *Le Passage du poème* and *Interrogation of the Threshold.*

6. Elsewhere I have compared these images with Derrida's conception of *brisure*.

7. Interview, *loc. cit.*

DENIS ROCHE

Michael Bishop

Over the past fifteen years the work of Denis Roche has increasingly aroused feelings of pleasurable surprise or, indeed, profound admiration. But it has also provoked, and continues to provoke, feelings of somewhat derisive incomprehension and open hostility. The latter feelings usually stem from the reader's concern upon being confronted with a poetry that seems with growing insistence to refuse all customary critical appellations and criteria either in its own suspected derision of such norms or in the sense that such critical blueprints, oriented as they usually are towards aesthetics, poetic 'consciousness' or some other form of 'discourse', lead necessarily and self-defeatingly to a negative, empty appraisal. To come to this (or any) poetry, however, demanding of it a particular conformity, imagining that it exists (and should exist) as more or less readily digestible fodder, as a substance that may be ultimately if not instantaneously reduced, is, it is arguable, not only to misconstrue the art of writing and the nature of the truly innovative poetic text, but also to unwittingly further undermine the already debatably productive role and function of the reader. To misinterpret or lightly dismiss the significance of the work of Denis Roche is, finally, to risk remaining blind to a crucial stage of the development - and, indeed, perhaps the survival - of poetic language in particular and written language and culture in general.

Without plunging at this point into a full description and discussion of the aims and techniques of Roche's poetic writing, it will be useful to immediately sample the flavour of his texts and observe some of the reasons both for the stumbling irritation and the strange excitement his work is varyingly held to occasion. It is not in fact difficult to put one's finger upon many of the formal features that contribute to the relative impenetrability of Roche's work. The text of his poems is dislocated. Its flow is discontinuous, destructive of anecdotality and causality - to a degree, moreover, that places Roche at a point of maximum distance in the post-naturalist shift away from broadly representational modes of art, language and being. The kind of elliptical symbolic or metaphoric discourse that readers might (in effect they invariably do) wish to haltingly decipher behind the 'surface' elision and compression of, let us say, Mallarmé's *Une dentelle s'abolit*, becomes essentially (in more than one sense of the term, as we shall see) impossible to establish in the case of Roche. The following poem - *énigme* from *Eros énergumène* (cf. EE, 77)[1], in itself a tantalising tongue-in-cheek quasi-Mallarméan pastiche, is a typical, if rather gently mannered example - even if its opening stanza seems to offer a purchase to the groping mind, our grip is rudely pried off by the second stanza:

> Interdit de près que le respect franchi
> Impose insoucieusement qu'il la vît nue
> Que sa splendide échine va, détale sur
> Lui, légèrement comme une personne embarrassée
>
> Pour elle c'est là, suspendue dans notre
> Répartition sur la réalité, parts d'
> Elégance, vers, pastiches de feuillets
> De l'ankylose et du sourire de l'imprimeur
>
> (EE, 87)

Moreover, many of Roche's poems, full of a vocabulary that runs from the colloquial and the mundane to the exotic, the invented and the scatological, are composed of (or engaged in a dialectic with, via title, epigraph and so on) quotations, snippets of real or imaginary conversations, debris and dross of all kinds - a rich (yet poor), a dense (yet empty) magma that sends out its powerful anti-lyrical and anti-metrical rhythms to its point of (anti-) climax. Another poem, the seventh of a series of 'Douze textes' from Roche's 1972 'farewell' - or rather, as he might say, 'rot is hell' - collection *Le Mécrit* gives an even better impression of this and of the final sensation of teeming virulence his work can create:

> 'pick-nick', jura le seigneur livre quand Contn proposa:
> nous avons la cuisine grillée et, portant-le hors des enceintes
> d'ses gonds après, mangeâmes couchés le long des courts dehors
> en se déployant au-dessus d'anacostia: rangs des paquets de
> mers d'enfants d'ordures tout ça le fait comme un projet grillé
> pétant il voit enfin le vrai morceau de phrase de Goethe 'un

> auteur bleu prend réellement la vie un peu plus sérieusement qu'un jaune' vers la mer alors le cavedas (cadenas, canevas, toua-toua!) d'strass, la revue de physique élancée sous le bras endosse l'appelant derrière, met le feu au capot, fouille les rideaux rouges en bordure, enf in il se déchausse pour entrer à son tour dans la mer d' ordure. Cure aiguë.
>
> (LM, 105)

Texts such as this are non-discursive amalgams pervaded by a number of 'energumen' rhythms that stride over the ruptures and suspensions. Roche's poems are, indeed, beset with a paroxystic tearing apart, a wild disfigurement, an apparently irrational and gratuitous automaticity. And yet they are also characterized by means of the very notion and fact of paroxystic rhythm and self-liberating, pulsional movement that all this implies - though this in particular escapes the unsympathetic critic -, by a strange coming together of what is torn apart, a dialectical interplay of textural units, an exemplary, non-arbitrary gesture of artifice which permits fragments to interact, 'produce' and construct, via the parodic, (self-) derisive interpenetration of revolution and convention.

The problems facing the reader of Roche's poems, are, then, from a certain point of view, quite considerable. But, of course, are they not in fact meant to be - though if so, for what reasons precisely? Moreover may such textual difficulties be resolved - and if not just what are we to do with the poem, how are we to react to it, to read it? Whilst answers to questions such as these will certainly be required, we must not at this juncture lose sight of the fact that, if the above and similar poems create a crisis for the reader of Roche, they also clearly reflect an experience of crisis on the part of the poet, whilst constituting simultaneously in themselves a poetic 'solution' to such crisis - and as it were, a passing-on of both crisis and solution. The thrust of this essay will thus be directed initially towards an analysis of the specific nature of the poetic crisis experienced, but will then reorient itself to assess the general aims growing out of this crisis, as well as the precise techniques employed to achieve them. This will leave as our final concern the discussion of Roche's tense but paradoxically salvatory articulation within his work of the forces of death and continuity, rotting and vital energy.

What becomes evident from the earliest stages of Roche's work is a distrust of the traditional language of poetry and a dismay at the use to which poetry is conventionally and moreover still presently put. Poetry that relies heavily upon the visual appeal of its typographical organization and that thus tends towards *lettrisme*, poetry, too, that is intended to reach us largely by virtue of the declamatory potential of its metrical rhythms - such poetry 'n'est qu'une contrefaçon de poésie' (EE, 15). Similarly, and perhaps much more significantly, Roche is vehemently antagonistic to what he calls 'le débordement de bas lyrisme issu du surréalisme, l'exploitation par celui-ci du fantastique et du rêve réitéré (écriture soi-disant non contrôlée) servant d'alibi à une sorte de logorrhée de l'imagination supérieure' (EE, 12). This does not mean, however, that Roche remains untouched by the work of certain Surrealists or that the power and function of a special kind of 'lyricism' escape him. As recently as 1966 in 'L'impératif de l'écriture' Roche is firm in listing Breton amongst those rare 'master-poets' whose influence continues beyond one's accession to the act of writing ('Dante, du Bartas, Guez de Balzac, Sorel, Pope, Sterne, Restif, Sade, Mallarmé, Breton, Pound, Ponge ... et dix autres qu'il n'est peut-être pas encore de bon ton de nommer publiquement' (IE, 27)); and his admiring respect for the unsentimental and lucid sensitivity of Michaux and Deguy to the relationships between language and being is undoubted, to the point of Roche's declaring in 1967: 'Deguy a mille fois raison quand il dit que "le poème moderne 'fait apparaître' ... Le poème est calligramme non point d'un contour 'imité' comme d'une bouteille ou d'une figure, mais plutôt de la configuration secrète de notre existence, de son rythme complexe"' (AP, 7). Despite such affinities, despite the fact that both Roche's theory and poetry may be situated, albeit at its extreme point of development, *within a tradition* that can be said to begin with Mallarmé and 'l'effort essentiel de retournement' of Lautréamont (EE, 11), shoot in different directions with Pound, Eliot and Dada and finally blossom in recent years in often significantly distinct but related ways with writers such as Pleynet, Sollers, Deguy, Noël, Steinmetz and Grivel -

despite all this, Roche finds himself, knows himself, to be anguishingly isolated in his poetic practice and theory. As early as 1963, with the publication of *Récits complets*, Roche is thus capable of sensing and foretelling the imminent demise of poetry: 'Il vient un jour où la poésie doit recommander son/Ame à Dieu le jour où les vaches se regarderont/ Avec étonnement où les arbres verts seront vernis' (RC, 80). Looking back ten years later not only has he no cause to change his view, but his whole effort of poetic production has transformed itself into a gesture of utter destruction. Writing used to be for the truly great poet, 'un combat d' idées, non un joli méli-mélo de mots ronflants, rimant à rime abattue' (BD, 38). Instead, today, poetry is an act of embroidery, 'tapisserie pour jeunes filles du couvent des oiseaux ... Plus rien à dire, à maudire' (*ibid.*). Poetic language has become a matter of camouflage and idealisation. Never does one hear the 'real cry' of the writer, 'tout ce qui crie dès que le cri prend son vrai sens', as Roche put it not too long ago in an interview with Betty Duhamel (*ibid.*). Poetry has ceased to be profoundly liberating, and has become largely incapable either of that authentic seizure of what Roger-Gilbert Lecomte terms 'l'image entrevue à la lueur d'un éclair, perpétuellement fuyante en-deçà ou delà du champ de l'attention' (RC, 17) or of appreciating, as Roche does from the opening pages of *Récits complets*, the extent to which this and indeed all problems of poetry boil down to 'un problème de signification' (RC, 12). From the moment Roche conceives of the act of writing as historically and personally problematical, his response to this dual crisis has always involved a recognition of the crucial and interlocking *poetic* functions of freedom and criticism, (cf. EE, 9-10) of the need to 'write oneself' with the most authentic, instinctually controlled immediacy and to realize within one's writing a lucid and incisive mode of self-reflexive, though non-discursive analysis of the act of writing (both as an individual and as a broad cultural phenomenon). If, then, as we shall now see, Roche increasingly regards poetry as a continuing but quasi-lifeless form of expression whose death he is willing to announce and even accelerate, we should not overlook - and we shall have good cause to later explore - the fact that Roche is always intrigued by the manner of putting together what is destructive, by writing as assembly, as that special 'rhythm' Deguy spoke of, a perhaps worthless and even horrible 'lien de création', (RC, 15-16, 17, n.1) but a mode of articulation that is exceptionally, 'marvellously', 'redly' his (cf. LB, 144).

The general aims that emerge from Roche's experience of what he feels to be the prevailing poetic and cultural crisis of our age are unambiguous and receive an increasingly violent and conscious articulation at the level of both poetic text and theory. Although it is clear that *Récits complets* is not conceived in a spirit of utter antagonism to 'poetry' and that it is from *Eros énergumène* (1968) on that the mechanisms of Roche's poetic practice begin to function with more particular efficiency, it is nevertheless evident, if we compare this poem from *Les Idées centésimales de Miss Elanize:*

ne ligne, des portraits de duchesses l'
Intelligence, bord d'un bateau que moi j'
Emmènerai chez cet anglais à ce mouvement
Qu'il et moi lui imprimons pour un vent
Sur la peau: je reviendrai à ce mouvement
Qu'il et moi, courbés sans souci de pudeur
(l'r de pudeur) ... à rire aux éclats,
A bouder saisie

(IC, 102)

with this brief text from *Le Mécrit:*

plusv plus vite encore le manège impénétrable
de ton con courant, air plus que parole plus
que nature, accidentel corps châtié qui s'envo

(LM, 118)

that, although the two texts/books reveal a certain appreciable distance travelled by Roche during the eight years between their publication, an overall constancy of purpose and practice is observable. Throughout his poetic output and with heightening intensity Roche has, in fact, sought to disturb, to destroy, to deride. It is these qualities of disruptiveness and disrespect that he has recently admired, for example, in Powys' *The Inmates*, in Vonnegut's *God Bless You, Mr. Rosewater*, in Heller's *Catch-22*, although unlike such writers Roche forces his work to function not merely at a socio-political level, but more radically at the level of *language's articulation* of culture. His act of poetic writing endeavours to 'conspuer la poesie' (cf. LM, 22), to despise it, to manifest against it, to spit upon it, 'l'avilissement strictement localisé/... constituant/ L'élément essentiel de ma langue', as Roche declares in *Eros énergumène* (p. 133). His poetry and the language of his poetry thus become in a fundamental way anti-poetry and anti-poetic language, directed to work against conventional poetic language certainly, but also ultimately, in *Le Mécrit*, anxious to remain hyper-critical and provocative in relation to his own ever-becoming language ('le mien ..., celui que j'élaborais en même temps' (JR)). It is with *Le Mécrit* in particular, also, that Roche's desire ultimately intensifies to a gesture of poetic torture (cf. LB, 177), where the poet not only demands but performs the death of poetry, causing it to 'rot' completely, bringing it to a point of what Roche terms, in *Louve basse*, 'glossolalie irréductible' (p. 185). The only poetic texts capable of producing this at first gently posited, but finally furiously pursued end, are those that 'détaillent et définissent une conjonction impérieuse du langage et de la réflexion', those that are capable of assuming a 'treatise-like' self-reflexive demonstrativeness (IE, 27). Only by virtue of such texts where language is furthermore made to adopt a truly self-revealing and self-critical posture, and convention and culture are made to fully speak themselves, will their various taboos be shaken; only via such a use/abuse of 'poetry' may the poet *betray* the cultural unconscious not merely of himself, but of an entire western poetic culture (cf. JR). Poetry for Roche thus becomes, as the painter Bernard Dufour says of their collaborative effort in the production of *Eloge de la véhémence*, 'une dénaturation de la convention poétique', just as painting for him becomes 'une dénaturation de la tradition picturale' (JR). In *Eros énergumène* Roche refers to such a process as one in which the poet deliberately aims to 'défigurer la convention écrite' (p. 11), to dis-occult the hidden grounds, procedures and devices by which it 'produces' by forcing it to become a 'succession de points de choc' with itself (IC, 123). Poetry thus comes to work against itself, the poet's task being to 'parler contre les paroles', as Roche quotes Ponge as saying, 'les entraîner avec soi dans la honte où elles nous conduisent de telle sorte qu'elles s'y défigurent' (EE, 10). Disfiguration and disfigurement: a radical platform for the destruction and betrayal of what is known as 'poetry' and the western 'culture' that underpins it.

If we look back over those poems of Roche already quoted in full or, indeed, if we select at random any other poem from Roche's entire opus, we are compelled to observe that, despite the intercalated presence of almost subliminal 'mini-messages', of small internally coherent or half-coherent fragments of sense, such fragments are incapable of cohering with any stable semantic continuity. Each discontinuous, amputated stump of sense eggs us on, but deflates, disappoints, destroys any notion or feeling of culturally acceptable poeticity. Nothing 'happens', nothing 'adds up', there is an absence of discursive sequencing that Matta refers to as the complete 'désintégration du donc'. Whilst obsessions and experiential data are everywhere in evidence, in teeming abundance in fact, it is by no means reasonable to characterize only the poet's cultural consciousness in terms of such data and, in any case, the latter resist reduction and tabulation, 'énigmes (qui) restent toujours sans solution' (IC, 18), imaginative elements that lack the fine tuning of semantic 'accomplishment'. Instead of a definitive substance, Roche offers a 'definitive dis-figuration' (cf. LM, 116), a continuous text plagued and subverted by a short-circuiting and suspension of meaning, 'la continuité sans vendange' (EE, 25), an act of production without a product.

All of the poems looked at reveal, therefore, with varying degrees of intensity Roche's efforts and techniques of dis-occultation and foregrounding of the centrality of language in writing and his revaluing and reconstitution of the notions of textual production and re-production-as-reading. The following 'Texte 3', from *Le Mécrit*, is given therefore not because earlier poems quoted illustrate inadequately the points we are to make concerning the techniques of Roche's poetic practice, but rather because it furiously proliferates within itself the latter's essential and culminating qualities:

qui moi me donne tant mangé à la mort &? QueuE
rapproche,t,elle à ce point de la mort gachettE
bien grasse tranche &et qu,elle entendait dit l&
homère con& un homme qui aimait le bonheur lacetS
le lacet c&est le bonheur aux viandes pourries l&
air gras de rOmana montrant son dôme naturel imbE
cile puis je pouvais entendre que même la fermièR
e était tombée au milieu de mon jeune quand&.
dans mon blême rêve = dans ma cuillère ardente eT
le tempsLfossile usurpe le pouvoir de ramper verS
une dupe une ersua une taupe tou&tes 3 lui fon tI
rant fortes révérences forts &u&cs à ne rien fouT
voyez-vous quand le con& fuit lentement quand l&H
éroine de la forêt pourceaux l&ont vue, tente encore = A
son adresse et toute cette forte tour gonfle poU
r rire et lance amène oeil et jardin foireuX
(LM, 144)

As is essentially the case with all of Roche's poems, 'Texte 3' performs a fundamental act of discrediting of the culturally crucial idea of stable or absolute meaning and focuses attention upon the notion - and act - of language as a movement of *Sa*, as a 'galaxy of *signifiants* in perpetual flux. Roche proffers his text (his 'genotext') not as a zone where the sign is sacrificed to signification, where the function of the flow of *signifiants* is to produce or even hint at a more or less solidified truth, a definitive *Se*, but rather as a space in which a process of production-transformation (*signifiance)* may be staged and an authentic exploration of the 'innocent' (but culturally enslaved) materiality of language conducted. The poem thus brings about an effective neutralization (and ridiculing) of its *signifiés*, of those idealized cultural referents or traces that correspond to the bourgeois and received idea of poetic language and writing in general (cf. JR). Whilst rendering painfully visible the rusty springs of the poetic imagination's traditional cultural code, the poem refuses all assimilation to any *code vraisemblable* by managing to 'évacuer les signifiés traditionnels au profit des signifiants' (JR). In this way the text critically dialecticizes its relation to the elements, procedures and rules of conventional poetic discourse, submerging the cultural referents, eliminating all perceptible figuration, in a flow of pure verbal *signifiance*. Decoding is manifestly out of the question, for we have before us only signifying 'husks', a materialization without content, an act of *scription* or *écriture* (as opposed to 'literature') operating at a pre-semantic, genetic level of linguistic performance no longer controlled by the perspective of some ultimate and, as Steinmetz has it, 'cabalistic' truth (JLS, 19). Roche's text deliberately breaks in this way the 'capitalistic', 'operator-mentality'-governed contract deemed to exist conventionally between poet and society: the consumer-reader finds that the comestible element has been withdrawn from writing and that he is obliged to digest the indigestible, or, as René Lacôte puts it, 'lire l'illisible!' (RL, 8). No longer can the reader sit back to be served and enjoy his meal in comfort, but instead he is obliged as it were to cook it himself (even though its indigestibility can offer him no more than a healthy feeling of dissatisfaction), to re-enact the 'geno-text', to become himself an endless producer of uncongealed meaning in its pre-semantic rhythms and with its wild air of mere potentiality.

'Texte 3' presents itself then, typically, as an exemplary space of destruction-cum-instruction in which the poet and reader may explore precisely that theatre within which voice and meaning operate. Roche creates a turbulently liberated montage of the (normally) culturally enslaved paraphernalia of language, though oddly one in which there is no movement away from itself, outside itself. Instead the poem's (language's) constituent parts jolt against one another, going nowhere, merely acting out their own factuality, flexing their muscles in a gesture of working that lacks all notion of working 'for' or 'towards'.[2] Despite its continuity (and even its moments of fusion), the text stops and stumbles at every turn, never permitting any accentuation of one element or *agissement* (cf. EE, 40) at the expense of another as in ordinary poetic discourse, and yet allowing each *signifiant* (which in Roche's poems may be a whole signifying sequence, borrowed or created, a phrase, a word, a letter or any other element of the writer's/printer's signifying code) to become a kind of nodal point in a network of interacting movements. In this way, although the text sweeps us on at a bewildering speed, every period, dash and comma, every 'misplaced' *or* untouched character, every syntactic, lexical or typographical feature, whether regular or irregular, thrusts upon us its oddly liberated and therefore utterly, pure available literality, just as together and simultaneously they all speak directly and violently Roche's derision and abuse of their customary, shackled and blinkered use. For as usual, in Roche's texts, everything in 'Texte 3' speaks its own degradation and its self-apotheosis, its strange potential, miserable and worthless as it may well be. Each ampersand, each word, each signifying element is in fact a plagiarised fragment in the sense that it is a functional factor of a conventional code of basic linguistic communication and of the generic code of poetry - and to this extent it is ridiculed by virtue of its 'evacuated', emptied, 'insignificant' state. On the other hand, however, partly to the extent that this very 'evacuation' is successful and partly to the extent that Roche manages to articulate all that he articulates in what he himself calls 'un ensemble rhétorique qui, lui, est nouveau' (JR) and in a language that *always*, from *Récits complets* to *Le Mécrit* or indeed *Louve basse*, obeys the writer's *personal* laws of 'order and adventure', the elements of language may be said to simultaneously take on a new power, a new forgotten independence that points, even if hesitantly, towards another mode of expression, outside 'poetry' and 'culture', yet establishing surely its own unpretentious, though 'jubilant' force.

All six 'texts' from the last part of *Le Mécrit*, like the 'Texte 3' under examination, conform most certainly to Roche's own devastating appraisal of the 'mis-written' given in a 1973 conversation with Betty Duhamel: 'Mécrit = mécompte, déboire, bévue = mévente, méconnaissance = mépris ou méprise = menstrues, mensualisation de l'esprit - mécène, méandre, méat urinaire. Tout ce qui crie dès que le cri prend son vrai sens, dès que la musique s'entend par-dessus les prés quand le vent de l'imbécillité cesse de souffler' (BD, 38). Most fundamentally 'mis-writing' is an act (mis-) calculated to reduce poetry to 'son point de plus extrême *méculture*, le point zéro, à l'évidence, de la poéticité' (LM, 139). It is a most serious act of mis-calculation in which the poet permits no erasure of error and, indeed, on the contrary, seeks to provoke his gesture of mis-production so that the disfiguring 'incidents de parcours' (JR) may proliferate, causing the text to function '*en moins*' (LM, 139), filling it with a dazzling, 'jabbering' (cf. LB, 197) multitude of lacks and poornesses that can only disappoint, mock and betray. In this way, 'Texte 3', like *Le Mécrit* in general, may be said to accumulate from a certain standpoint, nothing but *dross*, nothing but l'*entame*, that inedible waste habitually left on the side of the plate or thrown away before serving (cf. LB, 159). Culture and poeticity are reduced to and replaced by an alignment of 'merdes' (LM, 123) a flood of 'excremental misfortune' (cf. LB, 158), a precipitous and incoherent 'vomiting' in which Roche welcomes, seriously and yet with a lucid warmth and gleefulness, the bewildering defectiveness of his violent and impulsive mode of (in-) articulation and insists upon an absolute fidelity to what he terms, in *Louve basse*, his 'adhérences buccales' (LB, 144). And yet, whilst what retains our - and Roche's - immediate attention is the blusteringly destructive aura that surrounds his stunning (anti-)climactic gesture of 'mis-writing', we must not neglect the important fact that, for Roche, worthless, revolting and empty as such activity and the excremental traces it produces may indeed be, the only 'literary' and existentially worthwhile and necessary task confronting Roche involves *precisely* that very vomiting and *diarrhoea scribendi* of which we have spoken and which, in consequence, constitutes the tenuous thread of an ever-becoming and personally precious 'scriptive' minimality. It is to this notion of a broadly positively construed minimality that we shall give our final attention and it is here that we shall discover the extent to which Roche's writing is capable of constituting a 'solution' to the dilemma experienced - a solution, that is, both fused with and yet going beyond that offered by the act of poetic dis-figuration and de-construction itself. In this connection we shall need to become sensitive to the facts of continuing, change and jubilation in Roche's writing, though these are not the only elements of any solution eked out:

other factors remain, associated with naturalness, sexuality and openness, rhythm and 'pulsion', dancing, energy and living.

For the Denis Roche of *Le Mécrit* and *Louve basse*, 'poetry' as generally practised - and indeed, 'literature', with which it is now notionally, culturally fused- has become filth, 'ordure, RATS EN VRAC' (LB, 70), a decomposing corpse upon which poets and writers, those lingering privileges and prejudices of the past (cf. LB, 132), still blindly and contentedly fatten themselves like so many maggots. Moreover, it is understood in this regard that, even if Roche's own subversive act of 'mis-writing' divorces itself ideologically from such depraved gluttony by offering us a clear and yet 'starved' vision of the rotting flesh of literature's hulk, Roche is obliged, in order to achieve this, to live dangerously, to live in the proximity of death whilst seeking to avoid its grasp, to risk disease and pestilence (cf. LB, cover), boredom and utter *emmerdement* (complete excremental immersion) (cf. LM, 8), whilst struggling to denounce them and to release *simultaneously* from within something fragile and yet vigorous. He is in fact, and happily, 'pas tellement essoufflé au fond' (LM, 10), able, after the exhausting activity that reaches a certain culmination in *Le Mécrit*, to appreciate that he has miraculously managed to 'produire (s)on propre enseignement' (LB, -5), to reach the point where his obsessions and torment, like those of Artaud, have yielded the full measure of their sense and use and where - even more miraculously - 'l'impératif de l'écriture', which never ceases to plague and exhilarate Roche, is thus compelled, *naturally*, to manifest itself anew, to re-orient itself in order to discover new forms of any previous minimality he has succeeded in articulating, to expose him to the continuing danger and stimulus of his ever-becoming 'scripting' self (cf. BD, 39). In effect, Roche's abuse of language, both before and after *Le Mécrit*, is not merely underpinned by its coldly ideological demonstrativeness, but is, one might say, buoyed up by certain factors of *jubilation* at once superficially and integrally related to the written text, but in both respects personally significant and at least minimally salving to the writer.

Pleasure, the writer's 'monplaisir', should not, of course, be thought of as an objective and cannot be considered a valid criterion of writing. Roche himself is quick to acknowledge this: essentially it is a frill, a marginal factor of writing, as fundamentally worthless in his eyes as the cultural dross that constitutes the empty substance of his urgent demonstrations (cf. BD, 38). But it is clear, too, that, to the extent to which 'plaisir pour moi - véhémence du discours, rire du discours, jubilation du discours' (BD, 39), pleasure and jubilation - quite apart from any personally medicinal effect they may have - form a significant and highly salutary part of Roche's critical, de-constructive arsenal and, indeed, make themselves constantly palpable through the texture and tonality they produce in his work. It should be noted therefore that the equation written work → pleasure and jubilation, also functions inversely and that the character of Roche's writing would be deeply affected if the equation were disturbed. 'Mis-writing', disgusting and tiresome, as it may be, leads, oddly, to joy, but, more importantly, gleefulness, derision and jubilation also lead manifestly to a 'mis-writing' (cf. IC, III), which they suffuse with themselves - were this not so, Roche's work would be radically weakened, his adoption of incoherence as a mode of articulation would perhaps cease to thrill, the exultation (cf. LB, 204) and mental intoxication (cf. LB, 172) he (and his readers) may feel might evaporate, leaving him (and them) with a cold and flatly articulated intention.

A crucial factor in Roche's thinking - and in his use of language - hinges on a radical opposition of orthodoxy ('la triade habituelle Roi-Pouvoir, Bouffon-Ecrivain, Confesseur-Professeur' (LB, 110)) and freedom, collusion and self-adherence. To refuse the mechanisms of the 'tryad' is, moreover, not merely to withdraw and insulate oneself or even to confront and criticize. It involves, additionally, the establishment of an openness which permits a fundamental expression of *one's own* desire ('je me trouve là où le désir, *mon* désir me met' (LB, 118)), and demands an exclusive articulation of what one can and must write ('Qu'est-ce que vous voulez que j'écrive d'autre? Sinon cette fatigante oscillation du contenu de la gorge, trempant du cul, remontant à toute pompe, vomissant, renflouant, pâturant, picorant, crépitant, pimpant' (LB, 46)). To refuse oneself such an articulation is to repress oneself and one's language, to deny them a truly staggering coincidence, to bury them 'dans les sphériboles de l'arrière-garde, de l'avant-garde, de la garde, du lard, d'au-là, aidez-là, à dada, gagas go' (LB, 66) and to seal off that almost biological *textural openness* of which - and *which* - Roche speaks in *Louve basse:* "Je suis seul à fixer constamment ce quelque chose du quelque chose qui est la louve, principal personnage de mon histoire, et surtout sanie matricule du texte ouvert, flancs ouverts, parole jacassante ouverte et remplie, plaie ouverte' (p. 197). Any 'scriptive' solution will thus depend on a personal and correspondingly linguistic nudity (cf. LB, cover). Necessarily sexual and phantasmatic (cf. LB, 53), this nudity must be provoked and set free (cf. JR); what Roche calls the 'sanglantes raisons' (EE, 71) stored upon within him must be allowed to gush forth; a vast and monstrous act of menstruation, killing and blood-letting must be initiated - naturally ('et je suis aussi naturel que possible' (RC, 75) and immediately, in a hectic, vehement *élan* of 'self-redemption'. Writing, for Roche, is wasting both writer's and reader's time in expressing the pardonable, the admissible. His thus lurches towards the unpardonable, the *inadmissible* (cf. IC, 92; PI, 221). And, the voice he listens to and gives expression to, is not tidily cultivated, but 'la voix des sumacs sauvages et (d)es ronces qui forcent notre cave' (LB, 44), the voice to which we must always return, that 'hurlement originel, fantaisie déambulatoire, primesautière et sidérante' (LB, 42) that skulks within each of us, awaiting its darkly revelatory release.

Whilst offering, of course, a plurality and provisionality of meaning, this 'primordial screaming' is not fundamentally concerned with any kind of 'oulipian' promotion of its no doubt fascinating semantic polyvalence. The 'truth' of Roche's writing lies, not in the meaning of each successive textural layering, not even in a neat (but impoverishing) reduction of poem or other writing to theory, but rather in the nature and the how of its activity, in the fact of an adherence to a violent, raw and profoundly disturbing release of oneself and one's language. The texts of Denis Roche thus constitute, individually and collectively, that most authentic and plainly speaking calligramme of the writer's secret existential configuration and rhythm to which we alluded at the outset (cf. AP, 7). The strength and impact of Roche's writing come, in consequence, not from any linear, discursive structuring, but from the rhythmic, 'pulsional' activity it generates, from its ability to capture and explore the core of his language's - and our language's - volatile, 'energumen' reality.[3] The scriptive minimum with which Roche both culturally destroys, and yet operates a bare personal survival, constitutes in effect an astonishing feat of dancing, a dance of the self, a wild spinning and spiralling, a solitary whirling response to the pulsing energy within himself (cf. LB, 96-7). Roche thus reacts to an inner force 'qui me pousse, moi qui ai toujours horreur de ça, à *danser*, à danser *jusqu'à épuisement* ... l'arabesque effroyable et coupante de l'ecriture' (LL, 104). At once loved (for the torture it inflicts upon literature and culture) and abhorred (for the deleterious near-complete exhaustion it produces), the dancing out of the writer's and language's virulent energumen rhythms clearly remains a profoundly *vital* act for Roche. To furiously 'dance oneself out' may indeed induce a repulsive bout of vomiting, but then, on the other hand, to cease to listen and respond to such rhythms, to refuse to constantly vomit oneself and one's language, is, for Roche, to come face to face with death: 'Se non balla, muore! dit-on d'un tarentulé: "s'il ne danse pas, il meurt"' (LB, 105).

Roche would seem, then, to be locked into this screaming-pulsing-vomiting-excreting-swirling 'arachnéen comportement' (LB, 177) that is his writing. It would appear to be his starkest of salvations, as it is very nearly the most complete of (self-)destructions. To dance, to write, is to struggle to live - to struggle to live oneself and one's language out of recognition of one's fear of the ubiquitous manifestations of death. 'Je danse parce que j'ai peur, et je manie *jusqu'à épanouissement* ma carcasse d'avant en arrière et d'arrière en avant, de mes talons à mes orteils et vice versa', Roche declares, for example, in *Louve basse* (pp. 166-7) whose 'histoires qui n'ont de roman que le nom, qui n'ont en commun qu'un mâchage raisonné et vigoureux du mot *Mort*, ne sont que des substitutions dactylographiques du mot *Peur*' (LB, 119). Roche is in effect deeply preoccupied throughout his work with death, with death-as-language, death as the rotten language of a rotten literature, death felt moreover to be an omnipresent threat to himself and his own language. But it is precisely this same obsessed work, with its concentrated but freely melded activity, with what Roche has most recently called its 'états excités de langue et d'énergie ... qui captent' (APE, 35), that Roche opposes to death-as-the-language-of-poetry and -literature. Although the latter can offer no solution and indeed must be 'dragged' to the death to which they have already unwittingly surrendered, Roche's writing of himself now, his living of himself immediately, freely, through his language, his opposing of his life in terms of 'une langue toute rouge merveilleuse' (LB, 44) to the death that besets him - all such acts are capable of constituting a remedy to the universal sickness that infects and threatens to decimate all language. Whether or not Roche himself will see the apocalyptic 'victory' he anticipates (cf. LB, 117), is not important. What is clear is that he is, like few other writers today, intent on *living his full, frenzied potentiality*. To this extent he cannot escape writing and indeed, despite everyting, he has no desire to do so. 'Moi, je me lève dans ce livre pour tout voir', Roche roars out in *Louve basse*, 'pour être l'acteur autant que l'assistant, pour rire et danser comme jamais, *parce que je peux encore le faire*. Et parce que je ne pense pas que le rugissement des lions, le hurlement des loups, les fureurs de la mer démontée sont des parties de l'éternité trop grandes pour l'oeil de l'homme' (LB, 76). What little Roche salvages and contrives to propose - of course, beyond all claim to anything but a furiously intense and 'authentic' personal survival - must, certainly, be seen in relation to the considerable lands he has cleared, not to say laid waste.

The 'canine yelping' of Roche's writing is too intimately fused with a savage 'cynicism' (cf. LB, 69) for us to imagine that a line of separation could be conveniently drawn between the destroyed and rotting, the pulsing and surviving. In the long run, however, it will perhaps be more fully appreciated just to what extent Denis Roche's writing is not merely an elaborate and calculated dance of death, but, more importantly, the most ebullient and delirious celebration of life.

NOTES:

1. The following abbreviations are used throughout: RC: *Récits complets*, Paris: Seuil, 1963; IC: *Les Idées centésimales de Miss Elanize*, Paris: Seuil, 1964; EE: *Eros énergumène*, Paris: Seuil, 1968; LM: *Le Mécrit*, Paris: Seuil, 1972; LB: *Louve basse*, Paris: Seuil, 1976; IE: L' impératif de l'écriture', *Arts* (28.12.66), 27; AP: 'L'acte poétique', *La Quinzaine littéraire* (15.1.67), 7; PI: 'La poésie est inadmissible, d'ailleurs elle n'existe pas', in *Théorie d'ensemble*, Paris: Seuil, 1968, pp. 221-33; APE: 'Au-delà du principe d'écriture', *Tel Quel*, 67 (Aut 76), 25-37; BD: Betty Duhamel, 'Denis Roche, fossoyeur de la poésie', *Le Magazine littéraire*, 72 (Jan 73), 38-9; JR: Jean Ristat, 'Dénaturation, matérialisation', *Les Lettres françaises*, 1424 (23.2.72), 3-7; JLS: Jean-Luc Steinmetz, 'La mort de l'auteur de droit divin', *Le Magazine littéraire*, 47 (Dec 70), 19; RL: René Lacôte, 'Denis Roche', *Les Lettres françaises*, 1229 (10.4.68), 8: other useful critical essays and reviews not referred to here have been written by Jacques Roubaud, Charles Grivel, Hélène Prigogine, Veronica Forrest-Thomson, Marcelin Pleynet, Christian Prigent and Michel Deguy. I should also like to acknowledge the many valuable insights afforded by my conversations and correspondence with Yves Abrioux.

2. It is interesting to note in this regard and despite differences of emphasis a certain important parallelism between the thought and intent of Roche's writing and the influential work of Yvonne Rainer in the field of modern dance. See her article in *Tel Quel*, 63 (Aut 75), 78-85, and her book *Work 1961-73*, Halifax, Nova Scotia: Press of Nova Scotia College of Art and Design/New York: New York University Press, 1974.

3. See, in this connection, *Eros énergumène* (pp. 13-14), where Denis Roche looks to the time when it might be possible to examine writing (including his own) as the locus, the scene, of 'un ensemble de lois non (encore) connues régissant (...) des types de faits à dominante *pulsionnelle*.' The critic would thus be engaged in an examination of the rhythmic patterns of the text, the 'déroulement de l'écriture, rythme d'arrivée des enchaînements métaphoriques et des ellipses, rythme de déroulement de la lecture, rythme des thèmes, de leur apparition et de leur destruction, rythme des structures de discours, de leur arrivée et de leur disparition, rythme de disposition d'

étalement, d'enserrement, d'écoulement des textes imprimés, rythme de succession des pages et de leur imbrication possible et de leur succession comme autant d'*empreintes* (au sens biologique), toujours *fonctions d'un acte social qui est celui d'écrire et d'un autre acte social qui est celui de lire'*.

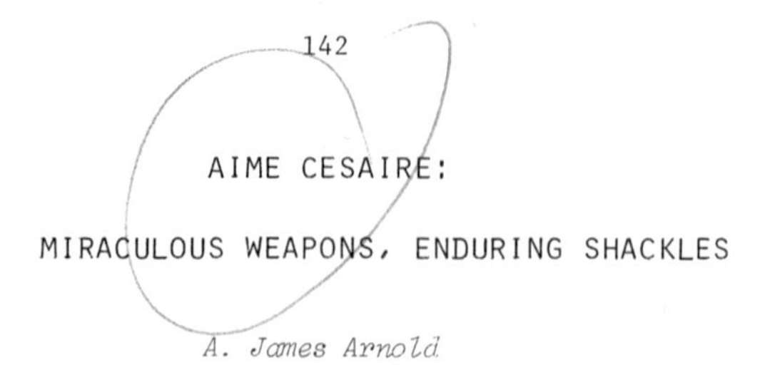

AIME CESAIRE:

MIRACULOUS WEAPONS, ENDURING SHACKLES

A. James Arnold

I. Is the Logos Black?

Aimé Césaire, the most versatile of the negritude poets, has probably had the greatest moral impact of any poet writing in French since Victor Hugo. His audience extends well beyond the confines of the little world of poetry readers; it includes a significant segment of the leadership of the emerging nations of French expression and, in English and Spanish translation, an important readership in the Americas as well. This is especially remarkable in that Césaire's poetics has never aimed at ease of access for the average reader. In a period when poetry has progressively retreated into one retrenchment after another - lately doubting its own most cherished prerogative, the capacity of language to express the condition of the self - Aimé Césaire has appeared to stand apart, untouched by the chronic desease of postwar literature.

In terms of current critical debate Césaire has seemed an unrepentant Cratylist, proclaiming the now scandalous message that the logos is alive and well, having taken up residence outside metropolitan France. As early as 1948 Sartre had announced that the logos - in the guise of Orpheus - was henceforth, and for the foreseeable future, black. This extreme statement of the case, for all its attendant Hegelian trappings (an 'anti-racist racism', etc.) has been sufficiently refuted to permit our dispensing with it here.

The fact remains, however, that with few exceptions - René Char being the best known today - the ancient privilege of the Word seems to have abandoned France for its current refuge in cultures-in-the-making, where a heroic will can yet oppose the principle of oppression. Lest this scenario begin to suggest the facile thematics of an eternal

Romanticism - nothing could be further from our real subject - an initial ambiguity must be noted. For the poets of negritude, the enemy was within as well as without. The politics of cultural assimilation which produced such marvellous 'specimens' as Damas, Senghor, Diop and Césaire, required the interiorization of the cultural arm of colonialism, the French language with its full weight of literary prestige: 'L'Europe patrouille dans mes veines comme/ une meute de filaires sur le coup de minuit. [...] Europe vieux chien Europe calèche à vers'.[1]

Aimé Césaire's poetry is born of the resistance of a self to this crushing weight. Ironically the resistance arose only at the point where further submission would have meant complete psychic disintegration. Here the term alienation applied to cultural products can keep its clinical connotation; poetry will not be 'mere' metaphoric expression; in the first instance it is a defence against madness. (see *inter alia* 'Le Noir et le langage', in Frantz Fanon's *Peau noire masques blancs*, 1952).

The colonized poet's relation to his language - if, as in the case of all the negritude poets, it be the language of the colonizer - is one of aggressivity. French became the language of the poetry of negritude only because there was no other choice. Thus, even when a poet like Césaire is at his most 'French' linguistically, a state of permanent hostility exists between the poet and his language, between the self and its means of expression. The 'revolutionary' project of Aimé Césaire has for many readers masked the dynamics constitutive of the poem. His longest and stylistically most complex poem, the *Cahier d'un retour au pays natal*, has been reduced to a 'flat prose' by one translator into English.[2] For analogous reasons one commentator has advanced the claim that this 'text' is not a poem at all.[3] Other readings which flatten out a poetics of considerable complexity include the 'Africanization' of Césaire by Jahnheinz Jahn (in *Muntu* and *Neo-African Literature*) and the archetypal patterns favoured by Lilyan Kesteloot (in *Les Ecrivains noirs de langue française*). Each presents a more or less recognizable profile of the author. Césaire did after all tell one interviewer 'Je suis un poète africain',[4] and in a letter to Kesteloot he affirmed his own belief in universal archetypes.[5]

For Jahn and Kesteloot, Césaire is one of the originators of neo-African literature, i.e. his poetics to be properly understood must be taken out of the complex matrix of contemporary French poetry. And yet Renée Riese Hubert has offered a short assessment of Césaire's contribution to contemporary poetry which places him squarely within a recent French tradition.[6] Although she does not allude to it, an article by Roger Bastide is apposite to her implied thesis.[7] Bastide, whose speciality is the ethnography of the black population of the Americas (*Les Amériques noires*), had, in *Présence Africaine*, drawn the provocative conclusion that Aimé Césaire is a (culturally) white poet. There is an important element of truth in this, sufficient at least to counter the thesis of Césaire the African propounded by Jahn. What Bastide has argued is that: 'L'Afrique de Césaire n'est donc pas une dictée de son inconscient mais une construction voulue de son imagination créatrice, faite avec des lectures - bref une image de nature ethnographique' (p. 16).

The first important study of Césaire by an African[8] confirms this by documenting a part of the source material from which Césaire drew. It is nonetheless undeniable that Césaire has on numerous occasions rendered a facsimile good enough to impress African critics. Marcien Towa, who was quite aware of some of Césaire's European sources, concluded his study of the important poem 'Les Pur-Sang' (in *Les Armes miraculeuses*) with the statement that 'la structure de "Pur-Sang" est parente de celle des cultes [agraires] africains'.[9]

The operative term here is 'parente', which directs us not toward sources in the positivistic sense but toward the poetic domain of analogy. Marcien Towa's conclusion is important in that it testifies to the rightness of Aimé Césaire's original wager: to overcome the effects of cultural assimilation by the reorientation of the language and the traditions of a European culture in such a way as to rediscover those universal aspects of symbolic behaviour which pertain also, if not especially or uniquely, to Africa. Césaire did not arrive at his goal in one giant stride. Some four years of tentative groping (1935-1939) were required to produce the original version of the *Cahier d'un retour au pays natal*. The text published in the August 1939 issue of *Volontés* is notable for the complete absence of those passages which have contributed most to the fortune of the poem since 1947.[10] Although Césaire has encouraged the legend that *Volontés* printed only 'fragments' of a poem - see most recently 'La Vie et l'oeuvre d'Aimé Césaire', *Poèmes* (p. 12) - there is nothing to indicate that the 1939 text was other than the complete poem as it then existed. Césaire seems unwilling to accredit or admit the notion that the poetics of the preoriginal *Cahier* is in any significant way different from that of the considerably longer postwar versions, although a careful collation of the texts proves that all the strophes, passages and lines written in a surrealist vein were added after 1939. I suspect that this relatively harmless deception was intended to reinforce Césaire's claim that he was writing surrealist poetry before meeting André Breton in 1941.[11]

II. Language and Styles in the *Cahier*

If the strophic organization reminiscent of Lautréamont and the thematic echo of Rimbaud's departure from Europe inform the *Cahier* from 1939 onward, providing it with a loose principle of associative structure based on figuration by anaphora, other aspects of the definitive text reveal the stitches testifying to several different poetic operations. Already in the 1939 version a peculiar syntactic inversion involves the systematic repetition of nouns in order both to heighten their effect and to render the flavour of working class speech:

> Et *le lit de planches* d'où s'est levée *ma race*, toute entière *ma race* de *ce lit de planches*, avec ses pattes de caisses de Kérosine, comme s'il avait l'éléphantiasis *le lit*, et sa peau de cabri, et ses feuilles de bananes séchées, et ses haillons, une nostalgie de matelas *le lit* de ma grand-mère.
>
> (P, 48)

Césaire's occasional use of this device draws our attention away from the narrative component of the *Cahier* to its poetic density. The systematic use of the weak coordinator 'et' in sequence, coupled with the anaphora of 'Au bout du petit matin', which regularly begins each new strophe, suggests an atmosphere of litany and of high seriousness which frequently recalls Péguy. Repetition of a single verb (*pédaler*) combines with a given noun (*nuit*) in the passage that follows to rhythmically reinforce the monotony and tenacity of poverty while according symbolic value to the mother's sacrificial activity:

> et ma mère dont les jambes pour notre faim inlassable pédalent, pédalent de jour, de nuit, je suis même réveillé la nuit par ces jambes inlassables qui pédalent la nuit et la morsure âpre dans la chair molle de la nuit d'une Singer que ma mère pédale, pédale pour notre faim et de jour et de nuit.
>
> (P, 47-8)

A few strophes of the 1939 text were parodic and for the reader who could recognize their model, mordantly funny. Césaire etches in his poetic acid the racist version of 'art nègre' disseminated by the likes of Paul Morand (*Magie noire*, 1929):

> Ou bien tout simplement comme on nous aime!
> Obscènes gaiement, très dousdous de jazz sur leur excès d'ennui.
> Je sais le tracking, le Lindy-hop et les claquettes.
> Pour les bonnes bouches la sourdine de nos plaintes enrobée de oua-oua. Attendez ... Tout est dans l'ordre. Mon ange broute du néon. J'avale des baguettes. Ma dignité se vautre dans les dégobillements ...
>
> (P, 60)

Césaire's adaptation of *humour noir* takes on even more vividly the colours of Lautréamont in this ferocious parody of the Antillean version of childhood paradise lost:

> ma reine des crachats et des lèpres
> ma reine des fouets et des scrofules
> ma reine des squasmes et des chloasmes
> (oh ces reines que j'aimais jadis aux jardins
> printaniers et lointains avec derrière l'illumination
> de toutes les bougies de marronniers!)
>
> (P, 70)

Compare the opening strophe of 'Pour fêter une enfance' by Saint-John Perse:

> Palmes!
>
> Alors on te baignait dans l'eau-de-feuilles-vertes; et l'eau encore était du soleil vert; et les servantes de ta mère, grandes filles luisantes, remuaient leurs jambes chaudes près de toi qui tremblais ...
>
> (Je parle d'une haute condition, alors, entre les robes, au règne de tournantes clartés.)[12]

Perse's stylistic signature, the parenthetical exclamation of praise, is both readily identifiable and mocked by the attributes Césaire gives his 'queens'. These are among the first efforts of the black Martinican poet to defeat the patrols of European culture within his veins.

The first version of the poem, moreover, is very straightforward about its subject: an alienated self sounds out the social conditions which generate a collective psychic disorder. Parodic devices render the state of personal alienation of the speaker while permitting the poem to remain in touch with social realities, however repugnant. The theme of negritude is introduced gradually as part of the inner dynamics of the poem: first in its racist connotations, which engender masochistic self-denial, then in a progressively sympathetic understanding which entails identification with the most abject manifestations of 'niggerness' and, finally, through the positive valuation of blackness assumed as one's ethnic and personal reality, as a triumphant, heroic affirmation. The 1939 text approximates the poetics of expressionism. It is concerned primarily with an emotional transformation of a mindscape which includes sometimes detailed and even graphic renderings of scenes from Martinican life. The dominant features of surrealism are not yet present in this original version of the poem; most particularly, the surrealist image is totally lacking. And yet the textural echoes of Rimbaud and Lautréamont certainly do reinforce Césaire's claim that these ancestors of surrealism were important to him before 1941.

After the second world war and some six years of writing surrealist poetry Césaire revised his *Cahier*. While he allowed the parodic elements to remain unchanged, he added substantially and stylistically different passages in which the surrealist ethos launched a veritable counter-attack against the causes of the black man's alienation: 'la folie qui se souvient/ la folie qui hurle; la folie qui voit/ la folie qui se déchaîne// Et vous savez le reste// que 2 et 2 font 5 ...' (P, 54). (Only very careful readers of Dostoyevsky will identify this last detail as a contribution of *Notes from Underground*). The surrealist simulation of *dementia praecox* is introduced thematically but not stylistically: '... nous nous réclamons de la/ démence précoce de la folie flamboyante/ du cannibalisme tenace ...' (P, 53). It was in the process of revising an earlier text that Césaire in 1947 introduced the surrealist logos into the *Cahier*: 'Je retrouverais le secret des grandes communications et des grandes combustions' (P, 49). This paraphrases the theory of the surrealist image; the remainder of the strophe exemplifies its practice: 'Je roulerais comme un sang frénétique sur le courant lent de l'oeil des mots en chevaux fous en enfants frais en caillots en couvre-feu en vestiges de temple en pierres précieuses assez loin pour décourager les mineurs' (P, 49). Césaire's originality, here and in most of his surrealist poems, is to temper orthodox theory by supplying a context in which the requisite *polysémie* can be imbedded so as to acquire a richness of stratification. In the same strophe his use of *dire* in the conditional has suggested to numerous readers the efficacity of Nommo, the African word magic discussed by Jahn in *Muntu:* 'Je dirais orage. Je dirais fleuve. Je dirais tornade. Je dirais feuille. Je dirais arbre. Je serais mouillé de toutes les pluies, humecté de toutes les rosées'. This stylistic introduction of an imaginary Africa adumbrates the goal, the aspiration toward which the entire poem strains with all its tonal diversity.

One of Césaire's most beautiful extended metaphors occurs in the next strophe of the *Cahier*. Its uninhibited eroticism is typically Césairean, uniting sexual desire with the aspiration to freedom translated as a concrete, maternal land and a transcendent, phallic sun:

J'ai des mots assez vastes pour vous contenir
et toi terre tendue
terre saoule
terre grand sexe levé vers le soleil
terre grande matrice girant au vertige ses fariolures de
sperme
terre grand délire de la mentule de Dieu
terre sauvage montée des resserres de la mer avec
dans la bouche une touffe de cécropies
[...]
il me suffit d'une gorgée de ton lait jiculi pour qu'en
toi je découvre toujours à même distance de mirage -
mille fois plus merveilleuse que tu n'es mille fois plus
natale et dorée d'un soleil que n'entame nul prisme-
une terre où tout est libre et fraternel ma terre.[13]

The Bordas edition of the *Cahier*, published later the same year from a further revised text, proceeded to combine the self-parody of the earlier version with the surrealist refusal of reason. Here the speaker assumes the role of a Voodoo priest (the *hougan* is merely mentioned in the two earlier versions) who would effect change through sorcery:

voum rooh oh
voum rooh oh
à charmer les serpents à conjurer
les morts
voom rooh oh
à contraindre la pluie à contrarier
les raz de marée
voom rooh oh
à empêcher que ne tourne l'ombre
voom rooh oh que mes cieux à moi
s'ouvrent

(P, 56)

Césaire continued to reinforce the surrealist aspects of his poem in the final revisions of the definitive edition of 1956, where for the first time one reads:

Des mots?
Ah, oui, des mots!

Raison, je te sacre vent du soir.
Bouche de l'ordre ton nom?
Il m'est corolle du fouet.
Beauté je t'appelle pétition de la pierre.
Mais ah! la rauque contrebande

de mon rire
Ah! mon trésor de salpêtre!

(P, 53)

Even a rapid review of the successive versions of the *Cahier d'un retour au pays natal* demonstrates the gradual 'surrealization' of negritude from 1939 to 1956. The dominant feature of Césaire's poetics during this period is his increased reliance upon the poetic word as a privileged mode of cognition.

III. Epiphanies and Other Miraculous Weapons

Between the original version of the *Cahier* and the 1947 versions Césaire had deepened his understanding of poetry as a means to acquire knowledge of the self. Some of his discoveries were then incorporated into the long poem which has had such a remarkable effect in stimulating ethnic and national consciousness in many formerly colonized nations. The full force of his new style would be felt, however, in the collection of poems *Les Armes miraculeuses*, written in Martinique during the war years and published by Gallimard in 1946. There is a unity of tone and style in these poems which has not characterized the *Cahier* since the postwar revisions. Césaire was pursuing in his own way, with the ethnic overtones attendant upon negritude and upon his status as a politically and intellectually colonized poet, the same quest which marked surrealism. Without minimizing the need for political and social change, he sought in his poetry to indicate the general direction consciousness must take to renew itself, to create the state of mind which might thrive in a new society. His priorities were, of course, in direct contradiction to the principles of Marxism, a situation which seriously complicated his representation of the French Communist Party, Martinican Section, in the national legislature from 1946 to 1956.

Césaire's poetics during this same period was irrationalist and even mystical. He has set forth his position in a paper delivered at an international meeting of philosophers in Port-au-Prince, Haïti, in 1944:

> Autrement dit, poésie est épanouissement. Epanouissement de l'homme à la mesure du monde - dilatation vertigineuse. Et on peut dire que toute grande poésie, sans jamais renoncer à être humaine, à un très mystérieux moment cesse d'être strictement humaine pour commencer à être véritablement cosmique.[14]

His ideal of poetic knowledge was primitivist, 'white' in the sense intended by Roger Bastide:

> Et voilà qui nous ramène aux premiers temps de l'humanité. L'erreur est de croire que la connaissance a attendu, pour naître, l'exercice méthodique de la pensée ou les scrupules de l'expérimentation. Même, je crois que l'homme n'a jamais été plus près de certaines vérités qu'aux jours premiers de l'espèce. Aux temps où l'homme découvrait avec émotion le premier soleil, la première lune. Aux temps où l'homme découvrait dans la peur et le ravissement, la nouveauté palpitante du monde.
> (PC, 158)

Read out of context this last sentence might be confused with the gentle humour of the author of *La Fable du monde* or *Premiers Pas de l'univers*. But, unlike Jules Supervielle, Césaire invested fully in the exploration and exploitation of the unconscious:

> Images héréditaires que seule peut remettre à jour aux fins de déchiffrement, l'atmosphère poétique. Connaissance millénaire enfouie. Les villes d'Ys de la connaissance.
> (PC, 167)

Césaire's harsh treatment of Christianity in the period since 1950 has led some commentators to conclude that he is an anti-religious poet. This is patently false. His satire of established religion, in the lyric version of 'Et les chiens se taisaient' for instance, is directed against the collusion between the Church and colonialism. Behind this critique stands a profound reverence for a 'natural' religion which Césaire projects on to Africa but which we now recognize as another creation of a poetic type. That Césaire initially conceived the poetic epiphanies of *Les Armes miraculeuses* transcendent and religious is indicated by another section of his paper on 'Poésie et Connaissance':

> Et parce que dans tout poème vrai, le poète joue le jeu du monde, le poète vrai souhaite abandonner le mot à ses libres associations, sûr que c'est en définitive l'abandonner à la volonté de l'univers.
>
> (PC, 164)

In this Césaire echoes textually Frobenius' *Histoire de la civilisation africaine*, the principal ethnographic source for Césaire's early ideas about Africa.[15]

Aimé Césaire incorporated these concerns in *Les Armes miraculeuses* by creating a myth of the hero who awakens to a new state of cosmic consciousness (in 'Les pur-Sang'). We may read the collection in terms of stages in the life of the hero. One group of three poems ('Perdition', 'Survie', 'Au-delà') indicates the ritual necessity of abandoning oneself, of surrendering to the will of the universe in order to survive spiritually. In this respect the hero of *Les Armes miraculeuses* is manifestly the persona of the author of 'Poésie et Connaissance'. 'Les Armes miraculeuses' follows 'Au-delà' in the collection, just as the battles of the hero follow his consecration. If we read the poems as interrelated in this way, the opening strophe of 'Les Armes miraculeuses', with its dense succession of *métaphores filées*, takes on a particularly rich resonance; we move backward to the preceding poems and we anticipate not only the development of this poem but the further evolution of the collection:

> Le grand coup de machette du plaisir rouge en plein front il y avait du sang et cet arbre qui s'appelle flamboyant et qui ne mérite jamais mieux ce nom-là que les veilles de cyclone et de villes mises à sac le nouveau sang la raison rouge tous les mots de toutes les langues qui signifient mourir de soif et seul quand mourir avait le goût de pain et la terre et la mer un goût d'ancêtre et cet oiseau qui me crie de ne pas me rendre et la patience des hurlements à chaque détour de ma langue.
>
> (P, 103)

We learn in conclusion that the hero's revolt must continue 'tant que nous n'aurons pas atteint la pierre sans dialecte/ la feuille sans donjon l'eau frêle sans fémur le péri/ toine séreux des soirs de source' (P, 105).

This quest for the original transparency of language ('la pierre sans dialecte'), for the natural understanding of the world by man ('la feuille sans donjon l'eau frêle sans fémur'), for the interpretation of all created things ('le péritoine séreux des soirs de source'), typifies several of the longer poems and occasional shorter ones ('Au-delà'). Several poems concentrate on the necessary violence of the revolt itself without the happy synthesis of poems like 'Les Pur-Sang' or 'Au-delà'. These poems ('La Forêt vierge', 'Autre Saison' and 'Jour et Nuit' are printed in series) share other features as well: the unrelieved typographical density of their lay-out intensifies the effect of the *métaphore filée*; the text of 'Jour et Nuit' echoes the title of 'La Forêt vierge', reinforcing the notion of intertextuality within the collection. Another sequence of three poems functions primarily to establish the role of ecstatic epiphanies: 'Phrase', 'Poème pour l'aube', 'Visitation'. These and some others share the type of closure that André Breton, referring to beauty generally, called 'convulsive ... explosante-fixe':[16]

> ... un assassin vêtu d'étamines riches et calmes comme
> un chant de vin dur
> (P, 96)

> l'aube irrésistible ouverte sous la feuille
> telle clarteux l'élan épineux des belladones
> (P, 97)

> ... et Ta très sauvage disparition
> tropicale comme une apparition de loup nocturne en plein midi
> (P, 98)

In the penultimate text of *Les Armes miraculeuses*, 'Et les chiens se taisaient', all the aspects of poetic language rapidly outlined above come together in a splendid dramatic poem which takes up nearly half the volume. The hero takes on the type of symbolic identity which permits him to remain midway between the lyric and the drama. 'Et les chiens se taisaient' is a tragic poem of the type described by Nietzsche in *The Birth of Tragedy*, a detail Césaire himself has acknowledged.[17] Le Rebelle, in the sacrificial action of his death, recapitulates the entire movement of *Les Armes miraculeuses*, sundering anew the veil of Maya. This poem also reveals another important facet of Césaire's poetics: it is fundamentally agonistic. His optimism is akin to Nietzsche's: hope lies on the other side of tragedy.

IV. Ambiguous Rhythms

Rhythm is an element of Césaire's poetics which has alternately charmed and shocked readers, depending on their willingness to see the traditional French prosody extended or drastically modified from within. Césaire's use of novel rhythms is intimately connected to the ecstasies and epiphanies in his poems. We may apply to his own practice this observation concerning the Harlem Renaissance poets, whom Césaire had studied with great interest. Of their contribution to contemporary poetry he wrote in *Tropiques* for July 1941:

> Car enfin, voilà une poésie qui n'offre pas à l'oreille ou à l'oeil un corps inattendu et indiscutable de vibrations. Ni l'éclat des couleurs. Ni la magie du son. Tout au plus du rhythme, mais de primitif, de jazz ou de tam-tam, c'est-à-dire enfonçant la résistance de l'homme en ce point de plus basse humanité qu'est le système nerveux (p. 41).

As a poetic device Césaire's rhythms are intended to deaden the conditioned reflex of critical intelligence so as to permit the desired abandonment of the self to the world. Although to my knowledge Césaire has never used the word trance in this connection, he was surely aiming for a trance-like effect in a number of his poems. As soon as we advance beyond broad generalizations of this sort, however, the ground for judgement becomes rather spongy and porous.

What of a poem like 'Batouque', for example? It is the most frequently mentioned of the poems which appear to have a peculiar rhythmic structure. (There are several which have the term 'Tam-Tam' in their title). In the original edition of *Les Armes miraculeuses* (1946) Césaire glossed the title in a note: 'rythme du tam-tam au Brésil'.

This authorial intervention, quite unusual for him, has led readers to assume a close relation between the structure of this poem and a specific drum beat. L. Kesteloot, commenting on a long and rhythmically frenzied passage which Césaire removed from the poem in 1970 (along with the note on 'Batouque'), supposed that the passage in question 'était le seul qui "collait" vraiment à la danse, que l'auteur avait traduite en danse de mots'.[18] From supposition to explanation is but a short step for this critic. She offers no more evidence for the explanation than for the assumption that the text is mimetic: 'C'est d'ailleurs pour cette raison qu'il l'a supprimée, pour cet aspect trop descriptif, pittoresque' (p. 85).

Bernadette Cailler has attempted something far more ambitious, an intertextual commentary of 'Batouque' and ritual ceremonies of traditional agricultural societies as reported by Malinowski and Lévi-Strauss. Her results enrich our approach to Césaire's text, but they are only partially successful insofar as they apply to the crucial question of metrics:

> 'Batouque', de rythme devient danse, et de danse devient corps, et de corps devient peuple. Bastide nous dit que cette danse est aussi bien profane que religieuse; elle appartient à tout nouveau du réel; elle brise les antinomies; elle mêle les hommes et les dieux, les mythes et la vie quotidienne: elle est cosmos [...] Le poète-magicien en fait la célébration d'une renaissance, celle des valeurs culturelles et spirituelles d'un peuple.[19]

This is indeed as far as we can reasonably go until basic research has been completed on Césaire's poetic rhythms.

V. Enduring Shackles

Les Armes miraculeuses is the high point of the triumphant phase of negritude for Césaire. The collection *Corps perdu* (1950) has a greater degree of coherence among the poems, but there are only ten in all, compared to the twenty-eight in *Les Armes miraculeuses* (twenty-nine in the definitive edition of 1970). The unity of inspiration of *Armes* had already been threatened when *Soleil cou-coupé* was published just two years later. During that period Césaire had encountered the first underlying realities of the colonial mentality in postwar France. A process of serious disenchantment set in, occasioning important modifications in his poetics which we can trace from *Soleil cou-coupé* to *Ferrements* in 1960. (The collection *Noria* which was released as the final section of Césaire's *Poèmes* in 1976 contains a number of occasional pieces; although some of the poems are significant individually the collection in no way alters our view of the curve of Césaire's poetic evolution.)

As a preliminary remark we observe a movement parallel to the general disappointment and growing bitterness that followed the wave of optimism felt by the entire political Left in France at war's end. Aimé Césaire's poetic productivity can be circumscribed historically between the prewar enthusiasm of the Popular Front and the first signs of the break-up of colonial empire in the late fifties. Paradoxically he ceased to write poetry at the very moment when the former African colonies began to gain their independence. An important lesson is readily drawn from this observation. The intensely, resolutely subjective poetics Aimé Césaire practised as his dominant mode was a strategy for survival in a world where social reality offered no acceptable grasp. When political conditions had changed, if not for Martinique at least for Africa, Césaire turned to the theatre. In his political plays written in the sixties (*La Tragédie du Roi Christophe*, 1963; *Une Saison au Congo*, 1967) one can follow the evolution of Le Rebelle as he comes to terms with the problem of leadership in a newly independent nation.

No serious critical attention has been given to the extent or the type of modifications Aimé Césaire has introduced into his poems after their initial publication, although this is a rich vein to explore in order to trace the direction of change in his poetic practice. We have already seen in the case of *Cahier d'un retour au pays natal* how important were the changes in subsequent editions. The privileged example for his postwar poetics is surely *Soleil cou-coupé*. Of the seventy-two poems in the original edition thirty were omitted entirely when the collection was re-edited with *Corps perdu* under the collective title *Cadastre* in 1961. The atmosphere of *humour noir* in the manner of Lautréamont is considerably reduced by the choice of poems omitted. The incidence of long sequences of *métaphores filées* is lessened by the exclusion of poems like 'Tournure des choses' and 'Déshérence'. The *topos* of monstrosity, which B. Cailler treats in some detail, is almost completely obscured by the exclusion of the poems in which it is articulated most explicitly: 'A l'heure où dans la chaleur les moines nus descendent de l'Himalaya', 'Attentat aux moeurs', etc. Some of the more provocative sexual metaphors disappear as a result of the same decision, as in 'Scalp': 'C'est vrai que j'ai laissé mes ongles en pleine chair de cyclone/ parmi le fracas des hannetons gros/ et jusqu'à faire jaillir le jaune neuf d'un sperme/ me jetant sous son ventre pour mesurer/ mon rut'.[20] But even more lyrical examples of surrealist eroticism were not spared. In 'A l'Afrique' Césaire sacrificed this passage: 'j'attends d'une attente vulnéraire une campagne qui naîtra aux oreilles de ma compagne et verdira à son sexe le ventre de ma compagne c'est le coup de tonnerre du beau temps les cuisses de ma compagne jouent les arbres tombés le long de sa démarche' (SC, 73). For this he substituted in 1961 the high-sounding, principled and revolutionary image: 'Famine et de toi-même houle ramas où se risque d'un salut la colère du futur frappe Colère' (P, 242).

One's overall impression on comparing the two editions of *Soleil cou-coupé* is that at the time when real change was taking place in the colonized world, the anarchistic posture of many of the original poems seemed to the poet out of place and inopportune. No longer was it enough for the logos to promise a Rimbaldian change in mankind, the Marxian injunction to first change the world took precedence henceforth.

The final poem of *Corps perdu*, the long and beautifully modulated 'Dit d'errance', opens with a retrospective glance at the heroic pseudomythology of *Armes*: 'Et pourtant que te reste-t-il du temps ancien// à peine peut-être certain sens/ dans la pluie de la nuit de chauvir ou trembler/ et quand d'aucuns chantent Noël revenu/ de songer aux astres/ égarés' (P, 89).

The nostalgic tone of 'Dit d'errance' occurs frequently in *Ferrements*, displacing to a considerable extent the militant provocation of the original *Soleil cou-coupé*. The title poem of *Ferrements* calls attention to the enduring shackles, remnants of the centuries-old history of colonialism and slavery: '... comme jadis/ esclaves arrimés de coeurs lourds/ tout de même ma chère tout de même nous cinglons/ à peine un peu moins écoeurés aux tangages' (P, 143). In a homophonic play on *ferrements* Césaire wrote 'Ferment' for the same collection. Whereas in the 1944 essay on 'Poésie et Connaissance' he had certified the Promethean character of poetry, in 1960 the poet is a Prometheus in chains: 'Séduisant du festin de mon foie ô Soleil/ ta réticence d'oiseau, écorché, roulant' (P, 176). And the sun, which in *Armes* had symbolized the hero's conquering will, appears in 'Ferment' ambiguously, metaphorically on the side of the eagle. The viscera of Prometheus suggest 'Viscères du poème', which metaphorically denies the former claims of heroic negritude: 'Peur dans l'écheveau fou je n'aurai que faire de chercher/ en tremblant/ le fil rouge de mon sang de ma raison de mon droit/ [...] je refuse ton pacte sa fureur de patience/ et le tumulte debout dans l'ombre des oreilles/ aura vu pour une fois sur la blancheur du mur/ gicler la noirceur de ce cri sans oubli' (P, 157).

Thematically, Césaire has, over a period of some twenty-odd years, moved from a tentative search for identity, to the triumphant affirmation of ethnicity, to a more reflective attitude toward the limitations of poetry. Stylistically, he has evolved from the expressionism of the early *Cahier*, through an unconditional surrealism, to a more personal and less dense poetic mode. The claims of the antique logos have been found to be excessive. Césaire no longer posits another, transcendent world to be revealed by the poem. But neither has he taken up poetry as a form of cultural criticism. In 'C'est moi-même, Terreur, c'est moi-même', we recognize Aimé Césaire in the voice of a wounded but very human fidelity:

> Les rêves échoués desséchés font au ras de la gueule des rivières
> de formidables tas d'ossements muets
> les espoirs trop rapides rampent scrupuleusement
> en serpents apprivoisés
> on ne part pas on ne part jamais
> pour ma part en île je me suis arrêté fidèle ...
> (P, 158)

NOTES

1. Aimé Césaire, 'Aux écluses du vide', in *Poèmes*, vol. I of his *Oeuvres complètes* (Fort-de-France: Désormeaux, 1976), p. 249. All reference to this edition of Césaire's poetic work will be made parenthetically in the text via the abbreviation P.

2. Emile Snyder, 'A Reading of Césaire's *Return to My Native Land'*, *L'Esprit Créateur*, X, 3 (Fall 1970), p. 198.

3. Michel Benamou, 'Entretien avec Aimé Césaire: Fort-de-France, le 14 février 1973',*Cahiers Césairiens*, 1 (Printemps 1974), p. 4. ('Au fond, *Cahier d'un retour au pays natal*, d'accord, ce n'était pas un poème mais un "texte" au sens moderne du mot' - Benamou's recollection of Césaire's reply to his question, the tape recorder having malfunctioned.)

4. Jacqueline Sieger, 'Entretien avec Aimé Césaire', *Afrique*, 5 (octobre 1961), pp. 64-67.

5. Lilyan Kesteloot, *Les Ecrivains noirs de langue française: naissance d'une littérature*, 3rd ed. (Brussels: Université Libre de Bruxelles-Institut de Sociologie, 1965), p. 238, note 26.

6. Renée Riese Hubert, 'Aimé Césaire, French Poet', *Dada/Surrealism*, 3 (1973), pp. 53-60.

7. Roger Bastide, 'Variations sur la négritude', *Présence afrique*, 36 (1961), pp. 7-17.

8. M. a M. Ngal, *Aimé Césaire: un homme à la recherche d'une patrie* (Dakar-Abidjan: Nouvelles Editions africaines, 1975), pp. 1-293.

9. Marcien Towa, '"Les Pur-Sang" (négritude césairienne et surréalisme)', *Abbia* (Yaoundé), 23 (1969), p. 81.

10. An important exception must be made for the strophe beginning 'Ecoutez le monde blanc/ horriblement las de son effort immense ...' which has not been modified since 1939. Césaire selected it as the epigraph introducing his collected *Poèmes* in the *Oeuvres Complètes* published in three volumes in 1976.

11. For a thorough discussion of this question see my essay '*Tropiques:* Surrealism in the Service of Negritude', in *Critical Perspectives on Aimé Césaire*, T. A. Hale, ed. (Washington: Three Continents Press [in press]).

12. St.-John Perse, *Eloges and Other Poems* (N.Y.: Pantheon Books, 1956), p. 6.

13. Aimé Césaire, *Cahier d'un retour au pays natal* (New York: Brentano's 1947), [p. 34]. I cite the original version of this passage, which was altered slightly in 1956: see P, 50.

14. Aimé Césaire, 'Poésie et Connaissance', *Tropiques*, 12 (janvier 1945), p. 163. Subsequent reference to this paper will be by means of the abbreviation PC. *Tropiques* was the cultural magazine edited in Fort-de-France by Césaire and a small group of young Martinicans from April 1941 to September 1945. Most of the poems collected in *Les Armes miraculeuses* first appeared in its pages.

15. Leo Frobenius, *Histoire de la civilisation africaine* (Paris: Gallimard, 1936), pp. 31, 211 and *passim.*

16. André Breton, *L'Amour fou* (Paris: Gallimard, 1966 [1st printing 1937]), p. 21.

17. In an interview with Ghislaine Préville cited by M. a M. Ngal, *op. cit.*, p. 181.

18. L. Kesteloot, 'La Poésie de Césaire', in Kesteloot and Kotchy, *Aimé Césaire, l'homme et l'oeuvre* (Paris: Présence africaine, 1973), p. 85.

19. Bernadette Cailler, *Proposition poétique, une lecture de l'oeuvre d'Aimé Césaire* (Ottawa: Naaman, 1976).

20. Aimé Césaire, *Soleil cou-coupé* (Nendeln: Kraus Reprint, 1970), pp. 46-47. Subsequent reference to this volume will be by means of the abbreviation SC.

'JE DANSE, DONC JE SUIS'
THE RHYTHM OF LEOPOLD SEDAR SENGHOR'S TWO CULTURES

Roger Little

The implications of the irony of an independent third-world writer having to use the language of his former colonizers to win an international reputation merit closer attention than they have perhaps been given. That irony is compounded when the writer is also a national leader, walking an inevitably delicate and no doubt on occasion dubious political tightrope. Flanked by the Scylla of sloth (induced by the fierce sun) and the Charybdis of charity (handed out by interested ex-colonisers and international do-gooders), he has to stretch his high wire, like Rimbaud, and dance. This is the dance of the poet, the unlikely balance, the feast of poised movement, the advance into stillness. Poetic 'success' cannot be measured in historical, political, social or other extra-poetic terms, but contextual considerations will inevitably colour our total assessment of Senghor as a poet.

Should we then argue, from his external biography, that the poetry traces the development of a sensitive, gifted and aristocratic young Serer through the schooling of alien missionaries (high-minded but profoundly misguided and alienating, should we add?), lycée and the Sorbonne to the much-prized *agrégation*, on to teaching French grammar and ever-increasing involvement with Senegalese politics culminating in his becoming president of the newly independent nation in 1960? Should we take a *taxi de brousse* to Joal-Fadioutt, where Senghor was born, do the last mile to the island by horse and trap, cross in a chartered dug-out to where, buried in millions of discarded cockle-shells, parched crosses mark the relics of an alien belief and fatuously stretch their arms for rain to swell the rice for the little native granaries on stilts across the *marigot*? However impressive the history, however pleasant the pilgrimage and powerful the image, they are poor substitutes, if we are literary critics, for looking at the poetry.

Its vocabulary and referents necessitate on the part of the reader a kind of bifocal vision combining awareness of both French and West African phenomena and traditions. Analyzed separately, each area offers stereotypes; linked, the interplay is novel, sometimes subtle and moving, and almost invariably horizon-broadening. If time has hackneyed that interplay by sheer multiplication, credit must be given Senghor for having been among the first to recognize and exploit the *prise de conscience* of the emerging black intelligentsia. That he did so in poems whose intrinsic merit is beyond dispute is important not simply in the historical development of the third world and its relations with the other two, but also with respect to man's whole aesthetic environment and sensibility.

To posit Senghor as mediator between two cultures is now a critical commonplace. To question the validity of his sweeping generalisations about 'Western' and 'African' society, as if Cairo, Cape Town and Cotonou were, like Aberdeen, Arles and Ankara, part of an undifferentiated black or white mass, is rather less common and certainly more necessary. To see as unhelpful in the long run and racist in the short his exclusive attribution of certain qualities, such as an inherent sense of rhythm, to his archetypal and therefore impossible 'African', seems a tasteless challenge to the (almost only) begetter of the renascence and new direction of modern poetry from Africa.

The African *cogito* of my title is close to one Senghor quotes with approval in his essay on 'L'Apport de la poésie noire au demi-siècle': 'Je sens donc je suis',[1] and represents the kind of interplay he is fond of between an assertion about his fellow-blacks and a sophisticated reference to the tenets of his acquired and by no means rejected French culture. Had a French-born intellectual such as Valéry said it (and it is by no means unthinkable that he might have done so), the *boutade* would have had a quite different effect. The very use of a metropolitan cultural reference in an assertion denying that culture access to dance, fundamental to the human body and mind, yet claimed for blacks alone, is an irony that cuts several ways. Independence entails dependence, not merely as a point of departure but in a perpetual dialectic.

A sense of rhythm is only one of several features of *Négritude* persistently reiterated in the pages of *Liberté I* as if repetition constituted proof.[2] Almost without exception, along with other eminently universal human qualities such as emotion and intuition, it is seen as the prerogative of black men: 'L'émotion est nègre' (p. 24); 'le Nègre [est] un être rythmique. C'est le rythme incarné' (p. 37); 'nous vous apportons, à vous, Européens, à vous Latins, la *raison intuitive*, par quoi se définit la Négritude' (p. 356); '... le rythme. Encore un don de la Négritude' (p. 410). Such appealing nonsense may serve short-term political ends (political in the broad sense): its generalisations appear both more naive and more dangerous as sophistication in inter-racial relationships increases.

That differences exist none will deny. That those differences occur in matters as fundamental to man's being as rhythm, emotion or intuition is questionable not simply in physiological terms but because such a suggestion ultimately connives at the very hierarchical concept of race against which Senghor's assertions are directed. Ordinary members of a technological society are geared to using the language of science and discursive reason; their whole training makes them belittle the language of poetry and intuition. Purposeful prose, cybernetic signs are not deflected by the cudgel of over-simplified rhetoric, but they can be subverted. And Senghor shows on occasion in his essays that when the essence of poetry is sensed, pigmentation takes its proper place as a matter, humanly speaking, of total irrelevance.

Sartre was right to call negritude 'un racisme antiraciste'.[3] Senghor's *faux naïf* rhetorical question: 'Comment voudriez-vous que nous fussions racistes, nous qui avions été, pendant des siècles, les victimes innocentes, les *hosties noires* du racisme?'[4] is better answered by a protestation that there was every reason to resent the domination of the 'roses d'oreilles'. The impassioned outbursts of Césaire, the seething resentment of others seem far healthier, far more 'honest' reactions than Senghor's improbable gestures of pacification and vision of a 'civilisation de l'universel'. To will oneself to be a *pontifex*, let alone a *pontifex maximus africanus*, is parlously close both to saintliness and damnation. The 'hostie grise' is a dangerous temptation.[5]

What modest measures may the poet take to insure his afterlife? I would venture to suggest that it is precisely by counterpointing rhythms sensed in two cultures that Senghor shows his mastery and poise, obliging his reader to assimilate the force of the other and thereby the force of the Other.

'*Plus de mots*. J'ensevelis les morts dans mon ventre. Cris, tambour, danse, danse, danse, danse!' Rimbaud's savage vision in *Une Saison en enfer* includes, after his taunting the bourgeoisie with being 'nègre', this wild cannabalistic self-projection which we take both as a symbolical stereotype of the 'primitive' and as an ironic caricaturing of that stereotype. Without the benefit of this irony, Senghor's evocations risk being simply a caricature:

> La danse est, pour le Négro-africain, le moyen le plus naturel d'exprimer une idée, une émotion. Que l'émotion le saisisse - joie ou tristesse, gratitude ou indignation -, le Négro-africain danse. ... Leur seul secret est de s'abandonner au rythme, cires dociles; de se laisser saisir et agir par l'Archétype, de vivre - non de jouer - leur personnage avec la vérité vraie de l'émotion.
>
> (*Liberté I*, p. 289)

Bodily expression of rhythm may be channelled into acceptable forms or frowned upon by different societies, but whether revealed in folk-dance, classical ballet or the bedroom mirror, delight in physical movement is surely universal. Stimulated by the rhythms of music, dance is, in the words of Maurice Béjart, 'un rituel englobant tous les sens, cérémonie, mystère, liturgie, orgie, orgasme, magie' (*ibid.*, p. 382) or again, as Senghor writes, 'le langage le plus complet. Il met en oeuvre tout le corps, ... tous les arts: poésie, chant et musique, peinture, sculpture et - naturellement - danse' (*ibid.*, p. 288). Although each time Senghor relates the capacity for dance to Africa, the impartial observer will see this as special pleading. Whatever affection we may have for jazz, it is only one musical form among many which encourage complex rhythmical movement. Senghor banks on its popularity to make his audience accept the following sweeping statement:

> Ce qui caractérise le rythme négro-africain, c'est précisément son caractère *vital*: la régularité dans l' irrégularité, l'unité dans la diversité, pour tout dire, sa variété sous son apparence de monotonie. Grâce aux *syncopes* et *contretemps*, dont les équivalents se retrouvent dans les arts plastiques, ce rythme exprime, plus que tout autre, la vie. C'est le fameux *swing* négro-américain, qui vient tout droit de l'Afrique et que souligne, ici, la polyrythmie des oeuvres négro-africaines.
>
> (*Liberté I*, p. 281)

African music certainly emphasizes its basis in rhythm (and swing is far from being the most complex example) whereas European music tends to be tonal. But melody without rhythm is scarcely imaginable: Senghor undermines his case by overstating it. And surely it is true of a particular brand of poet anywhere that, exchanging the tom-tom for his own cultural equivalent, 'il a besoin de se perdre dans la danse verbale, au rythme du tam-tam, pour se retrouver dans le Cosmos' (*ibid.*, 225).

The element of cultural specificity is not therefore fundamental, as Senghor would have us believe. It remains highly interesting, however, and not least because Senghor believes it to be paramount as regards rhythm in Africa: 'nulle part, le rythme n'a régné aussi despotiquement' (*ibid.*, p. 216).

> *Qu'est-ce que le rythme*? C'est l'architecture de l'être, le dynamisme interne qui lui donne forme, le système d'ondes qu'il émet à l'adresse des *Autres*, l'expression pure de la Force vitale. Le rythme, c'est le choc vibratoire, la force qui, à travers les sens, nous saisit à la racine de l'*être*. Il s'exprime par les moyens les plus matériels, les plus sensuels: lignes, surfaces, couleurs, volumes en architecture, sculpture et peinture; accents en poésie et musique; mouvements dans la danse.
>
> (*Liberté I*, pp. 211-2)

Where poetry is concerned, as Senghor makes clear by indicating specific instruments for many of his poems - kora, khalam, balafong and so forth - there is an interplay between accompaniment and text. More than once he states that the rhythm is governed not by the words but by the music: 'le rythme essentiel est non celui de la parole, mais des instruments à percussion qui accompagnent la voix humaine, plus exactement de ceux d'entre eux qui marquent le rythme de base' (*ibid*, p. 212). The complex rhythms of much African drumming act as a foil for the poem but tend to overwhelm its verbal rhythms and turn it into chant:

> Le rythme de base est marqué despotiquement par les gros tam-tams au son grave et par les battements de mains du public: d'autre part, visiblement, par les pas et gestes de l'athlète danseur. D'autres tam-tams, plus légers, et d'autres battements de mains brodent sur ce rythme, à contretemps et syncope.
>
> Les poèmes négro-africains peuvent être non pas déclamés, mais en quelque sorte *psalmodiés*.
>
> (*Liberté I*, p. 170)

The public and discursive nature of such poetry, designed for performance in a way perhaps analogous to that appropriate to the *Chanson de Roland*, is a far cry from introspective lyricism, the mainstream of modern Western poetry.[6] But one feature seems imperative: a strong clear beat, whether in *Beowulf* or the *Kalevala*, *El Poema de Mio Cid* or *Da Monzon de Ségou*.

For poems composed in heavily stressed or stressable languages such as Wolof, of which Senghor gives several examples, the reciter doubtless holds his own against the counterpointing of gorong, tama or mbalakh, and choric responses lend weight to the solo rhythms. The problem is compounded when a stressed language is replaced by an essentially unstressed one, when Wolof, for instance, gives way to modern French. Senghor is fond of the image of grafting French wood onto African stock so as to give new life to the old world (e.g. *ibid.*, pp. 230, 257). But grafting a rose on to a baobab is tricky, and the results are not necessarily beautiful. A more appropriate image from gardening might be the gradual naturalisation of imported seed or stock. For it is when Senghor perceives elements which French poetry has in common with his native traditions that he can transplant them and point to a family resemblance bridging the gap into which centuries of mutual incomprehension have driven so solid a wedge. In the standard French alexandrine, for instance, he singles out the binary pattern: 'le rythme binaire du vers classique peut rendre le halètement despotique du tam-tam. Il suffit de le bousculer légèrement pour faire surgir, au-dessus du rythme de base, contretemps et syncopes' (*ibid.*, p. 363). Few readers of classical French verse will, one suspects, be persuaded that even a single line conveys 'le halètement despotique du tam-tam': not only is the cultural transfer too distant, the French language scarcely admits of such tub-thumping. And against the syllabic count of the line with its special conventions relating to caesura, for example, or rhyme, the syntax of the sentence brings its cross-current to provide a regular but ever-changing interplay of rhythm and metre. 'L'unité dans la diversité', Senghor's reiterated designation for African poetic rhythms, applies no less to Racine.

When traditional French metre is sacrificed for freer forms, it is interesting to find Senghor homing naturally on the same binary rhythm and stressing the similarities between atavistic African texts and the work of Claudel and Saint-John Perse. Of the latter's prosody he writes:

> Ce que je veux souligner, c'est que, sous ses différents aspects, c'est le rythme binaire, celui de l'amble, le rythme même des *Forces vitales*: celui des jours et des saisons, du flux et du reflux, du battement du coeur, de la respiration, de la marche, de l'amour. Il est régulier, mais point monotone.
> (*Liberté I*, p. 335)

Negro rhythm is presented in almost identical terms elsewhere (e.g. *ibid* p. 80) and Senghor quotes with approval Jean Guéhenno's suggestion that 'les textes des cosmogonies *dogon* "ne sont pas sans analogie avec les poèmes de Claudel ou de M. Alexis Léger (Saint-John Perse)"' (*ibid.*, p. 219).[7] First in time and importance to influence Senghor from among

French poets was Claudel; first for his later output was Saint-John Perse.

Claudel's influence had been thoroughly assimilated by the time *Chants d'ombre* and *Hosties noires*, the first two collections, came to be written. And the prosodic lesson was doubtless learnt all the more readily because of the alien Catholic's urgent sympathy with the proselytising convert. It was only after 'la matière de deux recueils' was safely stowed in a drawer (see *Liberté I*, p. 334) that Senghor discovered Saint-John Perse. Even if the particular poem he first read, *Exil*, were not named (*ibid.*), the verbal echoes in *Ethiopiques* are sufficiently frequent and direct for there to have been no doubt.[8] There is doubt, however, about when Senghor first read the work. The evidence of the essay 'Comme les lamantins vont boire à la source' which stands as a postface to *Ethiopiques* and has therefore been reprinted in each republication and collection of that volume seems final and has never been questioned: 'à la découverte de Saint-John Perse, après la Libération, je fus ébloui comme Paul sur le chemin de Damas' (*ibid.*, p. 219). The *terminus a quo* would therefore be August 1944. But his essay on Saint-John Perse begins:

> Je me rappelle encore l'Evénement. C'était, sur ma table, un nouveau numéro des *Cahiers du Sud*, où j'avais publié un poème en 1938. Nous étions sous l'Occupation. Dans ce numéro, un poème, signé *Saint-John Perse*, avait retenu mon attention. M'avait foudroyé, comme Paul sur le chemin de Damas. Il s'intitulait *Exil*.
>
> (*Liberté I*, p. 334)

Exil indeed appeared in *Les Cahiers du Sud*, its first publication in Europe, in May 1942. 1942 also saw Senghor's return to teaching on the outskirts of Paris after two years in concentration camps. Copies of *Les Cahiers du Sud* would certainly have taken time to percolate through to occupied Paris, but hardly three years; and Senghor would scarcely think of a May 1942 issue as being 'nouveau' in late 1945.

If circumspection is necessary over such a matter, Senghor's registration of his reaction is consistent with the evidence and consistent *tout court*. There is a marked stabilisation of rhythm and construction in *Ethiopiques* as compared with the earlier work, and this is entirely in line with the prosodic differences between Claudel and Saint-John Perse. But Claudel's influence persists in the 'jaillissement du thorax': 'Plus surveillé chez l'auteur d'*Anabase*, dont la rhétorique concertée ne laisse rien au hasard, plus jailli du thorax chez Senghor, le ton de l'un et de l'autre est en rupture d'alexandrin, tout en respectant une métrique aussi discrète que rigoureuse'.[9]

Claudel's crucial shift of concentration from syllable-count to metre, from arithmetic to rhythm, has had important repercussions in French poetry but represents of course only part of a movement towards increasing flexibility of verse forms. By focussing on 'l'ïambe fondamental' in *Réflexions et propositions sur le vers français* and rapping the metronomic piano mistress over her knuckles for a change, he rediscovered a universal rhythm which would cut across national frontiers. Expounding the qualities of his poetic line in a letter to Eugène Marsan of 31 August 1907, Claudel wrote:

> Je vois que mon vers vous cause un certain étonnement. Pourquoi? C'est simplement le vers ordinaire libéré de la rime et d'un compte déterminé de syllabes, mais l'essentiel y est qui est une certaine réunion de sonorités et d'idées que comporte tel souffle. C'est la restitution de l'haleine puisée au blanc, une inspiration visible. Il constitue à la fois:
>
> l'unité respiratoire, comme en entendant parler et prêcher vous trouvez que les reprises d'haleine ne coïncident pas avec les points et virgules de la phrase, unité purement objective et logique. Par là il devient la mesure même de l'émotion et d'un débit plus ou moins saccadé ou régulier ...;
>
> c'est une unité musicale composée d'un rapport d'une grave et d'une aiguë ou ïambe, non pas fixes, mais à choisir par le lecteur au travers d'une riche modulation;
>
> c'est une unité intelligible qui permet de mettre plusieurs choses ensemble dans un rapport pur et nu sans l'attirail artificiel de la grammaire;
>
> enfin, c'est une unité psychologique ou amalgame de sentiments divers. ... Je pense toujours plusieurs choses à la fois.

> Enfin (point auquel je tiens particulièrement) mon vers n'a rien de neuf. C'est simplement le vers ïambique, dramatique ou lyrique, qui a toujours existé à côté du vers épique et narratif. ... Si mon vers ne peut se scander, il en est de même de celui de Pindare, de Plaute, des choeurs grecs et de Shakespeare (v. surtout les derniers drames)...[10]

Senghor's admiration for Claudel, fully expressed in *La Parole chez Claudel et chez les Négro-africains*,[11] includes, it would seem, acceptance of the term 'ïambe' applied more loosely than in classical prosody. Instead of meaning, in quantitative measures, a short syllable followed by a long, it is taken to cover a variable number of unstressed syllables followed, in French, by a tonally stressed syllable. It includes therefore not only the classical anapaest but peons and even longer 'feet' in which the stress falls on the last syllable. (Only exceptionally can French allow initial stress, which consequently always entails a special effect). The term *iamb* in this broad sense is less strictly binary than Claudel and Senghor would have us believe, since the unstressed part is elastic in length. But by drawing attention to stress rather than to arithmetic, Claudel allows and even encourages Senghor to declare: 'il faut lire les versets comme des "versets" négro-africains: d'une voix un peu monotone, mais non sans chaleur et en marquant fortement les blancs ou silences' (*La Parole chez Claudel* ..., p. 74). This emphasis on tonic difference is a first but decisive step away from normal stress patterns in French speech or verse.

Its consequences are important for our reading of Senghor.[12] We should be prepared to respect his pauses and allow for extra stress on syllables which can support and warrant it. Rhythmic drumming (which *faute de mieux* we must imagine) fills the silences and affords a richer sense of syncopation if an *attaque forte* is called for at the start of the following line. If such initial emphasis seems more frequent than is usual in French poetry, a further consideration might explain it. In the African languages with which Senghor is most familiar - Wolof, Serer and Fula - 'au lieu de l'ïambe francais, nous avons le dactyle. C'est que, si l'accent est d'intensité, il porte, ici, sur la syllabe radicale, pratiquement sur la première syllabe du mot, contrairement au français' (*ibid.*, p. 83). Just as vernacular speech patterns and accents influence an imposed or adopted international language when spoken, so it seems reasonable to suppose interaction at the level of rhythms of the written word. Diehards will denigrate and ridicule, but at worst they must grant, as Saint-Simon the memorialist did in other circumstances, that 'il faut toujours du fumier sur les meilleures terres'.

The French language was specifically entrusted with a universal mission in the eighteenth century, and it is precisely its international quality that fits it first and foremost, in Senghor's eyes, for use by writers who would otherwise have a majority of illiterates among their potential local, vernacular audience. Beyond being a partner in an arranged marriage of convenience, French is seen by Senghor as being, 'par excellence, une langue de communication: "une langue de gentillesse et d'honnêteté", une langue de politesse, de clarté, de rigueur' (*Liberté I*, p. 399; cf. pp. 358-63). If these are the dubious platitudes of the diplomat, they are also the moral imperatives of the poet. The greater the gulf between French and Negro culture, the greater the merit in building a bridge: 'vous comprenez, maintenant, pourquoi la littérature nègre d'expression française est une contribution importante à la *littérature généralisée:* à la *Civilisation de l'Universel*. C'est que, communicable par le fait qu'elle est écrite en français elle fait la *symbiose* des deux aspects extrêmes du Génie humain. Par quoi elle est *humanisme intégral*' (*ibid.*, p. 402). The word *chauvinism*, born in France, seems to have travelled with the colonizers' first ships.

Senghor's rhetoric rings hollow because it could apply to the confrontation and amalgamation of any two languages, one of which was rich in intellectual potential, with a wide range of concrete and abstract vocabulary, and the other relatively poor and largely restricted to the concrete. *Coincidentia oppositorum* has always been a fruitful dialectical source: 'Les valeur[s] latines, françaises, cartésiennes sont précisément à l'opposé des valeurs négro-africaines. De là leur *vertu*' (*ibid.*, p. 229). But Senghor also seems to ignore the truism that history is written by the conquerors and he therefore underplays the very merits of indigenous thinking in the vernacular, a language inevitably more completely adapted than any other to express the life of an African community until disrupted by colonization (whether by a European nation or by another African society). We would be rash to perpetuate the epithets 'uncivilized', 'primitive' or 'barbaric' in their all-too-common application to African societies: a 'civilization' that perpetrates the horrors of two world wars and shuts its orphans away in institutions has much to learn.

Yet neither should we succumb to the generous but naive reaction that assumes that black is better or in any essential way different. Senghor is right to underline the African's capacity for spirituality (though the absence of it would be astonishing). He may have a case in seeing rhythm as its root:

> C'est ... dans sa subjectivité que le Nègre, 'poreux à tous les souffles du monde', découvre l'objet dans sa réalité: le *rythme*. Et le voilà qui s'abandonne, docile à ce mouvement vivant, allant du sujet à l'objet, 'jouant le jeu du monde'. Qu'est-ce à dire, sinon que, pour le Nègre, connaître c'est vivre - de la vie de l'Autre - en s'identifiant à l'objet? *Con-naître*, c'est naître à l'Autre en mourant à soi: c'est faire l'amour avec l'Autre, c'est danser l'Autre.
>
> (*Liberté I*, p. 141)

> Le rythme, c'est cette spiritualité qui est exprimée par les moyens les plus matériels: volumes, surfaces et lignes en architecture et en sculpture, accents en poésie et en musique, mouvements dans la danse. Le rythme, c'est l'ordination qui entraîne tout ce concret, à quoi s'accroche notre âme émue, vers la lumière de l'Esprit.
>
> (*ibid.*, p. 80)

But whatever the means, is the end not one universally understood, experienced and appreciated? We are asked to marvel at a perception recorded by Fr Placide Tempels in his *Philosophie bantoue:*

> ... les Négro-africains distinguent 'ce qui est percu par les sens' - la matière, l'ombre, le souffle, c'est-à-dire le signe apparent de la vie - et 'la chose en elle-même': le *muntu* des Bantous. Celui-ci est l'essence même de l'être en soi, qui se définit par la *force* et se cache sous les apparences de toute manière douée de caractères

> singuliers, depuis le caillou jusqu'à Dieu.
>
> (*ibid.*, pp. 161-2)

Yet is such animism rare in philosophers from Thales to Ganges or in poets from Naso to Hugo?

I suspect that one virtue in Senghor has been unwittingly misled by another, greater virtue. Negritude has been suborned by Poetry. The political pressure on an African intellectual and leader to speak up for people too long oppressed is enormous. Senghor has done it powerfully, consistently and, as a pioneer, with staggering success. But when he parades his over-simplified generalisations about black (i.e. brown) as opposed to white (i.e. pink) people, he is in fact making a distinction not so much between them as between the poet - that is the sensitive, intuitive and imaginative person - and the non-poet, who lacks one or more of these qualities. Although he dismisses certain categories of men (as here mathematicians and scientists) in too black-and-white a way, the following juxtaposition of types provides an instance of his opposing mechanical non-poet and visionary poet:

> L'Europe, c'est la civilisation de la *raison discursive*: de l'analyse, de la mathématique, de la mécanique. Vos tentations, auxquelles vous avez parfois succombé, c'est la dichotomie et, partant, l'idéalisme ou le matérialisme. Vous avez trop souvent opposé l'esprit à la matière, la raison au coeur, la science à la foi - ou à l'art - pour ne pas vous être aperçus du danger. Le danger de créer un monde de machines sans âme, je veux dire sans chaleur humaine.
>
> Eh bien! la Négritude, c'est, essentiellement, cette chaleur humaine, qui est *présence à la vie*: au monde. C'est un *existentialisme*, pour parler comme vous, enraciné dans la Terre-Mère, épanoui au soleil de la Foi. Cette présence au monde est *participation du sujet à l'objet*, participation de l'Homme aux Forces cosmiques, *communion* de l'Homme avec les autres hommes et, par-delà, avec tous les *existants*, du caillou à Dieu.
>
> (*Liberté I*, p. 317)

Elsewhere Senghor equates this visionary capacity among black people with the basically European phenomenon of surrealism. He sees its qualities inherent in African languages, which express 'une pensée synthétique dans une syntaxe surréaliste' (*ibid.*, p. 143), and so in the patterns of thought and sensibility which lead towards the metaphysical. But he does make some distinctions (*ibid.*) and at a personal level, a poetic level, is glad to escape from 'la fatigante monotonie des procédés surréalistes' (*ibid.*, p. 341). For 'le Poète n'est pas comme M. Jourdain: si inspiré qu'il soit, il ne fait pas de la poésie sans le savoir' (*ibid.*, p. 300). Senghor's burden of knowledge is a heavy one. 'Sa tentation est de se taire devant la difficulté - l'impossibilité, sent-il - de dire l'ineffable' (*ibid.*, pp. 300-1). The sentence has an unmistakably confessional ring and enlists our sympathy on many counts, but mostly as the private cry of a public person.

'Nombril même du poème, le rythme, qui naît de l'émotion, engendre à son tour l'émotion' (*ibid.*, p. 224). That rhythm, born of an assimilation of Claudel's 'iamb' into the Serer or Wolof dactyl, grows through the binary line-structure of Senghor's writing as it absorbs French and native traditions, extends to that marvellous patterning of words which hints at the poet's deepest insights into the meaning of the universe. As history recedes, that vision will not lose its lustre, brighter indeed for sensing the rhythms of history, but beyond any question of colour.

NOTES

1. Léopold Sédar Senghor, *Liberté I: Négritude et humanisme*, Paris: Seuil, 1964, p. 141. Hereinafter abbreviated to *Liberté I*.

2. See for example, pp. 35, 37, 80, 111, 141, 169-71, etc.

3. Jean-Paul Sartre, 'Orphée noir', in *Anthologie de la nouvelle poésie nègre et malgache de langue française*, ed. L. S. Senghor, Paris: P.U.F., 1948, 2nd edn 1969, p. xiv.

4. *Liberté I*, p. 316, where Sartre is quoted.

5. The allusion is to Genet's *Les Nègres* and the character of Diouf:

   Le Missionnaire: Dites-moi, mon cher Vicaire, et l'hostie? Oui, l'hostie? Inventerez-vous une hostie noire? Et faite avec quoi? En pain d'épice, dites-vous? Il est marron.

   Diouf: Mais, monseigneur, nous avons mille ingrédients: nous teindrons. Une hostie grise ...

Le Gouverneur: Accordez l'hostie grise, vous êtes perdu, il exigera, vous verrez, de nouveau compromis, de nouvelles étrangetés.

Diouf (plaintif): Blanche d'un côté, noire de l'autre?

(Jean Genet, *Les Nègres*, Décines (Isère): L'Arbalète, 1958, p. 48).

Diouf it is who is dressed as a white woman during the course of the action.

6. The extant performance of epic in Africa could prove a fruitful source of information and comparison for mediaevalists. As an example of the living tradition, one might consult the Bambara epic *Da Monzon de Ségou*, ed. Lilyan Kesteloot *et al.*, Paris: Nathan, 1972 (4 vols).

7. Senghor's gloss is rather different from Guéhenno's. The latter's view, not unlike that of Proust's Céleste who thought Léger's early poems to be riddles, is not, however, without its similarities to Senghor's African way to the Other:

> J. envie les ethnographes. Les textes qu'ils recueillent et sur lesquels ils travaillent ne sont pas sans analogie avec les poèmes de M. Alexis Léger. C'est une sorte de gangue verbale confuse et obscure, une marne grise mais où des mots éclatent parfois comme des pépites d'or. Ils deviennent, ces mots, sous le regard plus attentif, toujours plus beaux, des images, des idées, des raisons qu'entrevoit le chercheur passionné, et, après lui, le lecteur en qui toujours veille le désir de toucher une fois au vrai monde. Ce ne sont rien que des mots peut-être, mais leur vague même et leur incertitude en font, pour qui les écoute dans une sorte d'angoisse, de plus sûres allusions à tout ce qu'il espère. Trop de clarté abolirait le charme.

(*La France et les Noirs*, Paris: Gallimard, 1954, pp. 74-75)

8. For examples, see Roger Little, *Saint-John Perse*, London: The Athlone Press of the University of London, 1973, p. 94.

9. Armand Guibert, *Léopold Sédar Senghor*, Paris: Seghers, Poètes d'aujourd'hui, 1961, p. 87.

10. Quoted *in extenso* in *Les Nouvelles littéraires* (22 Sept. 1966), p. 13.

11. Published in Dakar, 1973, by Les Nouvelles Editions Africaines, *La Parole chez Claudel et chez les Négro-africains* was read by Senghor to the International Claudel Congress held at Brangues in July, 1972. My page numbers refer to the original typescript.

12. I have considered one aspect of those consequences in a paper entitled 'A New Dimension to the Problems of Translation: The Case of Senghor' presented at the University of Sheffield in March 1976 and since published there.

TCHICAYA U TAM'SI

Gerald Moore

> Dure nuit! le sang séché fume sur ma face, et je n'ai rien derrière moi que cet horrible arbrisseau! (Rimbaud, *Une Saison en Enfer*)

A rather crude division of African poets working in the former colonial languages might place them in two categories, according to the way they interpret their relationship to the language used. In the first category would be placed all those who bring to their work an intense involvement with their indigenous poetic traditions and forms, so that many of the refrains, image-clusters and formal structures used in their own poetry are derived from those traditions. In such cases it is reasonable to assume that their first intense emotional involvement with words came through their participation in African verbal-musical events, rather than through the early study of a European literature. Thus they bring their minds to the reading of, say, Baudelaire or Yeats with an already clearly-formed idea of what poetry is in their own cultures.

Notable in this first category are certain important poets of Anglophone Africa, such as Kofi Awoonor of Ghana (the Ewe people), Mazisi Kunene of South Africa (the Zulu), Okot p'Bitek and Okello Oculi of Uganda (the Acoli), or the Nigerian poets Romanus Egudu and Okogbule Wonodi (the Igbo). Examples of this kind are rather harder to find among Francophone poets, perhaps because the assimilationist policies still followed by most of the former French colonies fifteen years after independence militate against the serious study of indigenous language and poetry. This intellectual climate also obstructs the sort of sustained involvement with this poetry by which young educated poets can produce work which extends their own poetic traditions into another language. Something of this kind does appear to have been achieved by the

Cameroonian poet E. Epanya Yondo in his *Kamerun! Kamerun!*, and the young poets collaborating with Sembène Ousmane on the Wolof revue *Kaddu* may be able to produce a genuine neo-Wolof poetry even in much-assimilated Senegal.

The example of Senegal's President, Léopold Sédar Senghor, has been extensively argued on both sides of the question; some commentators, like the late Janheinz Jahn, insisting that Senghor's technique in the praise poems (*Chants pour Naëtt* especially) is closely modelled on that of the traditional *griots* of the Western Sudan. They point to his use of parallelism; the accumulation of attributes around the person praised (like a worshipper piling up offerings around a shrine); the passionate, sustained, direct address to the object of praise; the long rolling vocal phrases of his verse; the absence of metrical regularity, stanzaic form or end-rhyme. Others, however, argue that many of these features can be found in the work of major French poets like Paul Claudel, Saint-John Perse and Charles Péguy, poets likely to have influenced him also through their fervent Catholicism or their search for a cultural universalism which would match the spiritual claims of their religion. Their use of the 'verset' has also been compared with Senghor's long, sonorous lines, which eschew the traditional prosodic devices of French poetry. Some commentators on the assumption that he is really a French poet masquerading as an African for political purposes, have even accused Senghor of exoticism for peppering his verses with the names of rivers, shrines and heroes which are meaningful to him but not the majority of his French readers. As in most academic controversies, the battle lines have been drawn up in rigid opposition, and doomed is he who has the temerity to venture into the No-Man's-Land between. But reason still prompts us to assert that a man who has dubbed himself 'un mulâtre culturel' is unlikely to have drawn his models entirely from one side or the other of these arbitrary cultural territories.

Our second category, much the larger of the two, would group all those poets who appear to have come first to poetry through an excitement with the works of French or English literature studied at school or university. Their early work is marked by imitation of certain chosen masters and only later, if at all, do they seem to reorientate their writing towards a native poetic tradition which has existed all the while outside the walls of their elitist institutions. Among leading Anglophone poets one might hazard here the names of Lenrie Peters, John Pepper Clark, Christopher Okigbo, Gabriel Okara and Mbella Sonne Dipoko; among Francophone writers, those of Birago Diop , David Diop, Joseph Bognini, Jean-Baptiste Tati-Loutard and Paulin Joachim.

It must be no surprise that this seems to have been the way through which Tchicaya U Tam'si passed to find, incredibly quickly, a voice and a tone entirely his own. Brought to Paris in 1946 at the age of fifteen, he was exposed at an even earlier age than Senghor to exclusively French surroundings and educational processes. What probably saved him as a poet was that from the Lycée Janson-de-Sailly he proceeded, not to the narrow elitism of the 'grandes écoles', but to several years of odd-jobbing as a warehouseman, farm-hand and restaurant porter. Only after the publication of his second book in 1957 did he move to one of the occupations usually associated with French-educated African poets, a writing and producing post in radio. But the initial move to France, no doubt well-intended on his father's part, left the deepest possible mark on his early poetry, which is charged with an overwhelming sense of loss. Whether literally or metaphorically, he feels deprived of a visible country, a mother and even of a genealogical identity. These are some of the recurrent themes throughout his first collection, *Le Mauvais Sang*, published in 1955 at the age of twenty-four. All his poetry, however, is haunted by the figure of his 'mère inconnue', and he reverts continually to the idea of something strange and alienated in his parentage:

> Né de mère inconnue, vénale
> Ma faute grandira l'oubli
> Je fus troqué contre le mal.
>
> (MS, 29)[1]

Is this the 'faute vénale' of the child whose birth coincides with his mother's disappearance, or is it some deeper and more mysterious sorrow? The figure of the father in his poetry is also enigmatical, charged with tension and perhaps with opposition. This is the father who brought the poet to Paris at the age of fifteen, and who thus both connects him with Africa (by his existence) and separates him from it (by his action). Tchicaya's father was the first elected black deputy for Moyen Congo to take his seat in the French National Assembly under the new constitution of 1946. It was for this reason that he came to Paris and brought the young Tchicaya with him. Perhaps for the same reasons, of social and political ambition, he had earlier taken Tchicaya away from his natural mother and had denied the child all knowledge of her existence or identity. In the ironical poem 'Entendu dans le Vent', which describes a visit to a fortune-teller and ends with the words 'Monsieur, je voudrais voir comment sont vos viscères!', we find these lines, again heavy with deprivation:

> Ouvrez votre bouche et vos mains: des cancrelats!
> Je ne vous vois ni père, ni mere, ni frères ...
> (MS, 34)

Tchicaya's second and third collections, *Feu de Brousse* (1957) and *A Triche-Coeur* (1960) are haunted by the figure of 'l'enfant' or 'l' orphelin', who wanders everywhere seeking the tree or root of his origin, the source of his very being. The same orphan figure meets us already in the concluding poem of *Le Mauvais Sang* written, like Rimbaud's poem of the same title in *Une Saison en Enfer*, in prose:

> Fleuve non mer non lac non, arbre oui arbre mauve à l'endroit du soleil rond, arbre la nuit mille et mille lucioles en font un diamant brut comme la naissance et j' ouvre mes bras pour me chercher une mère-Misère! Pitié! Splendeur! Clopin-clopant infernale cadence! fleuve mer lac non non viendra l'orfèvre je fermerai mes bras pour retrouver un coeur de pierre. Crève donc! ...
>
> Ils marchent à pas lents des orphelins nus de honte comme si avec le sens que nous avons du monde il est permis à des orphelins privilégiés d'être sans père. Quelle comédie ...
> ('Le Signe du Mauvais Sang', MS, 46-47)

In this passage we note the bitter word-play not only on *mer/mère/misère*, but also on *père/pierre*. The theme of an infant cursed with ill even in his very birth is present here, not only in the words *Clopin-clopant* (Tchicaya has a clubfoot) but in the opening arms of the newborn child, which close upon a stone.

This particular theme is taken up in another poem of his first collection, 'Le Mal':

> Ils ont craché sur moi, j'étais encore enfant,
> Bras croisés, tête douce, inclinée, bonne, atone.
> Pour mon ventre charnu, mon oeil criait: aumône!
> J'étais enfant dans mon coeur il y avait du sang.
> (MS, 31)

Tchicaya's blood, it seems, is 'mauvais' in a double sense. The orphan's blood carries the heritage of a bitter destiny founded in ill, but it is also the 'gros sang' of a new race, full of a rebellious urgency which breaks and remakes the physical world. Perhaps it is this 'gros sang' in both senses which makes Tchicaya recognize, in Arthur Rimbaud, a companion both in ill and in world-shaping poetic creativity. Rimbaud, though born in and of Europe, felt himself always displaced there because of his 'mauvais sang'. Rimbaud's too was an orphaned adolescence of revolt and restless departures. He yearned for a pagan identity which would renew his existence under tropical suns, far from the sick, war-torn Europe of 1870-71. Fate had ensured that he play a part in that Europe and he spent his brief life in endeavouring to change that role, at whatever cost in isolation and pain. This feeling of kinship with Rimbaud is asserted not only in the choice of title for Tchicaya's first collection but in a specific passage of a slightly later poem, 'Le Forçat'. Here again Tchicaya refers to some scandalous feature in his origins (the words 'famille heureuse' are clearly ironical) and to the sense that something in his inborn destiny has deprived him of nationality. Perhaps only in the age of slavery could a black man growing up in Paris have found a context nonsensical enough to contain him (or so I interpret the cryptic final line of the passage). The exemption from military service, which would follow from his physical disability, only reinforces this profound sense of *dépaysement*; a sense which haunted Rimbaud also:

or donc moi j'aime sans contrainte.
je le sais bien,
il n'y a pas d'amour
sans lutte de crasses.

ma crasse à moi c'est ma situation
de famille heureuse

prétentions
pour le scandale dans ma famille
je m'avoue une sourde parenté de corps
avec un certain arthur
- mise à part la révolte -
à cause de mon passé

signe particulier
exempté de service militaire
n'ayant plus de patrie sur aucune
planisphère
depuis l'abolition de l'esclavage

(FB, 89-90)

One of the final poems in *Le Mauvais Sang*, entitled 'Le Gros Sang', also elaborates upon the idea of a blood whose 'badness' is now only an ironic way of referring to its strength and rebellious urgency. Here the associations with some profound guilt, approbrium or scandal are shed, and the poet is ready to burst his bonds:

J'ai disloqué les vents puisqu'il faut qu'on m'entende
Pour retrouver blessant les désirs qu'on me vende
Je suis l'acier trempé, le feu des races neuves
Dans mon gros sang rouge écument troublants des fleuves

(MS, 43)

But does the connection with Rimbaud extend beyond a biographical identification? A more precise formal influence might be seen at work in this first volume, *Le Mauvais Sang*, in which there are also traces of a Verlainian elegance. Certainly some of the poems of this first book suggest a *submission* to French nineteenth century forms and conventions. Here, in a way uncharacteristic of his later work, Tchicaya writes predominantly in regular stanzaic form (generally in sonnets or in quatrains with a predominance of twelve-syllable lines) and in rhyme. He also makes much greater use of punctuation and of sentence-structure than in his later poetry. On the other hand, certain poems, such as the last poem of the volume, 'Le Signe du Mauvais Sang' (see the passage quoted above, beginning 'Fleuve non mer non lac non ...'), whilst perhaps acknowledging Rimbaud's *Une Saison en Enfer* in their prose form, mark a linguistic departure in their unbroken flow and freer association of sounds and images. The poem 'Le Forçat', quoted above, suggests a similar departure in the cryptic placing of words or phrases which 'open out' in the following stanza, as is the case, for example, with 'prétentions' or 'signe particulier'.

By the time Tchicaya publishes his second collection, *Feu de Brousse* (Caractères, 1957), he has moved decisively away from this relative conservatism of prosody and form. If we wish to chase influences, we might adduce a direct one from the French *Surréalistes*, or an indirect one through the work of Aimé Césaire. However that might be, Tchicaya swings into his new volume with an amazing sustained *élan*, a torrent of freely associating images which flow backwards and forwards within the poems, without the barriers of punctuation or capitals to separate them or demarcate their areas of reference. The occasional mannered weaknesses of the earlier poetry are avoided, by the absence of any regular demand for a formal gesture of conclusion. One example from *Le Mauvais Sang* may serve to illustrate such weaknesses:

Belle pluie, douce pluie
Je t'attendrai demain
Si je meurs - d'Ennui

(MS, 13)

The heavy emphasis thrown on 'Ennui', and the rather self-conscious parading of urban morbidity, are both reminiscent of late nineteenth century Parisian poetry.

In *Feu de Brousse* the individual poems are much longer than before and each is shaped as it emerges, upon the page, rather than being submitted to the demands of any previously selected model. The poems are also more unified within the whole volume, making it in effect one sustained poem. Indeed, the poet has indicated as much by sub-titling it a 'Poème parlé en dix-sept visions'. Here, to give an idea of these new qualities in Tchicaya's work of the later 'fifties, are the opening lines of the first poem, 'A Travers Temps et Fleuve':

> Un jour il faudra se prendre
> marcher haut les vents
> comme feuilles des arbres
> pour un fumier pour un feu
>
> qu'importe
> d'autres âges feront de nos âmes
> des silex
> gare aux pieds nus
> nous serons sur tous les chemins
>
> (FB, 51)

It will be noted that the poet here fulfils a vision only glimpsed in his earlier work, the vision of a manifold physical existence which corresponds to, transforms, intermingles with all the elements of the world around him. Even more striking examples of this identification with the physical world will be quoted from his later poetry, but the process is certainly at work throughout *Feu de Brousse*.

Given the unity of the collection, it may be more rewarding to quote extensively from one of the 'visions' which exemplifies the special qualities of this new style, arrived at without any apparent transition, than to attempt any comprehensive account of a volume running to some eighty pages. In the poem 'Présence', which forms the seventh vision of the book, Tchicaya unfolds a number of themes which are to dominate his next two collections also. In the opening lines we find one of the most striking of all his expressions of physical identification with the river, forest and ocean of his native Congo. The very strength of this impulse towards physical unity may be seen as a product of his exiled situation. Then follows one of the many ambivalent references to Christ, a figure with whom the poet feels indissolubly linked and even implicated. Christ was betrayed by his own companions, but also by his followers, who systematically destroyed the Congo Kingdom and enslaved, brutalized or exploited its inhabitants in his name. The stench of this historical betrayal clings inescapably to Christ himself. But the figure of the sacrificed god retains nevertheless an extraordinary fascination for the

the exiled poet who has also both betrayed and been betrayed by his country; 'betrayed' because he does not fully share its experience, and 'been betrayed' because robbed by destiny of this fuller Congolese experience. Thus Christ appears in his poetry as a 'fétiche cloué', a description which is not a mere insult or reduction but an acknowledgement of his profound, intimate relevance. The image stuck all over with nails is also a common feature of the sculpture of the Bakongo, Tchicaya's people. The nails in Christ's flesh are, Tchicaya tells us, 'mes vices'. The gentle forgiving Christ is mocked as 'a fakir', the prophet of an 'invertebrate religion', but it is to music of Christ's slow sadness that the poet chooses to waltz his poem.

These references, gathered together from various parts of *Feu de Brousse*, *A Triche-Coeur* and *Epitomé*, are necessary to build up a picture of the complex, ambivalent and even contradictory image of Christ and Christianity as it emerges in the whole corpus of Tchicaya's work. And each specific reference, as in stanza 3 of 'Présence', is best seen as a facet of that complex image. Indeed, the same is true of any of the master images of this poet, which gradually deepen, enrich and complicate their total meaning as they recur in new situations, moods or applications. Thus, one could not say definitively what Tchicaya means by 'j'ai suivi mon fleuve', because here the river is internalized, thereby stressing its analogous relationship to the bloodstream, whose salt content matches that of the rejuvenating ocean, whose waters thrust and mingle in those of the Congo. The river is here the companion of the poet in his wanderings and in his search for rebirth. But in a poem such as the great threnody 'Ils sont morts' from *Epitomé*, the river is more externalized, as the tragic process of Congolese history itself. It is the war dead of 1960-61 who are mingled with its transforming waters, rather than the poet, who stands upright upon its shores to memorialize them in his fragile, but still delicately restorative linguistic act.

So much by way of preparation for some of the recurrent *leitmotifs* which make their appearance in this poem, some of them for the first time:

Présence

1 N'ayant pas trouvé d'hommes
sur mon horizon
j'ai joué avec mon corps
l'ardent poème de la mort
5 j'ai suivi mon fleuve
vers des houles froides et courantes
je me suis ouvert au monde
des algues
où grouillent des solitudes
10 Aux solitudes ouvrez les halliers
Au soleil
ouvrez ma chair
Au sang mûr des révoltes
le sperme réel par des souffles m'assimile
15 aux levures des feuilles et des tornades

ma chevelure rêche à tous les vents
s'arc-boute
mes mains humides à tous les germes
portent mes pieds profonds à toutes les latitudes
20 à toutes les latitudes
la mort lente avec ses soleils richissimes m'assimile

présence truquée
je serai perfide
puis dieu des armées
25 le christ m'a trahi
en se laissant trouer la peau
qui voulait qu'on fît la preuve de sa mort

christ traître
voici ma chair de bronze
30 et mon sang fermé
par d'innombrables moi cuivre et zinc
par les deux pierres de mon cerveau
éternel par ma mort lente
poisson coélacanthe

35 un parfum de verveine et de biche
me tourmente et j'entends tard naître des voix
dans le jour
le jour passe le zénith
avec un savant cortège de cigales
40 si je m'écoutais c'est le moment de l'adieu
mais non j'ai encore une tâche

(FB, 69-70)

The imagined process of death in the magnificent opening lines is one forced upon the poet by his isolation in a white world which cannot share his concerns or comprehend his anguish. The sense of isolation grows still deeper in *Epitomé*, when feelings in the West begin to run high over the Congo tragedy, but in a direction absolutely inverse to those of any radical, informed African - more especially any Congolese African. But these earlier lines give us already a powerful impression of the poet's inner exploration of a body, a physical 'presence', which is his only link with the landscape and people of his own country. And since death is above all the process by which we mingle our elements with those from which we came, it is this process which dominates the opening stanzas of the poem. But the impression is far from deathly, for the imagery of 'sperme réel', of 'levures' and of 'soleils richissimes' stresses that the path is one of renewal - poetic, linguistic at the least, but in fact more sweepingly significant - rather than of utter disappearance. Here, moreover, we might note in passing, Tchicaya finds qualities of sound and rhythm in French which perfectly evoke the physical and metaphysical processes at work in the poem. This is especially evident in lines 7-21.

Connected with this belief in the total suggestive power of the human body is the common practice of multiple metre in African dance. Robert Farris Thompson has shown (*African Arts in Motion*, University of California Press, 1975, pp. 14-16) how multi-metric dancing, where each part of the body is moved to a different rhythmic strand in the music of the orchestra, is matched by similar characteristics in African sculpture and in the complex sounds of many African instruments (e.g. bells or vibrating wires attached to stringed lyres and bows). He goes on: 'Ideally speaking, multiple meter in the dance is a means of articulating the human body more fully than is possible in ordinary discourse; it makes a person blaze as a living entity at the center of understanding.' In fact, Tchicaya often moves from imagery of physical auto-exploration to imagery of dancing, moving the whole body in sadness, exultation or praise:

Christ
je valserai au son de ta tristesse lente.

It is this pagan, organic conception of death and rebirth that is contrasted in the third stanza with the dualism of Christianity, which can conceive of a death of the body and an immortality for the soul alone. The frail body of Christ may be pierced, but the poet's body is cast in bronze, as though the mortal clay were only a mould into which the hot alloy of the blood is poured. Thus the poet is rendered eternal, not by separation of the soul, but by 'ma mort lente'. Like the coelacanth he will lurk unguessed at in the deepest oceans of Africa, stirred by the currents of rebirth.

In the final stanza there is an awakening to mundane reality which reminds us of a similar process in the submarine imagery of Eliot's 'Prufrock':

> We have lingered in the chambers of the sea ...
> Till human voices wake us, and we drown.

The experience of abrupt awakening when the self is scattered is equally disorienting for both poets. In Tchicaya it stirs an impulse towards departure, and with this stifled impulse the poem closes.

The transition from the concerns of *Feu de Brousse* to those of *A Triche-Coeur* is marked by a sharper concentration upon the quest for origin. The new collection, published in 1960, is dominated by the poet's search for the 'clé des songes', introduced in the very first line. The search is conducted exclusively beside the waters of the Congo, but the passionate restlessness of the seeker is gradually transformed into the positive discovery of resurrection. The familiar images of orphan bereavement occur again and again early in the sequence. In the second poem, 'Etiage', we find:

> ma tête à moi est un soc agraire
> mais sur ma terre
> pas une ornière pas un sillon
> où est le giron de ma mère
> que j'y mette ma tête haute
> avant la nouvelle lune
> et la marée haute
>
> (TC, 110)

African standards, Tchicaya is able to see his personal situation as something transcended by the fate of others apparently more 'typically' Congolese. So, the superscription to the poem 'Ils sont morts', already referred to, invites the poet to wash off his deep sense of personal guilt in the waters which carry the Congolese dead to the sea:

> Vivez; lavez votre opprobre
> Ils sont morts

But at other times, where the poem is imaginatively situated in Paris rather than Kinshasa, Tchicaya ironizes his own situation and contrasts it with the other forms of 'betrayal' offered by his Congolese brothers, whose caution and bourgeois commitment leave the nation to the care of foreign powers even more rapacious than the classic colonists of Belgium:

> ... une pluie grise suffis[ant] à tous les rêves
> me contraign[ant] à ce besoin d'être faussaire
> saintement sicaire
> malgré l'équinoxe
> malgré moi
> malgré les sortilèges des sourires
> de mes frères d'obédience nègre
>
> Et puis
> qu'en dites-vous de ce silence
> du côté de ma propre conscience?
>
> (E, 42)

and in the very next poem

> Je suis extensible comme tout coeur honnête
>
> (E, 43)

It is this ironic note, this ability to situate his concern in relation to the complex of African attitudes towards the Congo crisis, which prevents any sense of Messianism from overwhelming Tchicaya's poetry even at its most passionately involved. If he sees himself here as the poet of his people, he is incapable of castigating them without seeing the ambiguities of his own situation. The perception of these ambiguities is far more honest in his work than we shall find it in other exiled patriots like Birago Diop and Léopold Senghor. When the Parisian situation of writing is evoked in their work, it is invariably lamented as something and again a few lines later:

ouvrez le giron de ma mère
que j'y mette ma tête chaude
et béni soit le pain qu'on m'ôte
bénie soit la soif qu'on m'ôte

(TC, 113)

We may note here also the skilful use of half-rhymes, both internal and final - *agraire-terre, sillon-giron, ornière-mère* - which bind the poem tightly together.

In a later poem, 'Equinoxiale' the same pattern of images (head as ploughshare, breast as earth, moon as sexual symbol associated with intercourse, menstruation and childbirth) is taken up and reworked as a kind of spiritual biography of the mother in death. Here it is the moon which takes the newborn child and the woman who wages war upon it. The opening lines are full of a moon-bathed stillness which grips the tableau of death:

La lune répandit
tout le sang d'une femme
en guise d'holocauste
aux étoiles de mer

la lune prit l'enfant
d'une femme
crêpant de sa lumière
bleue de mort les cheveux
de cette femme-mère ...

une femme la même ...
tint tête à une lune
meurtrière et maudite
elle guerroya vainqueur
portant à ses chevilles
une lune en tribut ...

(TC, 127)

Fighting against the moon's innate influence towards death and negation, the woman opens her 'sexe musicien' to the ardent blackening of the sun's rays. Intent upon a new fructification of 'la tristesse de sa terre ouverte', she wrestles the crescent moon into the 'shape of a ploughshare', and the furrow thus opened within her becomes a shining river of rebirth.

The transformation of the images of death, stillness and negation which dominate the opening lines of the poem into the great hymn for 'un sillon pour écrire l'éternité' which closes it, makes this one of Tchicaya's strongest and most complete visions of wholeness and continuity. And the resurrection here achieved by the dead mother becomes a means enabling the poet to separate himself from the 'orphelin ma complice'. The orphan becomes now, not his current, but his dead self, from which the poet bursts and rises in a triumphant assertion of immortality. Thus in the next poem, 'Le Corbillard', we find:

l'orphelin est mort dans l'orage

and

Le corbillard passe sous ma fenêtre
j'ouvre mon coeur pour le saluer
le vent bruit aux feuilles des arbres
et c'est à peine si je me souviens de ma vie
orphelin ma complice

One other feature of *A Triche-Coeur* is a greater element of childhood recollection and autobiography, often using imagery of a highly sexual character, a kind of purging through poetic release of his obsession with something scandalous or obscure in his begetting:

puis
une pucelle idiote m'ouvrit son sexe
pour pisser sur ma douleur déjà purulente
dieu seul sait comme j'ai joui
et revenant sur mes pas plus vaillant
je ne rencontrai que des arbres
qui portaient les fruits les uns des autres
arbres quand même
mais pas un membre de ma famille
sur leurs branches

(TC, 121)

It seems almost fortuitous that Tchicaya thus resolves a part of his personal dilemma before embarking on his more active involvement with that of his people. It is already suggested in 'Equinoxiale' that the mother's vindication of her flesh will be that of the suffering Congo also. The poems in the main sequence of *Epitomé* (published in 1962 but evidently written mainly in 1960) each carry a superscription identifying them with particular phases or events of the struggle which raged on the banks of the Congo in 1959-61. In the midst of this period, Tchicaya was for three months Chief Editor of the Zaire daily *Le Congo*, published in Kinshasa. He was thus an anguished and immediate witness of Patrice Lumumba's virtual imprisonment in his own capital; the ambiguous role of Dag Hammerskjold and the United Nations in that affair; and its culmination in the attempted escape, capture, torture and martyrdom of the Prime Minister, who seemed to carry to the grave with him all hopes of a genuinely united and independent Congo. The first part of *Epitomé* reads like a poetic diary of these events, in which their initial impact is recreated, their meaning sought in the deeper perspective of all other events suffered by the same or other colonized peoples. The vision nurtured during these perilous but heady days in Kinshasa was something very different from the American-dominated dictatorship which later rose upon the wreck of Lumumbist hopes. It could even be dreamed, as Tchicaya dreamed in some of these poems, that the Congo's five centuries of anguish since the Portuguese arrival might be resolved at last into the possibility of freedom and unity for peoples divided more by rival colonialisms than by the wide waters of the river. The poet taunts Christ to share to the full the specific agony and division of his people, wrought by such 'Christian' slavers, colonizers and intriguers:

> Marche sur ce chemin de mon peuple où je boite
> Tu me diras en quelle Egypte geint mon peuple
> Mon coeur n'est pas le désert parle ô Christ parle
> Est-ce toi qui mis l'or vif dans mon vin de joie
> Te dois-je mes deux sources
> Et mon âme et mon coeur ...
> Dis pourquoi souffrirais-je d'aimer par coeur
> Un arbre de vie mort fleurissait mon oubli.
>
> (E, 62-3)

Contemplating the dead of the Congo, and viewing their deaths in the perspective of a colonial history peculiarly disastrous even by inescapably imposed on the poet, who yearns helplessly for the village hearths of Martinique or Senegal. It is time that we recognized the existence of a sentimental pastoralism in black poetry quite as evident as it is in that of Europe. Tchicaya's protective irony accepts that there is an element of choice in his exile, which answers the choice of those 'at home' who fail to match all the challenges of the hour with adequate courage or commitment. The poet can even mock himself as being:

> plus français que Jeanne de Lorraine

and therefore, perhaps, all the better equipped to recognize the compromises and betrayals of others.

This quality of self-irony in Tchicaya's language grows even stronger in his last two published collections, *Le Ventre* (1964) and *L'Arc Musical* (1970). The first is a volume still dominated by the Congo experience. The belly turned uppermost in the acts of love, birth and a watery death, becomes here the crucial image whose poetic meanings must be allowed to express their full *horror*, before being made to yield also their potentialities for renewal. Even more than *Epitomé*, these poems are driven by an impulse to understand and come to terms with, imaginatively and linguistically, the experience of those terrible months in the Congo. In this respect they might be compared with the 'Massacre' sequence in Wole Soyinka's *Idanre* (1967), which is similarly engaged with the mind-beggaring facts of massacre and civil war in Nigeria. Soyinka uses imagery of harvest to deepen our sense of everything that is abortive and dismaying in the spectacle of a new nation tearing itself apart. This is a seed-time which sows only violence and reaps only the victims of it, heaped by tractors into putrid lakes or common graves:

> There has been such a crop in time of growing
> Such timeless noises when we longed for sighs
> Alone of petals, for muted swell of wine-buds
> In August rains, and singing in green spaces.[2]

Instead of contrasting the Congo's harvest of death with the vital harvests which independence might have brought to fruition, Tchicaya muses intensely over the distended bodies of the slain, striving to see within them the lineaments of rebirth, as well as denial and decay. And once again it is often his own body that he uses as interpreter and mediator for this experience of death:

> Je me tords le ventre,
> Ni l'iode ni le goémon
> ni les algues n'ont eu
> autant de suavité dans la caresse
> que mes lèvres naguère
> avant qu'il ne fût fait à la terre
> l'affront d'un galop de chacals
> hélas ventriloques!
> Le ventre,
> partout avec cette chaleur
> pestilentielle des vieux charniers.
>
> (V, 18)

Here, even the very warmth of the living belly links it with the hot stench of putrefaction. In the last lines of the same poem, the 'music' of the spilling blood at Kin(shasa) is compared with that of the fountain which plays in the bishop's palace. The flakes which darken the sky above the city are the parachutes of the returning Belgians which snowed upon the city only a few weeks after independence. In these terrible days, there is even a certain safety in death; once again it is the 'squelettes ardents' which display the quality of warmth in the midst of this white blizzard of death. Is it the poet's sense of complicity - as an *assimilé* normally resident in Paris - which makes him 'armé à blanc' to withstand this new assault from the skies?

> Rien n'est plus seul que le ventre
> et le coeur!
> Seul de cette solitude
> dont les saillies écorchent les plaies vives;
> arrachent les dents de lait
> dans la première désillusion du coeur!
> Il faut être du côté de ces musiques
> d'où dégouline le sang
> alors que l'on ne vit jamais
> l'âme se répandre avec le sang
> à Kin!
> Or que le ciel soit sale de ce floconnement
> seuls des squelettes ardents
> sont sûrs de ne pas répondre à l'appel

or moi je suis armé à blanc
pour me perdre dans le moindre assaut
de rire
ou dans ces musiques
d'où dégouline le sang
à Kin!

(V, 20)

In this passage there appears to be a juxtaposition developed between the essential solitude of the living sentient being ('le ventre et le coeur') and those who are 'du côté de ces musiques', linked with the continual bloodletting of those days. Ironically, the poet situates himself (since he is 'armé à blanc') with these collaborative forces, as he had done earlier in several poems of *Epitomé:*

Le roi bafouille: je jouis
je suis extensible comme tout coeur honnête

(V, 18)

Alongside this ironic portrayal of the poet as someone who, despite himself, has inescapable elements of complicity and 'obédience nègre' within him, there develops another comparison. Far more than *Epitomé*, these poems are haunted by the martyred figure of Patrice Lumumba. No Congolese leader since his murder (which begins to take on more and more the lineaments of another C.I.A. job) has gathered into himself so many aspects of the struggle for a meaningful Congolese and African unity; for the use of the Congo's wealth to free rather than to subdue its people; for any real departure from the five-century history of foreign manipulation and exploitation, which is practically the only relation the Congo has ever known with the West. The *internalization* of these processes, under the protective cover of a client black government, is not what that whole struggle was about. But in 1960-2 it was still possible to hope, despite Lumumba's death, that it might be otherwise resolved, since the Lumumbists were still in arms and were still far the largest elected party in the country.

In these poems, then, the physical exploration of experience is conducted through the broken body of Lumumba as much as through

Tchicaya's own physical witness. It is what *dies with* Lumumba that remains uncertain at the time of writing; hence, perhaps, the offer of a 'Flamenco funèbre' for the burial of the fallen leader, whose death may mark only a phase of a developing struggle. It is notable, too, how the themes of betrayal, martyrdom and flogging link Lumumba here with the images already developed of Christ and of the betrayed/betraying poet himself:

Il tombe avec les fléaux
Puis quatre ou six planches
les compagnons sont dehors
à moins qu'une fosse commune
sous le mince éboulement de terre
à peine pour égarer le sexe
dans tous ces cris -
alors que mon ventre n'est chaud
que de vin!
Il tombe avec les fléaux!

Oui! (un oui strident
pour ce ferreuillement
d'âmes, d'axes et de flots!
Flamenco funèbre pour lui!

(E, 43)

After all, the poet is able to force out a painful cry of assent, even if 'le Oui déchire la gorge du ramier!' A myth can sometimes wield more positive force than its own progenitor, and one has only to recall how the dead Lumumba instantly became the hero of a thousand anonymous ballads, funeral dirges, broadsheets and passionate recitations up and down the length of Africa to perceive the meaning of this 'Oui' across the twelve years which already separate us from it.

It will be seen that the poetry of *Epitomé* and *Le Ventre* is on the whole more public in its concerns than the intensely self-communing volumes that preceded them. And this more public orientation of Tchicaya's poetic voice is matched, particularly in *Le Ventre*, by a slight simplification of style. A more stanzaic form reappears on the page, after the boiling cascades of images which pour through *Feu de Brousse* or *A Triche-Coeur*, and there is a return to a limited use of punctuation, capitalization and sentence form within each poem.

Tchicaya nevertheless continues the search for the tree of his origins, he pummels and dissects his own belly to find the meaning of rebirth within the giant fact of death in the Congo of those years; the great river flows as ever through his language, carrying, changing and delivering up the burden of a tragic historic experience. Thus all the elements of continuity are present; only the poet's preoccupations begin to take on a more representative character; he is both literally and imaginatively closer to the experience of his people than the brilliant young Parisian poet of the 1950's.

This quality of passionate involvement makes possible the assertion which ends the long dialogue poem 'Les Corps et les biens':

> Qui vivra
> Verra le Congo
> A cheval sur le Congo
> ou flottant parmi les jacinthes d'eau
>
> (V, 131)

It also forms the sombre magnificence of the final poem 'Le Ventre reste', into which Tchicaya gathers many of the themes of the whole volume, with a focus of extraordinary intensity and power. Here the dead of the Congo become 'les voyants', every one of them prophesying the Congo that shall be, after the anguish and loss of our day. Their posture is that of love and birth as well as death, and there will be 'biens' from these countless 'corps' which scatter and disfigure the land. Just as Soyinka's imagery of harvest, even of the aborted harvest, nevertheless reminds us of the green harvest that can, should and ultimately must be; so Tchicaya's long physical exploration of death and martyrdom leads him at last away from despair:

> Certes le ventre demeure chaste
> sous un trésor d'os blancs
> puis ouvert au chant d'un combattant
> perdu corps et biens
> dans les flammes de sa passion ...

Certes, il reste le ventre
Est-ce plus souillé que chaste?
A cause de certain bris de coeur/
L'amour pour l'amour
est aussi désolant que le reste.
Mais l'amour la vie
celui qu'on donne du ventre
la terre s'en charge
Dieu merci les voyants tombent
le plus souvent sur le dos
le plus souvent les bras ouverts
le plus souvent
le ventre face au ciel!

(V, 133-4)

Tchicaya's next collection, and the last to appear, marks another change of direction or emphasis within the stream of development of his consciousness of the social - and not just personal - function of the language of his poetry. This collection, *Arc Musical*, was published as part of the two-volume Collected Works issued by Pierre-Jean Oswald in 1970. In some ways it marks a move towards African poetic tradition, since the poet here conceives of himself more as a *griot*, a poet-musician who sings as much through his instrument ('arc musical') as through his voice, but one who is compelled to practise his craft in an alien city and for an alien audience. The imaginative centre of his work now seems to have shifted once again to Paris and the situation of the exile is ironized in a way reminiscent of his earlier work, where 'ma cité' referred usually to Paris rather than to Kinshasa or Brazzaville. Although the regime of the author's native République du Congo is a leftist one and represents something closer to the ideals of 1960 than what has emerged across the river in Zaïre, it seems that he nevertheless prefers to experience it as an annual visitor rather than as a citizen. He retains his post on the permanent staff of UNESCO (with special responsibility for teacher-training facilities in Africa), his apartment in Paris and his 'maison secondaire' in the Ile de France. The intense excitement and immediacy of his work of 1960-64 gives way, therefore, to a more lyrical vein and at times to an ironic poise, a kind of protective detachment. Characteristic of the first might be these lines, which still carry the conviction that everything must be experienced through the channels and structures of the body. The poet already carries his death:

> Attachez une pierre à ma mort
> que j'ai lourde sur le corps
>
> (TC, 126)

his 'généalogie improbable'; his tyrannous mistress with her grinning fakir of a Christ. Let fraternity be built also into the walking skeleton which informs his poems:

> La fraternité fut un mot
> j'en fais un os de plus
> à joindre à mon squelette
>
> (AM, 117)

The detachment, which is only another aspect of the saving laughter which pours through *Epitomé*, here takes the form of a professional skill; if the poet's language cannot any longer serve to warn or to terrify, perhaps it can at least be compelled to entertain:

> Des mots qui font tache d'huile
> me venaient quand ma bouche en feu
> sur ton front laissait une trace d'aube
> j'étais facteur d'orgues et de balafon
> pour un chant à la mesure de chaque espoir
> Mais les épis sans discernement se laissaient battre
>
> Malheur à l'oiseau ivre!
> A quoi bon japper?
> C'est l'arc musical
> qu'il faut jouer en ce pays
>
> (AM, 110)

The use of the bow harp here as something which stands between the poet and the listener, the art to some extent detachable from the artist, has also been prepared for in the figure of 'le passant' who moves mysteriously and enigmatically through the pages of *Epitomé*. 'Le passant' is a foil to the poet's own desperate existential involvement, as the harp here is his linguistic skill rather than his mortal life.

Allied perhaps to this withdrawal into a recognizable traditional role as the professional poet-singer, is an even greater economy and precision of form than Tchicaya had already achieved in the previous two volumes. The poetry is at times almost tersely controlled; there are few of the great 'cris de passion' earlier saluted by Senghor.[3] The poet is less totally self-exposed by his language, but for that very reason his sarcasm can be even more deadly. Tchicaya had already written in *Epitomé*:

> mon rire de sicaire
> singeant le roi féroce
> fit rire le bourreau
>
> (E, 90)

Here that laughter often pierces more than it scalds. Tchicaya now once again inhibits a society where his passionate concern for the victims of racism and imperial ambition, whether in Louisiana, Algeria, Vietnam or the Congo itself, can appear eccentric to those who still clutch an illusory white security and complacency. The shape of the world is simply very different when viewed from the Quai d'Orsay than from the shores of the River Congo. This is something that even the most sympathetic and informed white too often fails to realize. And it creates an acute problem for the exiled poet, even when he knows that many of his eventual readers will be in the black world. It is the immediacy of human response and equally shared response that he must lack. His words are obliged to function in something of a vacuum and he knows it. There are glimpses, too, of a more intimate pressure upon the poet to surrender the Promethean fire of his art and lapse into the 'douceur de vivre' that Paris knows so well how to supply:

> Une Chair rendit ma chair triste
> Un feu fit mon âme liquide ...
> Un amour à peine plus suave
> que la mort du juif que j'ordonne
> me promet la paix du coeur
> pourvu que je rende le feu volé
> et reprenne mon sang à la nuit.
>
> (AM, 134)

In the same vein, he promises to 'rendre moins nocive ma quête d'un refrain' and concludes with a wry gesture of submission:

A chacun sa révolution
moi je tourne sur ma pipe
je rêve des yeux atteindre
mon dos afin qu'élargi
il soit votre seul esquif.

(AM, 115)

Tchicaya's evocations within his poems of an auditor who responds and is responded to, began with the many dialogue poems in the later pages of *Epitomé*, and in *Le Ventre*. There too they had the effect of placing the poet's hot heart in a cool perspective, almost the perspective of an unintelligent radio interview (a medium in which Tchicaya himself worked 1957-60). They also provide a means of offering the most cryptic of replies to the questioner:

- Vos espoirs légitimes?
- Un! la mort!
- Et après?
- Etre paien au renouveau paien du monde ...

(E, 94)

Many of the poems in *Arc Musical* also seem to offer more insight into what the poet seeks immediately in his life; the search is less cosmic, less all-embracing than the whirlwind which drives through *Feu de Brousse*, for example. Instead of tree, river, blood or sun, we have attempts to define the sort of faith which might be acceptable to the poet, the sort of house he wishes built for him by faith. The very titles of the poems - 'Collecte du Sang', 'Communion', 'Funèbre', 'Noces' - reveal this incessant use of religious imagery (particularly that drawn from the Eucharist) and this urge to move beyond mockery of the bourgeois, compromised Church and Christ of *Epitomé* towards a definition of his own creed. In 'Pourquoi donc dieu est-il mort' he sings:

Je voulus que ses deux mains
sur ma tête fussent mon toit étanche;
son baiser un second soleil
sa bouche une seconde porte
...
à cause de la chair périssable
j'oublie l'esprit du vin qu'il chantait
mieux que moi m'aidant de mon arc
son chant funèbre mon chant de gloire!

(AM, 112-3)

Much of the poetry in *Arc Musical* is in fact very close to the traditional dirge poetry of Arica with its frequent use of refrains; its general reflections on the inescapable sadness and pain of existence; its more specific reflections on the nature of the poet's art and his isolation among men who cannot share his intensity or participate in his vision.[4] Such a note predominates in one of the finest poems of the collection, 'Legs', which, although not placed at the very end, might stand as a testamentary conclusion to it. Here the imagery of the ardent earth yearning to console and consume the poet is not an example of his exploration of death as a means to intenser life. The poem is, rather, about a kind of immortality specific to the artist, and its tone is more valedictory than exploratory:

Et comme toujours
la terre plus ardente
à nous vouloir dociles
dans ces flancs sans lait
nous langera d'humus.
Et si cet art ne me suivait
là où sont les manes
Ceci est mon testament:
Je vous lègue le feu et le chant.

It would be easy in writing of *Arc Musical* to lament an apparent drawing-in of the poet's horns, a retreat from the extremes of expressive intensity reached in his middle period. But we must remind ourselves that Tchicaya U Tam'si, despite his extensive *oeuvre* of six thickish volumes of poetry in the fifteen years 1955-70, is still only in his middle forties and has not lost that ability to develop and extend his art which all the earlier volumes have evidenced. It is unlikely that any poet could have long sustained the pitch of self-communion and interaction with the suffering world about him which produced the poems of 1960-64. 'Legs' is certainly not a genuine testament, but rather a device within the particular fabric of *Arc Musical*. For, although I have stressed the underlying continuity and unity of Tchicaya's work, there is a sense in which each separate volume reveals an internal structure and unity of its own. That Tchicaya has already moved far beyond the mood and immediate concerns of *Arc Musical* is apparent in the announcement that he has already completed another volume of poetry (*La Veste d'intérieure: suivi de Notes de Veille*); and a full-length play on Chaka the Zulu, presented at the Avignon Festival in August 1976.

On a recent visit to Dakar, where Tchicaya was elected first President of the African Writers' Union, I was able to read through the unpublished manuscript of 'La Veste d'intérieure' and to form an impression of two definite currents within it.[5] The first is a satirical assault on the regimes which now predominate in Africa, some sixteen years after the Annus Mirabilis of 'flag independence' in 1960. Many francophone states have fallen into the hands of veterans from the French colonial armies, whose political training for independence consisted of killing their fellows in Algeria, Madagascar or Vietnam. This is hardly an auspicious formation for the president of an autonomous modern state, and the resulting regimes are often a good deal less subtle and sophisticated in their operation of client status than the governemtns of such experienced politicians as Houphouët-Boigny in Côte d'Ivoire or Léopold Senghor in Sénégal. Tchicaya's travels in Africa have made him a connoisseur of such military regimes, where the common man's relationship with the forces of order and exaction has scarcely changed since colonialism, and certainly not for the better. A poem like 'Cri' speaks for all those who still cherish a better vision for Africa:

> Voici les caciques
> Les macaques d'hier
> Les princes d'aujourd'hui
> s'épouillant se dépouillant
> m'épouillant t'épouillant
> poux le cul par terre
> peuple - souverain - les - masses,
> à coup de slogans on sodomise
>
> 'Mangeront-ils' demain
> demain est un jour suspect

Here is a return to the more direct and public manner of *Le Ventre* with Tchicaya as the articulate witness of his age and all that it brings to his fellow Africans. Tiring of his long exile, Tchicaya now speaks of returning to his homeland. Perhaps the imminence of this return already lends a certain urgency to these poems, in which he again obliges language - a 'foreign' language powerfully and poignantly appropriated - to bear the weight of Africa's contemporary reality.

But the intimate dialogue, ranging from tender eroticism to anger and renunciation, which has been a current through all Tchicaya's work, flows still in the new collection. In 'Le Corps' it achieves a new perfection and economy of form; a poem whose language is like a mask, to be viewed from many angles:

> Je grave des cils sur tes lèvres
> on les verra de loin
> scintillantes du bleu des vagues
> ainsi salées de lumière
> L'inférieure surtout qui mouille
> quand le mot amour passe
> le zénith ou les canicules
>
> Mon baiser te refait
> l'oeil clair
>
> Tu redeviens racine
> Ton corps te ressemble.

The process of transformation here is continuous right into the last line, which startles and illuminates the poem, controlling its shape and its direction to culminate in that single rooted image of fulfilment, 'Ton corps te ressemble'. The next few years in the specifically poetic development of Tchicaya's use of language promise to be as rich as any that have preceded.

NOTES

1. From the poem 'Jadis'. The following abbreviations are used throughout: MS: *Le Mauvais Sang*; FB: *Feu de Brousse*; TC: *A Triche-Coeur*; E: *Epitomé*; V: *Le Ventre*; AM: *Arc Musical*. Reference throughout is to the following editions: *Le Mauvais Sang, suivi de Feu de Brousse et A Triche-Coeur*, Honfleur/Paris: Pierre Jean Oswald, 1970; *Arc Musical, précédé de Epitomé*, Honfleur/Paris: P. J. Oswald, 1970; *Le Ventre*, Paris: Présence Africaine, 1964.

2. 'Harvest of Hate', *Idanre*, Wole Soyinka, London, Methuen, 1967, p. 50.

3. Preface to 1st Edition, *Epitomé*, Tunis, P. J. Oswald, 1962.

4. I am thinking particularly of the collections made by Kofi Awoonor (*Guardians of the Sacred Word*, Nok Publications, New York, 1974) and Okot p'Bitek (*The Horn of My Love*, Heinemann, London, 1974). These dirges, respectively from the Ewe peoples of Ghana-Togo and the Acoli of Northern Uganda, give some indication of features common to the genre in many other parts of Africa also.

5. I am grateful to M. Tchicaya U Tam'si for permission to quote from the manuscript.

THE POWER OF THE WORD IN MARIE-CLAIRE D'ORBAIX'S EROSION DU SILENCE

James W. Brown

During the past twenty-five years feminist poetry in Belgium has multiplied at an enormous rate, gaining a literary ascendancy which it had never before enjoyed. Like her contemporaries Liliane Wouters, Lucienne Desnoues and Andrée Sodenkamp, Marie-Claire d'Orbaix sings in an intense lyrical voice and endows her imagistic universe with feminine charm, imagination, and simplicity. Quite evident too in her poetry is the thematic of maternal love, which in its expansiveness and continuity embraces past, present and future in an attempt to come to terms with life and death. These, and many other feminist themes are to be found in Marie-Claire d'Orbaix's poetry, but with the publication of her third collection of poems entitled *Ces Mots vivront dans ta vie* she begins to focus on the means by which this love is transmitted and sustained, that is, on the specific functions of the language of poetry in both expressing and resolving the Eros/Thanatos antinomy. *Erosion du Silence* (Brussels: André de Rache, 1970), Mme d'Orbaix's fourth collection of poems and the subject of this essay, represents a linguistic *prise de conscience*; it is a collection of poems about language in which the poet views words not just in their potential to communicate and signify, but also in their capacity to commune with the very essence of things. Because Marie-Claire d'Orbaix considers that language functions to concretize man's relationship to God, she accentuates all forms and nuances of communication which lead to this desired reification: communion, then, is modelled on the speech act.

Moreover, in elaborating this model, Marie-Claire d'Orbaix reduces the constituents of the speech act to a primordial unity in which addresser, message and addressee are made homologous so that they can enter into a dialectic which is at once immanent and transcendent. In other words, she does not limit the so-called message of the communicative act to its referential function but rather she demonstrates in these texts that it is generated by and is co-extensive with the process of dialoguing. Under these circumstances it is quite understandable that the only voice one hears throughout the entire collection is that of the addresser, the textual *Je*, who is ever conscious of language and its nodical function. In many of the texts of *Erosion du Silence* the poetic voice uses language to speak about language: fundamentally, it performs a metalingual function which aims at semantic and structural clarification. Poem, therefore, is transformed into meta-poem: it doubles as a reflection on the process of signification and on artistic creation, thus affirming itself as a coalescence of the epistemological and the metaphysical.

For purposes of analysis the title of the collection may serve as the key to the semiotic universe of these texts by virtue of the fact that it suggests the theme of geological erosion while simultaneously positing a reading which focuses on the process of communication. As a transformational model the title informs the reader that the semantic core of the poems of *Erosion du Silence* is the process of communication; it may be represented schematically as follows: *Erosion du Silence* → *Parole (écriture, chant, musique,* etc.*)* → *Communication avec l'Etre*. Marie-Claire d'Orbaix has purposely constructed a surface paradox (i.e. silence yields sound, language and communication are born of silence) in order to be able to juxtapose two semantically distinct fields at the deep textual level. Moreover, the possible contradictions inherent in the title (the process of erosion presupposes the *presence* of something to be eroded whereas silence occurs as *absence*) prepare the reader for many unexpected fluctuations in connotation and they point to the process of semantic reversals which occur throughout the entire collection: all connotative polarities remain, but with a shift in negative and positive charge so to speak. This initial propensity for semantic realignment accounts for all subsequent reversals and, at the same time, it also engenders several systems of stylistic features which function as metonyms of the process of erosion.[1]

At this point it seems both necessary and desirable to take up each of the textual transforms of the given semantic in order that they may be analyzed individually and then related to the semiotic network of the text as a whole. Furthermore, this methodological procedure has been adopted in an attempt to adhere as closely as possible to the structure of *Erosion du Silence* itself, whose parts enter into a dialectic which progresses toward a final synthesis or 'Credo'. To begin with, the paradigm of the speech act obviously functions at the linguistic level of the text, as previously mentioned. But even more importantly it also serves as the generative basis for the thematic of erosion. This primary metonymical extension allows the poet to exploit all the similarities between the act of communication and the process of erosion: in both cases opposing elements enter into a dialectic which evolves by means of permutations and realignments only to terminate in a new formal arrangement. Geologically and figuratively, erosion connotes transaction - all forms of transaction signal interdependence, all ensure communication. The geological configuration which informs the poems of *Erosion du Silence* is reflected at both the surface and the deep textual levels in such a way that a change in one of the poetic structures of the text produces an effect upon the entire system.[2] According to this principle the thematic of erosion governs the stylistic structure of the entire collection: on the one hand, it accounts for the obvious geological imagery at the surface level; on the other hand, it explains the seemingly paradoxical transformations which occur at the deep level.

It will not be necessary to elaborate on the geological imagery at the surface level of *Erosion du Silence* because the poet has chosen to employ certain lexical items which clearly denote erosion. In many of Marie-Claire d'Orbaix's poems, for example, the human body is likened to the earth; both undergo the effects of erosion: 'Rien ne révèle en mon sillage/ La femme en pleurs des profondeurs,/ Et toi qui me sillonnes, Amour,/ Ignorant la tempête ultime,/ Et toi qui me sillonnes, Amour,/ Ne descends pas en mes abîmes ...' ('Tempête', p. 12). Similarly, the earth-body motif motivates the lexicon of 'Sang du Songe - Songe du Sang': 'Coulez, coulez mon sang dans mes terres fertiles/ Où bondit le soleil, où se glisse le froid;/ Irriguez-moi le coeur, cette éphémère ville,/

Et suivez ces ruisseaux qui sillonnent ma voix ...' (ES, p. 49). More importantly, however, the title is actualized in another series of lexical images which centre on the major theme of *Erosion du Silence*: *parole*, in its capacity to break down the barriers to communication, constitutes a positive erosive force, and, for Marie-Claire d'Orbaix, it further becomes an ontological necessity:[3] 'Laissez-moi déchirer le silence, ...' she implores in 'Légende du Silence', cognizant of the fact that silence is eloquently eroded in the song of the poet.

Indeed, the texts cited above betray a certain ambivalence in the poet vis-à-vis the agents and the effects of erosion, for in all of them the process of erosion carries both positive and negative connotations. As regards the latter, the destructive potentials of erosion are revealed in many of the poems comprising part three of *Erosion du Silence*, titled *Cycle de la Mort*, in which the poet's fear of death and disintegration become apparent in a series of images belonging to a larger aquatic motif. Water, in its elemental instability and fluidity, terrifies Marie-Claire d'Orbaix: 'Que tout est flou dans ma pensée,/ il me semble que je m'efface/ comme une légère buée/ sur la vitre du temps et espace ...' ('Buée', p. 53). This fear is also apparent in 'Sur l'Eau': 'Sur l'eau j'ai peur,/ suis fille de la terre,/ fille des sillons sages./ O bateaux, vifs sillages,/ remous et balancements,/ instable élément,/ je tremble sur vous perfides' ('Sur l'eau', p. 59). Ultimately, the liquid element is the metonym of the poet's horror of atomization, because without 'liens' and 'algues', without the binding force of language, the cosmos dissolves into a mass of amorphous and meaningless matter.

It should now be evident that a denotative reading of the lexical items in *Erosion du Silence* is activated by and conforms to the thematic of erosion; such a reading, though superficial in the non-derogatory acceptation of the word (i.e. treating superficies), is the necessary prelude to a profound intelligence of these texts because it creates a false sense of security in the reader. On the surface the stylistic structure of *Erosion du Silence* is static; by its very usualness and its expected images (verbs like *sillonner*, *mordre*, *déchirer* are, for example, totally predictable in a context of erosion) it gives the impression of order, thus functioning as the mimesis of an unchanging geological configuration. At the deep textual level, however, a dynamic force shapes and reshapes the semantic universe of these texts. Here the power of the word as logos is felt in all its awesome beauty; language lies at the very centre of the production of meaning, its semic eruptions are capable of eroding, transforming, and reversing surface structures. Marie-Claire d'Orbaix, with profound insight into the rapports between spirit and matter, natural phenomena and language, exploits to capacity the metonymical similarities between the processes of poetic and geological structuration. The thematic of erosion, for instance, is represented at the deep textual level by a series of images whose function is to actualize the semes *interior* and *exterior*, in themselves metonyms of the process of erosion as well as of the act of communication, both human and divine. This semic model is first realized in a network of images whose connotations become negative when associated with interiority, positive when related to exteriority. Imagistically, then, the thematic is developed according to a system of opposing geological configurations which may be schematically represented first as (A/B), then as (B/A) and which, as the result of many transformations finally interact and become mutually supportive ($A \leftrightarrows B$).

The ostensible semic opposition between interior and exterior is expressed ontologically as the poet's relationship to the cosmos, and semiotically as man's dialogue with the Divine. In the first part of *Erosion du Silence*, entitled *Cycle de l'Amour*, Marie-Claire d'Orbaix describes a universe wherein love predominates and manifests itself as the harmonious and melodious relationship between corporeal and celestial bodies. In 'Poussière Stellaire', for instance, the poet intentionally mixes metaphors in order to arrive at the cosmological ground of being, heralding as it were the orchestration of all phenomena: 'J'écoute en ma poussière stellaire/ Flamber l'écho des mille lumières,/ Je touche sur toi leurs vibrations/ Et sens tournoyer les horizons ...' (ES, p. 13).

The title of several of the poems in this part (e.g. 'Sirène', 'Sonatine') further suggests the balance and serenity of a universe infused with music.

The prevailing ambiance of harmony and restraint in *Cycle de l' Amour* is offset in part two where dissonance and hyperbole function as the poetic mimeses of realignments caused by tumultuous geological forces. The title of part two, *Cycle du Silence*, betrays a fundamental paradox, for in these texts the word has a ferocious resonance.[4] Language erupts, wreaking havoc upon the benign equilibrium evident in *Cycle de l'Amour*, destroying, in a succession of connotative reversals, the initial semiotic stability which the poetic voice had previously created, undermining itself in order to recover its primordial innocence. The erosive force of language in this part is felt principally in those images which actualize the semes *interior* and *exterior*, themselves metonyms of erosion and communion. The semic model is first realized paradigmatically in the poems belonging to *Cycle du Silence* by a series of images whose connotations are negative when associated with interiority and positive when related to exteriority. The model, a formal quintessence of the entire semiotic universe of *Erosion du Silence*, accounts for the semic, thematic, and communicative transformations of these texts into an imagistic pattern which may be represented in the following analogy - interior: exterior: earth: cosmos: man: God. In short, this model serves as the generative base for the numerous systems of oppositions occurring in *Cycle du Silence*.

In the first series of images the poetic voice gives the reader linguistic reassurance of the stability of his world. Connotations conform to traditional literary patterns which oppose, in a positive to negative manner, such poetic commonplaces as sound to silence, music to noise, light to darkness, life to death. The echo of such imagistic banalities tends to neutralize the word by subjecting it to a seemingly endless series of repetitions; sameness eschews subversion by language. 'Oasis, the first poem in *Cycle du Silence*, has an almost hugolian resonance in its metaphorical structure, with its characteristic horror of the void and anxiety produced by discordance: 'Dans le chaos qui bêle/ Dans le bruit dont j'ai peur .../ Donne-moi ton silence,/ Ton soleil roucouleur,/ Belle oasis où dans/ Un hiatus en fleurs' (ES, p. 23). In this poem Marie-Claire d'Orbaix is content to merely prefigure the magical power of the word to perform the impossible - to animate nothingness. Logical paradox in a verbal construct (i.e. 'le chaos qui bêle') serves to nullify the ostensible negative connotation of the word *silence* in the title of the collection since noise will obviously not suffice as an alternative to silence. Cacophony must be superceded by harmony so that only the melodious word, the *chant* of the poet will prevail. This concept of a musicallity which infuses the word with life receives its most eloquent expression in 'Chanson d'Eté', the poet's paean to the sun, from which emanate light, life, and speech: 'Paroles, chantez chaud/ Quand miroite la plume,/ Vous coulez d'elle où brûle/ Un or de toréro' (ES, p. 26). Likewise, 'Chanson' reaffirms the alliance between the sun and the word and expresses their vitality: 'Encore un poème au soleil,/ Encor un petit palpitant/ Qui, dressant le bout de l' oreille,/ Me vrille d'un oeil arrogant./ Je sais le sens du silence/ Si long, si lourd à porter' (ES, p. 27).

The struggle to purge the self of its internal chaos, to escape from the prison of silence, is nowhere better articulated by the poet than in the texts entitled 'Tempête' and 'Exorcisme'. Both of these poems demonstrate Marie-Claire d'Orbaix's ability to exploit a large number of images of geological space in their role as metonyms of the interior and the exterior. Once again in a manner reminiscent of Hugo's, the poet associates misery and anguish with viscosity and density:

> Il se cache au-dessous des eaux
> De grands remous, de grands vertiges
> Quand la colère sous-marine
> Ebranle et brûle ses échos.
>
> Il se cache au-dessous des eaux
> La chute, un jour, d'une colline,
> Quand la colère sous-marine
> Eveille un feu de vieux chaos.
>
> ('Tempête', p. 12)

The marine setting here designates the poet's body as the locus of the upheaval, a synechdoche which is made possible by the poetically familiar technique of having the sea serve as the mirror of the soul. Appropriately, the final three stanzas of the poem reflect the first three: 'Il se cache au dedans du coeur/ De grands remous, de grands vertiges,/ Quand s'entremêlent ces clameurs:/ Où êtes-vous Seigneur? Qui suis-je?' (ES, p. 12).

'Exorcisme' complements 'Tempête' and completes the series of poems whose imagistic patterns relate the interior to the exterior in a negative to positive way. Most of the opposing semes in this associative network appear in 'Exorcisme', a poem whose very title suggests the imminence of a reversal and a release from the anguish of isolation by means of a ceremonial designed to ensure deliverance. Because the semes of the connotative system so far discussed coalesce in 'Exorcisme', the poem will be quoted in its entirety:

Toi, dans ta caverne d'échos
Toi, dans ton antre de silence,
Toi, qui sais le pouvoir des mots
Et le pouvoir de leur absence,

Dégèle aux gouffres du gosier
Le premier bruit d'une parole,
Relève, degré par degré,
Ce murmure que l'ombre immole ...

J'offre les cordes de ma voix
Pour une lente résurgence,
Si l'air s'écorche contre moi
Le supplice des sons commence.

Cueilleront-ils en cette chair
Assez de sang, assez de souffle,
Pour émerger de leur hiver
Et s'évader, zébrés de foudre?

Ah! je crépite de leurs cris,
Le coeur secoué par l'orage
Et lance les mots engourdis
Qui brûleront les lèvres sages.

... Toi, dans ta caverne d'échos,
Toi, dans ton antre se silence,
Tu m'as rendu pouvoir des mots,
Tu m'as rendu vie et présence ...

(ES, p. 28)

A ritual practice such as an exorcism is a type of semiosis - in this case the rite may be accomplished through the medium of language, the channel which permits communication between the interior and the exterior. 'Exorcisme', then, disrupts the stasis established thus far in the connotative system of the poems just discussed. A verbal journey begins here in which th word is set in motion, bound on a course of emergence and release, destined to be revivified when it reaches the surface. This verbal exorcism - the necessary pre-condition to successful communication - is performed within the sanctuary of the poem; for the poet the text is a symbolic pilgrimage in the journey from darkness to light.

'Exorcisme' serves as a transitional text vis-à-vis the associative patterns of images belonging to the opposition between interior and exterior. Up to now the reader has been safely enclosed within a metonymical framework whose connotative parameters are both familiar and expected. However, in a seemingly contradictory sequence of poems in *Cycle du Silence* the poet subverts the prevailing semantic by reversing expected connotations: silence - and by extension all images of the exterior - now carry positive affective qualities whereas harsh and unpleasant sounds connote negative phenomena. A process of figurative materialization corresponds to this connotative reversal and further mimics the spatial realignments which occur as part of the thematic of erosion. As stated previously, the word *silence* in the title of the collection is materialized by virtue of its inclusion in a syntagm whose semantic tone is first set by the denotative force of the word *érosion*: this kind of semantic contamination allows the poet to generate a series of images based on substantialization or personification of the non-material. The poetic word eludes all verbal logic in its capacity to transform silence into material substance as may be evidenced in the title chosen for certain poems, e.g. 'Les Branches du Silence', for example, or 'Légende du Silence'.

Several poems reveal this technique of semantic oxymoron in a strikingly similar and condensed manner. In nearly all cases the production of images has its generative origin in the transformation of an absence into a presence. In 'A l'Orée du Bruit' the poet personifies silence in such a way that the connotations heretofore established in the first series of poems have undergone a complete metamorphosis: 'Un petit silence naît/ Tout appeuré dans l'oreille,/ Tout chiffonné de soleil,/ Sortant du cocon du bruit.// Flocon de lumière/ Aux creux de l'être,/ A l'orée de la nuit/ Il vient naître' (ES, p. 35). Silence is now associated with light, whereas noise occupies an oppressive spherical space. Similarly, in 'Plage' the poet transforms silence into material substance, once again assigning a luminous existence to it, situating it at the exterior of the 'gouffre', and finally denuding it of a possible negative affectivity: 'Une plage blanche,/ Une page de silence,/ De grands remous de calme/ Sur la stridence de l'âme:/ La lumineuse mort du bruit/ Couvant les noirs vacarmes' (ES, p. 34). The transformational processes achieved by means of personification and substantialization unify in 'Chant de la Parole' wherein the poetic voice juxtaposes two metaphorical operations in an attempt to increase the semantic range of their common tenor. Having resolved - or rather overstepped - the initial paradox of materializing silence, the poet now creates a new contradiction which is both permitted and sustained by virtue of the fact that it exists as text only. 'Chant de la Parole' is a prose poem which attains a level of semantic density analogous to certain texts of Rimbaud's *Illuminations*. In the first stanza, for example, reference is partially blocked by the poet's use of pronouns having no antecedent in the given text:

> On le déchire, le déchiquette, le troue à chaque instant ... Il y a le rire des femmes qui le fait voler en éclats, le ronflement des moteurs qui le ronge en rond, le grignotement continu des voix, le claquement des pas qui le fend, la grêle des sonneries qui le fissure en cascades ...
> (ES, p. 38)

The verbal system (i.e. *déchirer, déchiqueter, trouer*, and so on) prompts a decoding of the pronoun *le* (whose antecedent, *silence*, may easily be deduced at the intertextual level) according to its materialized objective function; in context *le* represents the transformation of silence into a thing, but conclusive identification of the referent is subsequently undermined by contradictory verbal systems. The series of verbs beginning with *déchirer* would suggest that the object in question is a cloth or possibly a sail; but in the next series (i.e. *voler en éclats, fendre, fissurer*) this reading is nullified because these latter actions are generally associated with hard, rigid objects. Even though the referent may be characterized by its material existence, a fundamental disparity remains - *le* encourages a reading based on the semic opposition between softness and hardness as attributes of the same object. The second stanza of the poem carries this discontinuity one step further. The poet now confirms that the referent of *le* is *silence*, but in this present context silence is personified:

> Il y a tout ce qui abolit le Silence, la grande voix du Silence qu'il nous faut lever à notre bord, malgré leurs ouragans, leurs assauts le flagellant ...
> (ES, p. 38)

Obviously the paradox is intentional: by violating the laws of logic it enables the poet to create a verbal synthesis and to find a unit in language which dissolves all contradictions and permits access to the Divine. 'Chant de la Parole' draws to a close with a reaffirmation of the poet's belief in the metaphysical function of poetry:

> Alors, lorsque toute neuve, elle sera tendue sur notre vie, alors, lorsque palpitera, épanoui, le Silence, nous entendrons Dieu, nous trouverons notre première et finale Joie, et dans la vibration vierge de cette Joie, de cette Voix, nous oserons hisser au sommet du Silence, l'étoile de la Parole.
> (ES, p. 38)

In phase three of the connotative sequence of *Cycle du Silence* the formal and thematic oppositions between silence and sound are overcome in a larger synthesis which views them both as bi-polar coordinates of the same axis. The ostensible sound/silence dichotomy which results from the poetic practice of reversing the connotations of a given seme is not so much paradoxical as it is interactional. In other words, the two terms of the opposition are not irreconcilable but rather, as the title suggests, they form part of the same structure. From this viewpoint the texts of *Erosion du Silence*, much like the relationships established between individuals, may be read as a series of transactions which culminate in a desired interaction. Schematically, the dynamics of the sound/silence dyad may be represented as follows: (A-/B+ > A+/B-> A+-/B-+). It might be added, moreover, that this formal interaction between semes also pervades the thematic structure of *Erosion du Silence* where it has a triple mimetic function. First, it is the textual analog of geological erosion; second, it represents the linguistic act of communication; third, and most importantly, it signifies divine communion.

Marie-Claire d'Orbaix in her profound wisdom as a poet has seen, felt and understood the metaphysical necessity of silence, the *sine qua non* of all poetry and the ground of all being. Silence - a Janus-like figure, simultaneously the beginning and the end of all discourse - must violate any linguistic code based on semic discreteness in order to reduce all distinctions to an essential unity. Silence neither nullifies nor contradicts speech; it is its source. All poetry inevitably presupposes a poetics of silence. No one understands this better than Marie-Claire d'Orbaix, who proves to be an expert at unmasking the semantic function of silence. For Marie-Claire d'Orbaix silence is not only the state of being against which speech posits itself, it is also an ontological necessity because she exists by and through her very discourse: 'Je parle, donc je suis; j'écris, donc je suis.' ('Du Poète et de Son Outil', *Le Thyrse*, 1967, p. 3), she exclaims jubilantly while simultaneously acknowledging that *halo de silence* to which words lend their structure and shape.

Though the poet must endeavour to overcome silence in order to exist, he wins only ephemeral and tenuous victories in his battle with words. In the end the poet must always return to silence, glorifying its very ambivalence, protecting and nurturing it so that it can be reborn as a new poem:

> Un petit silence naît
> Tout apeuré dans l'oreille,
> Tout chiffonné de soleil,
> Sortant du cocon du bruit.
>
> Flocon de lumière
> Au creux de l'être,
> A l'orée du bruit
> A l'orée de la nuit
> Il vient de naître.

('A l'Orée du Bruit, p. 35)

Silence conceived as the ground of all being is nowhere more evident than in the poems of *Erosion du Silence* which equate it with the very essence of things. In 'A l'Orée du Bruit' it assumes a human form, but in 'Poème de Pierre' and 'Fleur de Repos' its presence also permeates the material universe where it is treated first as mineral substance 'Je vous offre enfin ce silence/ Qui mimera le minerai' (ES, p. 37); then, in a delicate but crystalline floral metaphor, it becomes the source of universal existence, 'O mort, fleur du repos,/ Corolles de silence,/Retour à la sève, à l'essence' (ES, p. 45).[5] Having identified silence with cosmological existence, having returned to the source, the poetic voice is now co-extensive with the Word. This final synthesis which Marie-Claire d' Orbaix so carefully constructs between sound and silence can only be achieved as the result of turmoil and realignment: language must be turned inside out and stripped of conventional meanings in order to expose its essential infrastructure, which is itself grounded in the silence of divine enunciation.

Once the poet has hushed all the superficial chattering which serves to fill the void for much of mankind, once he has unveiled the emptiness which underlies routine conversations, then he can hear the voice of silence which in its turn must be gently eroded in order to ensure true communication. In the face of silence the poet has words at his disposal, words which have been regenerated, spiritualized, and consecrated by their journey back to the source, words which now emerge in all of their sacred glory, words which spring forth as the *Verbe*. Viewed from this perspective the semic reversals which characterize *Cycle du Silence* underscore the poet's awesome powers of creation and his ability to manipulate words at will and to assign cosmological values to them. *Parole* emanates from silence: in its ceaseless flow it simultaneously confirms and annihilates the void from which it comes. Rarely is the concept of the word as Logos more consciously affirmed than in these texts: throughout the entire collection the poetic voice consistently, at times evangelistically, persuades the reader of the word's potential as the shaping force which determines the physical and semantic structure of the universe, its power of appropriation by naming: 'Toi, qui sais le pouvoir des mots/ Et le pouvoir de leur absence, ...' ('Exorcisme', p. 28).

From chaos comes logos. Throughout *Erosion du Silence* the power of the word is evidenced in the stylistic structure, or rather structuration, of these texts, most of which accentuate a creative process that may be characterized by an almost unlimited freedom in the production of images. The creative liberty of the poet is terrifying and exhilarating because of its very ambivalence, governed as it is by an immutable necessity while at the same time expressing itself as an inevitable contingency. Marie-Claire d'Orbaix's cosmogony, then, manifests itself at the textual level of her work as the coded transformation of a semantic which equates the word with divine power by means of a series of stylistic devices which are appropriate for rendering this idea. Thus, a fundamental metonymy suggests a *Weltanschauung* according to which the poet's power to appropriate by naming is tantamount to stating that the universe is contained in the Word. At first this particular vision of the universe seems to run the risk of fixing the cosmological order by avowing the presence of the Word while simultaneously rendering it inert. The Word indeed appears to hold things together, to serve as a stabilizing and binding force; such is the case, for example, in 'Feuilles' where the poet underlines its graphic existence in order to assign to it a sort of permanence: '... Parfum des mots clouant la vie/ Au linteau d'une page,/ Je vous retrouve, fous et sages,/ Que l'écriture auréola' (ES, p. 57); and in 'Chanson', one of many poems in which the poet compares words to ligaments: 'S'il revient ce soir encor/ Poser aux sables de mes pensées/ Les algues des syllabes nouées/ Puis-je guérir de ma mort?' (ES, p. 44). More often than not, however, this ostensible verbal inertia is superseded by a series of kinetic images which function to make the word dynamic by accentuating its generative powers. Several poems, for instance, describe the physical universe in terms of sound vibrations: 'Quand nous dévalons comme des astres/ Au coeur des abîmes endormis,/ Dans une chute immobile et vaste/ Qui nous sépare et nous réunit,/ J'écoute en ma poussière stellaire/ Flamber l'écho des mille lumières,/ Je touche sur toi leurs vibrations/ Et sens tournoyer les horizons ...' ('Poussière Stellaire', p. 13). The notion of the universe as *Verbe* becomes even more apparent in those texts where the poet assigns a sonorous existence to the human body. In 'Vitre' the physical separation of two lovers is vocalized as a plaintive cry emitted by the flesh: 'Miracle de la vitre,/ Ton visage m'est offert!/ L'instant brûle et palpite/ Des mille cris de la chair' (ES, p. 16); similarly, in 'Dune', Marie-Claire d'Orbaix conjoins *écriture* and *chant* in a stunning graphic image which silhouettes the grace of the human form: 'Lorsque tu écris/ A larges enjambées/ Le chant de tes jambes,/ Lorsque je vois le ciel toucher la dune,/ Et le vent gonfler haut ta robe,/ ... Je te chante et te salue,/ Toi qui écris sans vocable,/ Les souples syllabes/ De tes jambes nues' (ES, p. 20).

The poems in the preceding section have portrayed the poet as a musician because of his inclination to describe the universe in terms of an ultimate harmony. However, the poet's musical virtuosity is finally subsumed in the all-comprehensive logos principle according to which the Word becomes the generative base for both formal and biological existence. The function of the poet as adumbrated in 'Oasis' and 'Les

Branches du Silence' is to posit sound against nothingness, to structure sonorous and graphic forms in the face of chaos: 'Oasis, oasis,/ Je t'écris, je t'épelle/ Avec tes trois voyelles/ Et tes deux sons sifleurs ... Je t'écris, je t'appelle/ Dans le chaos qui bêle/ Dans la nuit dont j'ai peur ...' ('Oasis', p. 23). The divine nature of the poetic voice manifests itself in the poet's consciousness of his own creative act at the moment of creation.

Consciousness emanates from the void in the form of logos just as the breath flows from the lungs to produce words. The poet's power to give and sustain life is encoded in a final series of images which are based on the 'breath of life' motif. Once again, Marie-Claire d'Orbaix simulates a generative process wherein the poet's voice becomes the animating force which infuses stillness with movement. In this group of texts she actualizes the 'breath of life' motif by means of opposing imagistic systems in which figures of immobility are rendered as material or spatial entities with the consequence that they function as metonyms of silence. In the second stanza of 'Plage' the poet associates sound and space by means of phonetic similarities, then confirms their identity in the next line by focusing on their common sense of immobility: 'Une plage blanche,/ Une page de silence,/ En fragile immobilité' (ES, p. 34); in 'Nuits' also, the poet depicts stillness as an elongated, plane surface, 'Alors soudain s'érige/ Ce pont entre les rives/ Des heures de lumière/ Et s'allonge une steppe de silence/ Entre la mort du jour/ Et sa résurgence ...' (ES, p. 18). Images which oppose stillness derive from the power of the poetic voice to breathe life into empty forms and thereby to endow them with movement. This process of animation equates the word with life itself in 'Les Mots français': 'O mots français que j'aimais/ Je vous gonfle de vie à jamais' (ES, p. 39).

A discussion of the logos principle would not be complete without underlining the importance in linguistic terms of those elements of the communicative act which comprise its very necessity: namely, the obvious but essential addresser/addressee polarity. We shall conclude this essay with a brief examination of the process of enunciation in

Erosion du Silence and, for the sake of simplicity, we shall limit our remarks to the fundamental significance that Marie-Claire d'Orbaix attaches to the pronominal system employed in these poems. In the very first poem of her volume the poet establishes the tone and form of the linguistic exchanges which occur throughout the entire collection; 'Offrande' sets the enunciation pattern in terms of a *Je/Tu* relationship, thus positing and fixing the central theme of a communication achieved by means of verbal and physical interactions: 'Je vous offre ce livre/ Où je me suis livrée,/ Le bon grain et l'ivraie/ Ah! je m'en délivre' (ES, p. 7). By virtue of the primary ontological hiatus between the *en-soi* and the *pour-soi* implied in the addresser/addressee dichotomy, the linguistic component of these texts - herein defined as a kind of dialogue simulation - is made co-extensive with its thematic counterpart, i.e. the process of erosion which unfolds as a struggle between opposing geological forms.

The rather evident technique of dialogue simulation which occurs at the surface level of *Erosion du Silence* functions through normal referential channels. In many of these poems the poetic voice addresses itself to an identifiable *Tu*, though admittedly this process does not comprise a true dialogue because *Tu* never responds. This one-sided dialogue is not at all unusual in poetry; generally it serves as a pretext for the writing of the poem itself. The best examples of this kind of dialoguing may be found in those texts which are dedicated to a specific person, that is, where both interlocutors are named or evident. In other texts, however, the dialogue simulation takes place but it eschews any possibility of extra-textual referentiality since the *Tu* is a pure fiction, a textual construct: the poet now dialogues with an artifact, a product of his own creation. In 'Oasis', for instance, the *Tu* is generated entirely at the linguistic level: 'Oasis, oasis,/ Je t'écris, je t'épelle/ Avec tes trois voyelles/ Et tes deux sons siffleurs ... (ES, p. 23). This retreat from the domain of normal reference serves to spiritualize the dialogue by forcing it to play itself out on the mystico-metaphysical stage. At the deep textual level, however, the *Je/Tu* dichotomy echos the poet's perpetual dialogue as a kind of synecdochical appropriation of the world by means of his voice, a voice which simultaneously creates and incorporates the 'other'. The importance of the dialogue form becomes quite evident in a poetics which envisions the world as part of a divine pronominal system wherein the coordinates 'I' and 'Thou' become the basis of an ultimate spiritual reality.

The relationship between 'I' and 'Thou' is certainly the most fundamental bond which the poet established in *Erosion du Silence*, for it marks the presence of a continual heavenly discourse and a perpetual transaction which is both formulated and affirmed in language. As infra-text the *Je/Tu* dialogue recalls and reflects the nature of the Christian faith, which is itself maintained by the very tensions arising out of the contradiction between an apparently existential duality and a supposed essential unity:

Ils veulent tout vérifier
De l'admirable Parabole:
Le Lieu et l'heure et les paroles...
Ah! s'ils pouvaient revoir les plaies,
Capter l'écho de l'agonie,
Filmer ce mort qui les survole,
Scruter les phrases de sa vie
Et jauger l'auge où il est né ...

... Parfois je sens dans ma poitrine
Le dialogue originel
Entre le cri de leur famine
Et la nourriture du ciel.

('Credo', p. 67)

Thus, at the deepest level, *Tu* becomes a metonym of the exterior; metaphysically, it can be equated with the entire cosmos and the Supreme Divinity. It is in this sense that one can understand, after Marie-Claire d'Orbaix's fashion, that man's relation to the universe is contained in a pronominal system which induces him to seek God precisely because He is the 'other'; that is, to incorporate him into oneself. Indeed, binary categories make the dialogue possible; the very articulation of the pronoun *Je* implies my presence, your absence. You are absent *in me*; I call you into being by means of language but at the same time you are that entity by which I confirm my own being.[6]

In the act of communication the spiritual journey of man is represented. The very morphology of the word 'dialogue', composed of the elements *dia* and *logos*, reveals a process of mutual shaping. Word world, and meaning are completely relational, forming as they do the interacting elements of a cosmological co-production. Viewed from this optic, the linguistic structure of *Erosion du Silence* supports its thematic structure and vice versa: the former, which occurs as the *Je/Tu* dialogue, may be called algorithmic in nature because all the referential multiples of each of these pronouns are ultimately reduced to their lowest common divisor - the divine dyad; the latter, which is actualized in the process of erosion, might be described as teleological due to the fact that erosion figures as part of Nature's design to unify all things so that they may commune with one another. The overlapping which takes place at all structural levels of *Erosion du Silence* is itself a kind of dialectic which proceeds through the various cycles of the collection and terminates in a synthesis: appropriately, the final poem is entitled 'Credo'.

At the ultimate stage of communication poetic discourse is abandoned for a signifying system wherein the emphasis shifts from the speech act as a human convention to a kind of universal hieroglyphic. In this sense the universe constitutes a text, 'la Grande Bible' as Hugo so aptly called it, which the poet deciphers through his interpretations of Nature's signs.[7] In *Derniers Poèmes*, the final section of *Erosion du Silence*, Marie-Claire d'Orbaix's belief in a cosmological semiology reveals itself in 'Chrysalide', a text in which words and celestial stubbles coalesce: 'Nous regardons d'un oeil aveugle/ La moisson mûre du cosmos,/ Soudain le ciel est plein d'éteules/ Qui se comptent à petits mots ...' (ES, pl 63). 'Champ de Blé-Chant du Blé', the poem which best characterizes the articulation of the Divine Message in natural signs, is too long to be quoted in its entirety but it should be mentioned that it expresses how acutely the poet senses the divine presence in Nature's bountiful fruits and thus equates her spiritual quest with 'sa faim humaine et sa faim de Dieu'. In the final lines of the poem, which correspond to the thematic of the harvest, her appetite is sated as she listens to the divine voice deliver its message:

> Blé bondissant de coteau en coteau
> Vous êtes notre cri le plus chaud,
> Je l'entends s'assouvir et s'engranger
> De ma bouche aux horizons rassasiés,
> J'entends crépiter les épis de mille crèches
> Pour la clarté de la première promesse
> J'entends la meule mûrir le grain
> Où tourne le message divin ...
>
> Eteules, griffez-moi les genoux
> Je célèbre Noël en plein Août,
> Et je moissonne un pain universel
> Dans cette gerbe écrasée de soleil ...
>
> (ES, p. 66)

The closing verses of 'Champ de Blé-Chant du Blé' suggest that in the poetics of Marie-Claire d'Orbaix communication is ultimately superseded by communion and that the final goal of dialogue is the total identification of the communicants. Language - in its mundane communicative function as well as in its spiritualized semiotic function - is the elemental binding force which depolarizes all things and makes love possible. As symbol of this unity, Christ on the Cross becomes the paradigm for a universal semiosis since he represents the paradox and the resolution of the paradox. Crist *is* the Word become flesh, the total identity of *signifiant* and *signifié*, for as the poet so humbly concludes:

> Je ne veux rien vérifier
> De l'admirable Parabole:
> Je crois en l'unique symbole,
> Je crois Dieu sur parole,
> Ma foi s'incruste au Crucifié.
>
> ('Credo', p. 68)

NOTES

1. I have chosen as my methodological point of departure the semantic system of analysis proposed by Riffaterre in a recent article entitled 'Paragram and Significance', *Semiotext(e)*, I, 2 (Fall, 1974), p. 74, where he views the text as an expansion of a semantic nucleus:

> The model I propose for the lexical paragram is the expansion of a matrix. Contrary to the verbal sequence thus generated, the matrix is semantic ... And the paragram generated by the matrix is lexical, being made out of words related grammatically instead of being phonetic or graphemic as in Saussure's paragram. So that instead of having fragments of a word scattered along the sentence, each embedded in the body of a word, we get words or groups of words, each embedded in a syntagm, whose organization reflects and exteriorizes the inner semantic configuration of the nuclear word or trigger word or semantic given.

Riffaterre's theory of the semantic paragram, moreover, is especially relevant to the stylistic structure of *Erosion du Silence*, which is largely metonymic:

> To arrive at a definition of the semantic paragram, or even at the concept of such a paragram, I started from three facts of literary utterance. One, that the literary text is built up by expansion from units of meaning smaller than the text they generate. Two, that such derivations are self-sufficient, since they do not refer to non-verbal referents; but the focus to which self-reference should point is replaced by an empty space, leaving the verbal referent that is the paragram, unspoken, while enabling the reader to circle around it. Three, that the words actualizing the derivation are never literal statements, but indirect ones, metaphorical or metonymic.
>
> (*Ibid.*, p. 73)

2. Once again, I refer the reader to Riffaterre's article (see n. 1) where he discusses the effects of lexical transformations on the given semantic:

> There is no point of departure preceding other developments of language, but rather displacements: any nuclear semantic component functions as if it were a suppressed symptom whose suppression causes it to pop up elsewhere in the text with a flourish of other symptoms, that is, of other synonyms periphrastic or not. The text behaves like a neurosis.
>
> (*ibid.*)

3. In a short treatise which appeared before *Erosion du Silence*, Marie-Claire d'Orbaix had already formulated some interesting ideas on the ontological and epistemological functions of poetry which seem quite pertinent to this study:

> Ainsi le poète use de la parole gravement, comme d'un instrument de connaissance de soi et des autres; il sent qu'il existe, il sent que l'univers existe lorsqu' il le dit. Tout son travail, tout son bonheur résulte d'un double mouvement: d'abord une mise à l'écoute du monde qui l'habite et du monde qui l'entoure puis une mise en ondes de ces mondes. Sans cesse se fera ce va-et-vient, ce perpétuel échange sur le plan de l'être.
>
> ('Du Poete et de Son Outil', *Le Thyrse*, 1967, p. 4)

4. The paradoxical structure of *Cycle du Silence* is not only intentional but it also represents the poet's attempt to seize and evoke totality by means of the word:

> 'Ce qui reste à jamais à dire', d'énormes domaines au dedans et au dehors de nous doivent être déchiffrés, défrichés, allais-je dire, d'énormes domaines attendent la voix des poètes. Toutes les choses nouvelles qui n'ont pas encore été chantées attendent d'être brassées dans la pensée des poètes et moulées dans leurs phrases.
>
> (*ibid.*, p. 5)

5. In an essay entitled 'Le Mythe aujourd'hui', written nearly twenty years ago, Roland Barthes perceptively noted the fascination with silence which characterizes modern poetry. Barthes argues that contemporary poetry is a retrogressive semiotic system because it uses language (the sign) in an attempt to destroy - or get beyond - language. The word-sign is transformed into the word-thing, it is a return to the very essence of existence:

> En somme, de tous les usagers de la parole, les poètes sont les moins formalistes, car eux seuls croient que le sens des mots n'est qu'une forme, dont les réalistes qu'ils sont ne sauraient se contenter. C'est pour quoi notre poésie moderne s'affirme toujours comme un meurtre du langage, une sorte d'analogue spatial, sensible, du silence. La poésie occupe la position inverse du mythe: le mythe est un système sémiologique qui pretend se dépasser en système factuel; la poésie est un système sémiologique qui prétend se rétracter en système essentiel.
>
> ('Le Mythe aujourd'hui', in *Mythologies*, Paris: Editions du Seuil, 1957, p. 242)

6. I should like to call the reader's attention to Todorov's comments on the need to develop a theory of the personal pronoun within descriptive poetics, if only because this eminent critic for once observes the necessity of stepping outside of the literary text itself, into the domain of the ontological function of such a pronominal system:

> Le *je* signifie le relatif isolement de l'homme dans son rapport avec le monde qu'il construit, l'accent placé sur cet affrontement sans qu'un intermédiaire ait à être nommé. Le *tu*, en revanche, renvoie précisément à cet intermédiaire, et c'est la relation tierce qui se trouve à la base du réseau. Cette opposition est asymétrique: le *je* est présent dans le *tu*, mais non l'inverse. Comme l'écrit Martin Buber: 'Il n'y a pas de *Je* en soi, il n'y a que le *Je* du mot-principe *Je-Tu* et le *Je* du mot-principe *Je-Cela*. Quand l'homme dit *Je*, il veut dire l'un ou l'autre, *Tu* ou *Cela*.'
>
> (*Introduction à la littérature fantastique*, Paris: Editions du Seuil, 1970, p. 163).

7. Marie-Claire d'Orbaix's conception of nature and signification closely parallels that of the 19th century Illuminists, and more especially the theory of *correspondances* which prevailed in 19th century occultist poetry: natural phenomena are *not* fortuitous and meaningless, but rather they represent the articulations of an unspoken language in which the sign enjoys a total restitution, that is, the unification of formal and semantic components:

> ... every phenomenon of Nature is a word in the divine language. Objects do not merely exist, they also signify and are endowed with spiritual meaning. Such was the doctrine of correspondence. All that the first man saw and touched in nature was a living Word, and Language was thus born from the contact of human sensitivity with the mute symbols of the created world, the signs or characters in the divine language which God had addressed to men.
>
> (Gwendolyn Bays, *The Orphic Vision*, Lincoln, Neb.: University of Nebraska Press, 1964, pp. 44-45).

GASTON MIRON

John Beaver

Among the poets of the postward generation in Québec whose work reflects the development of a new cultural consciousness, Gaston Miron is the most public and yet the least published. In the nineteen-sixties, the years of the 'Quiet Revolution' that transformed an ultraconservative and inward-looking society into one which expresses more confidently and more powerfully a sense of its autonomy, Miron acts as a catalyst and organiser, occupying the centre stage as much through his activity as editor and publisher as through his poetry. Co-founder of the Hexagone group whose poems define the new historical and geographical entity in the word 'le pays', he sees as a major duty the establishment of the financial and material means through which poetry can address itself to the public. In 1957, he writes, 'Il appartient aux poètes de sauver la poésie non seulement spirituellement mais aussi dans sa matérialité',[1] and the dual role he ascribes to himself has made him an almost legendary figure in Québec literary circles. As *animateur*, he sees the encouragement of new cultural expression as an integral part of the 'salvation' of poetry in Québec; and any approach to his poetry must take into account his intense commitment to the social revolution of the nineteen-sixties, a commitment that, among other things, guaranteed his imprisonment under the War Measures Act during the October Crisis of 1970.[2] Social activism has also contributed to the fragmentary nature of his work. In all, he has published three collections of poetry: *Deux sangs* (1954), written in collaboration with Olivier Marchand, was the first of the Hexagone publications. *L'Homme rapaillé* (1970) contains poems from his first book, poems written during the 1960's, and a number of articles. More recently, he has published *Courtepointes* (1975), a collection of poems written and reworked from as early as 1954.

Miron's poems are guaranteed to frustrate literary historians since they are rarely published in definitive form. Even in his most complete collection, *L'Homme rapaillé*, a number of poems are designated as fragments and extracts, part of a work in progress, continually subject to revisions. Unlike Gatien Lapointe's epic *Ode au Saint Laurent* (1963) or Paul Chamberland's *Terre Québec* (1964), Miron's poems do not root the Québec experience within a clearly defined context, although thematically they refer to the same experience of cultural re-creation. Instead they perpetually question both the cultural context and the nature of poetry. Miron constantly searches for authenticity, both in socio-cultural terms and in terms of the language which is to be the vehicle of his cultural expression. It is therefore not surprising that in a society undergoing rapid and critical transformation, one of its major poets should characterise himself as transitional, provisional and problematic, that the fundamentally interrogative character of his poems should reflect the cultural 'pre-text'. The Québécois has yet to be politically and socially defined, recognised in his independence by the international community; the authentic Québécois poetry that would constitute the fully integrated expression of the new culture is still to be discovered. For this reason, Miron refers to his activity as an 'art pré-poétique' (HR, 129), often going to the extent of deriding himself, of refusing to accept the definition 'poet', preferring to see himself as victim, clown, fool. As long as the socio-political situation defines him as 'colonisé', he argues, there can be no authentic poetry; his language will inevitably reflect the alienation that has characterised the Québec experience. To give the impression that Québec culture is alive and well would be to deny that social reality:

> Quant à moi, je refusais toujours de publier mes poèmes en livre, bien que j'aie consenti à les donner à des revues qui oeuvraient dans une perspective d'indépendance, j'aurais fait, croyais-je, le jeu de ceux qui prétendent sans broncher que nous avons tous les moyens de nous réaliser en tant qu'être au monde de culture française (être nous-mêmes), dans le statu quo d'un système où aucune motivation socio-politique ne vient rendre nécessaire la pratique de cette culture.
> (HR, 117)

Poets in French Canada have been acutely aware since the conquest of 1759 of the need to discover an authentic literary voice. Politically and economically dominated by English-speaking Canada, culturally overshadowed by France, the French-Canadian writer has until the Second World War been faced with a problem that Octave Crémazie analysed pessimistically in 1867:

> Plus je réfléchis sur les destinées de la littérature canadienne moins je lui trouve de chances de laisser une trace dans l'histoire. Ce qui manque au Canada, c'est d'avoir une langue à lui. Si nous parlions iroquois ou huron, notre littérature vivrait. Malheureusement nous parlons et écrivons d'une assez piteuse façon, il est vrai, la langue de Bossuet et de Racine. Nous avons beau dire et beau faire, nous ne serons toujours, au point de vue littéraire, qu'une simple colonie; et quand bien même le Canada deviendrait un pays indépendant et ferait briller son drapeau au soleil des nations, nous n'en demeurerions pas moins de simples colons littéraires.
>
> (Lettre à l'abbé Casgrain, 29 janvier 1867)

Literature in French Canada has traditionally followed one of two paths. On one hand, the imitation of French models expresses the attempt to become'universal', with the result that poetry has become separated from its immediate and particular environment. On the other hand, a strongly regionalist tradition has sought to portray the picturesque rural elements of the Québec landscape. In neither of these two traditions is there integration between poet and milieu, a dynamic relationship through which may be forged a true sense of identity with Québec space. Miron is well aware of these two colonial reactions when in 1965 he writes: 'Je m'efforçais de me tenir à égale distance du régionalisme et de l'universalisme abstrait, deux pôles de désincarnation, deux malédictions qui ont pesé constamment sur notre littérature' (HR, 117). This situation prevails until the postwar years when an upheaval in literary values signals the arrival on the scene of a new generation that seeks to integrate poetry with the major currents of the modern age. The new generation, of which Miron is one of the principal spokesmen, represents a new and socially mobile class that challenges the traditional authority of the clericobourgeois elite. The literary expression of this traditional elite is essentially one of detachment and defensiveness. It attempts to maintain a linguistic and cultural fortress in order to guarantee its survival. The new generation, however, sees this mentality as sterile, reflecting a colonial ghetto that stifles creativity and modernity. The literary revolt of the writers of the 'forties and 'fifties is an image of the challenge that a new class issues to the older order. The flowering of this revolt can be seen in the Quiet Revolution[3] and the birth of the independantist movement.

Miron's arrival in Montréal in 1947 from Ste Agathe-des-Monts, a resort village in the Laurentian hills, mirrors the general contemporary shift in Québec from a rural to an urban milieu and the attendant upheavals which strike not only at previously held values, but at the roots of language itself. Montréal, 'grand comme un désordre universel' (HR, 38), reflects the social, and therefore linguistic, humiliations of Québec, the 'condition de colonisé' which Miron has to first recognise and identify before he can begin the process of redefining the Québec imaginative stance. He becomes acutely aware, during his early years in Montréal, and later during a stay in France, that literature in Québec and therefore Québec society itself is victim of linguistic as well as political confusion, and that, as poet, his main effort should be to clarify and identify the nature of the malaise:

> Je croyais que les conditions normales à l'existence et à l'épanouissement d'une littérature n'étaient pas réalisées ici: nous étions condamnés à une littérature d'en-deçà, de moribond. La perversion sémantique à l'échelle nationale en faussait la communication et la rejetait dans l'irréalité.
>
> (HR, 116)

For Miron, Québec is faced with problems of a semantic nature. Its present contradictions will only be resolved when language is freed from the historical and social conditions that have defined it as a sub-language. In 1965, he published the *Notes sur le non-poème et le poème*, typically designating them as *extraits*; these may serve as a starting-point for our analysis of his experience of language and of the problems facing the poet in Québec.

'Je parle de CECI' (HR, 122), he writes, and the unspecified nature of the demonstrative pronoun reflects the initial vagueness that hinders his attempt at definition, the malaise of 'un homme cerné d'irréel' (HR, 125). Defined by a language that separates him from reality, that has created a screen of nuance and accretion and predetermined the structures of his experience, he sees poetry as struggling against a pervasive linguistic darkness:

> Le non-poème
> c'est ma langue que je ne sais plus reconnaître
> des marécages de mon esprit brumeux
> à ceux des signes aliénés de ma réalité
>
> (HR, 122)

This situation echoed in the *Monologues de l'aliénation délirante*:

> ravageur je fouille ma mémoire et mes chairs
> jusqu'en les maladies de la tourbe et de l'être
> pour trouver la trace de mes signes arrachés emportés
> pour reconnaître mon cri dans l'opacité du réel.
>
> (HR, 59)

'Dualisme linguistique', 'quotidienne altérité', 'vacuité', 'ce qui sépare', such are the characteristics of a language whose signs do not correspond to Miron's search for integration. When he refers to the 'signes aliénés de ma réalité' or speaks of 'la trace de mes signes arrachés emportés', he is setting in opposition two languages. One is the authentic voice rooted in the specific images of his space; the other, a colonial voice which inhibits the development of his vision (and that of the collectivity) by accepting the social and political status quo and confirming itself as colonial:

> Je parle seulement pour moi et quelques autres
> puisque beaucoup de ceux qui ont parole
> se déclarent satisfaits
>
> (HR, 122)

Miron must therefore struggle against a colonial mythology whose metaphors no longer reflect the political and social reality; he must clear the ground so as to create a territory in which may be rooted and grown a new linguistic and social order. 'Je dis que la langue est le fondement même de l'existence d'un peuple, parce qu'elle réfléchit la totalité de sa culture en signe, en signifié, en signifiance' (HR, 124), he states. Unless Québec can create its own specific universe, its inhabitants will continue to be marginal and semi-human, evolving in a world of unreality and irrationality.

Miron traces the alien sign system that has determined the Québec language back to the historical situation; and it is a historical sense that informs to a considerable extent his notion of the function of poetry. The Conquest of 1759, the trauma that gave birth to the French Canadian, was an historical event over which he had no control. Since then, history has always been made elsewhere. The French Canadian has been determined by'les autres', and the 'non-poème', 'qui sépare le dedans et le dehors en faisant des univers hostiles l'un à l'autre' (HR, 122), is evidence of the weight of colonial history upon him. Miron illustrates this in abrasive fashion:

> Longtemps je n'ai su mon nom, et qui j'étais, que de l'extérieur. Mon nom est 'Pea Soup'. Mon nom est 'Pepsi". Mon nom est 'Marmelade'. Mon nom is 'Frog'. Mon nom est 'dam Canuck'. Mon nom est 'speak white'. Mon nom est 'dish washer'. Mon nom est 'floor sweeper'. Mon nom est 'bastard'. Mon nom est 'cheap'. Mon nom est 'sheep'. Mon nom ... mon nom ...
>
> (HR, 127)

The historical role of the Québécois is that of an object named, rather than of a creative subject naming and ordering his world. History has pre-ordained a world in which the specific and personal is devalued. Miron juxtaposes collective history and personal history, showing how the latter is negated by the former: 'Je suis malade d'un cauchemar héréditaire. Je ne me reconnais pas de passé récent. Mon nom est "Amnésique Miron"' (HR, 126). The past as determined by the Conquest distorts and controls the linguistic and social life of Québec; the authentic, immediate experience is masked. On the other hand, the victim is also imbued with possibilities of re-creation:

comment faire qu'à côté de soi un homme
porte en son regard le bonheur physique de sa terre
et dans sa mémoire le firmament de ses signes

beaucoup n'ont pas su, sont morts de vacuité
mais ceux-là qui ont vu je vois par leurs yeux
(HR, 126)

Against the 'non-poème', 'mon historicité vécue par substitutions' (HR, 122), 'la dépolitisation maintenue de ma permanence' (HR, 123), Miron seeks to establish the authenicity of the poem which will inaugurate a new cosmology, a new history; the political independence of Québec will be accompanied by the emergence of the poem, which Miron sees as an historical event:

Poème, je te salue
dans l'unité refaite du dedans et du dehors
o contemporanéité flambant neuve
je te salue, poème, historique, espèce
et présent de l'avenir

Le poème, ici, a commencé
d'actualiser
le poème, ici, a commencé
d'être souverain
(HR, 123)

For this reason, Miron sees his work as 'anté-historique', an 'art pré-poétique' which anticipates the independence that will give birth to true poetry.

The title of Miron's two last books indicates to us the function of poetry as he sees it: 'rapailler' has been defined by Miron as 'ramasser la paille qui a servi à protéger les champs de la gelée, mais qui peut encore servir'.[4] *Courtepointes* similarly evokes the notion not only of collecting but of piecing together, creating out of deteriorated and rejected material a significant language and a significant human being. The task that Miron sets himself is one of cleaning, trimming, paring language, so that space may be cleared for the work of reconstruction to take place. In 'La Marche à l'amour' he refers to 'ma vie en friche' (HR, 36), equating his task with that of the pioneer clearing the land for cultivation. In the midst of semantic and linguistic confusion, Miron seeks to revalue his own language and create a space in which it may grow and develop into a 'universal' language. Under these conditions it will express the totality of his experience. Compared to 'international' French, his language, though rooted in his native Laurentian village, has not yet achieved its full range and subtletly. In Montréal, the sub-language 'joual',[5] contaminated syntactically and semantically by English, betrays at every turn its colonised origins. The language that Miron seeks is therefore one which will be at the same time specific, derived from the particular images of his native place, and raised beyond the partial, regional, colonial barrier, to an expression which will be equal to other languages that express their culture independently and completely.

Miron's early poems published in *Deux sangs* (1954) as well as *La vie agonique* (written between 1954 and 1959), reveal the dimensions of the dilemma out of which he writes. In Miron's experience a number of characteristics determine a colonised language. In the first place, a considerable dichotomy exists between inside and outside, between the 'je' and the word, between self and reality; 'je marche dans mon manque de mots et de pensée' (HR, 81), he writes, and while this, to a greater or lesser extent, is the dilemma of any poet, for Miron it has a more acute significance: it reflects the impossibility of writing under the present sociopolitical conditions. Language has become a stranger to experience: Miron refers to himself as 'déphasé et décentré dans ma coincidence' (HR, 58), to the language of his poetry as 'ces mots dehors' (HR, 11), 'ma part d'incohérence' (HR, 43). Such incoherence is the result of the disparity between word, reality and self, a rift that prevents him from adequately synthesising experience, and is less a reflection of personal failure than of the effect of colonialism on language.

Language thus affected becomes emptied of content and significance. One striking characteristic of Miron's early poems is the high level of abstraction. Dominique Noguez has commented on such abstract words as 'poésie', 'réalité', 'aliénation', 'contemporanéité': 'il est en effet résistance. Résistance linguistique, car les mots abstraits jouissent d'une sorte de privilège et de prestige: purs, scintillant dans leur candeur éthérée, ils paraissent moins accessibles que les autres aux souillures et au parasitage idéologique'.[6] This may be so, but because of their abstract nature they are devoid of the substantial physical attributes that guarantee presence and significance. When Miron speaks of 'ma poésie' in interlocutory fashion he speaks to something yet unattained or unfulfilled:

> ma pauvre poésie toujours si près de t'évanouir
> désespérée mais non résignée
> obstinée dans ta compassion et le salut collectif
> (HR, 76)

or when evoking a sense of loss he is imprecise and vague as to what has been lost:

> je parle de ces choses qui nous furent volées
> (HR, 34)

And, indeed, we frequently find Miron attempting to characterise the various elements that prevent his writing poetry by the use of demonstrative forms - 'ça', 'ce que', 'ceci' - that lack clear and precise identification. In the cycle of love poems, *La Marche à l'amour*, Miron evokes the figure of a woman in much the same way as he refers to poetry, and with a similar reference to the power of the 'non-poème' to abstract:

> Je finirai bien par te rencontrer quelque part
> contre tout ce qui me rend absent et douloureux
> (HR, 36)

Absence both of a sense of reality and a sense of his physical presence creates at times in the early poems a language that in its abstraction can only hint at the world Miron is seeking. *Pour retrouver le monde et l'amour* (1954), whose title expresses the fundamental aim of Miron's poetic practice, somehow fails to achieve clarity and precision because the language lacks the concrete, substantive elements that would attach it to immediate reality. Hence the special quality of an abstract vocabulary 'raised' to almost heroic proportions:

nous passerons très haut par-dessus les clameurs
et tu ne vivras plus de perfides rumeurs
or loin des profiteurs, des lieux de pestilence
tu entendras parler les mages du silence
alors tu connaîtras la musique à tes pas
et te revêtiront les neiges des sagas

(HR, 19)

Hence, too, the characterisation of his land:

'démuni, il ne connaît qu'un espoir de terrain vague' (HR, 49)

A dichotomy between the form and the substantive content of the poem is typical of a poetry alientated from its milieu: and we shall see later how Miron rediscovers the essential images with which he replaces the semantic emptiness of abstraction.

Among a number of other important characteristics of the 'non-poème' we might mention one which, allied to the insubstantive nature of the abstract nouns, involves a particularly frequent use of the past participle to designate the object situation of the *colonisé*. Thus poetry is determined by circumstance:

Ma désolée sereine
ma barricadée lointaine
ma poésie les yeux brûlés

(HR, 23)

and the poet, 'défoncé enfoncé' (HR, 26), paralysed by the alienation of language and substance, uses the past participle to underline the object status by which he is defined:

moi je gis, muré dans la boîte crânienne
dépoétisé dans ma langue et mon appartenance
déphasé et décentré dans ma coincidence

(HR, 58)

Moreover, we may observe here another significant characteristic of the 'non-poème', namely the use of the absolute and intransitive verbal construction. 'Je gis' is one example of this; there are many others, among which a particularly local use of 'refouler' as an intransitive verb stands out:

ta vie refoule dans son amphore (HR, 10)
je suis ici à rétrécir dans mes épaules (HR, 58)
à vivre mon angoisse poudrait (HR, 12)

A language unable to come into viable contact with the outside world reflects the political and social isolation of Québec. Miron's language struggles against dislocation and cacophony, the 'désordre universel' of Montréal, the 'opacité du réel', the 'folie mouvante' of a total semantic and syntactic disorder:

Car le péril est dans nos poutres, la confusion
une brunante dans nos profondeurs et nos surfaces
nos consciences sont éparpillées dans le débris
de nos miroirs, nos gestes des simulacres de libertés
(HR, 61)

celui qui n'a rien comme moi, comme plusieurs
marche depuis sa naissance, marche à l'errance
avec tout ce qui déraille et tout ce qui déboussole
dans son vague cerveau que l'agression embrume

comment me retrouver labyrinthe ô mes yeux
je marche dans mon manque de mots et de pensée
hors du cercle de ma conscience, hors de portée
père, mère, je n'ai plus mes yeux de fil en aiguille
(HR, 81)

The last line of the second of these quotations, from *Les Années de déréliction*, is characteristic of colonial language. We frequently find in Miron's poetry the expression of a man, who, in his words, 'frissonnait dans les parallèles de ses pensées' (HR, 61). The parataxic and litanical structure of the poems indicates the sense of two realities existing side by side but never meeting. The opening lines of the 'Monologues de l'aliénation délirante' similarly show us a syntax working through conjunctions which indicate a temporal-sequential, rather than a causal logic:

Le plus souvent ne sachant où je suis ni pourquoi
je me parle à voix basse voyageuse
et d'autres fois en phrases détachées (ainsi
que se meuvent chacune de nos vies)
puis je déparle à voix haute dans les haut-parleurs
crevant les cauchemars, et d'autres fois encore

déambulant dans un orbe calfeutré, les larmes
poussent comme de l'herbe dans mes yeux
(HR, 58)

Alternatively, we see the parallelism of alienation in the litanical structure of 'les siècles de l'hiver':

pays chauve d'ancêtres, pays
tu déferles sur des milles de patience à bout
en une campagne affolée de désolement
en des villes où ta maigreur calcine ton visage
nous nos amours vidés de leurs meubles
nous comme empesés d'humiliation et de mort
(HR, 51)

In many poems from the *Vie agonique* cycle, as well as from the early poems, the prevalent atmosphere is static. There is no sense of progression, the syntax frequently falls apart and the poems are inconclusive.

Nevertheless Miron attempts in a number of ways to carve out a significant space for poetry, to create a valid world out of his colonial chaos. Resolution of the contradictions and dilemmas of colonialism depends largely upon two major areas of activity. One is to cultivate a lucid and critical awareness of the dangers and effects of semantic perversion; hence the strongly didactic vein. Miron even assumes the role of clown and fool in order to reach the public, and to un-name and un-invent both self and world. At this point may begin a second activity, the naming and rediscovery of a new world and the structuring of a cosmology around the physical and substantial images of the Québec space.

'Les poètes de ce temps montent la garde du monde', Miron writes in 'Recours didactique' (HR, 61). More specifically, within the context of the struggle against a colonial mentality, the first necessity according to Miron's socio-poetic logic is to develop a clarity and lucidity that will clean language. It is no doubt for this reason that the image of the eye and of seeing assumes a particular significance in his poetry. 'Réduction', one of Miron's early poems, shows the poet in the role of vigilant critic, a first step in the process of denunciation:

je n'ai plus que mes yeux de z-yeux
tout ailleurs dans mon corps est ténèbre
(mes yeux de z-yeux
- en tout et pour tout)
(les bulletins annoncent
qu'aucune localisation n'est en vue)

pourtant je vois ce que je vois
(HR, 27)

In the same collection of poems Miron forcefully evokes the idea of the poet 'sounding' the depths of his darkness, alert and attentive:

soudain je suis debout contre l'air égratigné de mouches
à feu
je suis droit à l'écoute comme un fil à plomb
je comprends que nous ne serons plus jamais des hommes si
nos yeux se vident
(HR, 31)

In 'La Marche à l'amour', the 'mince regard qui me reste au fond du froid' (HR, 36) is his last link with reality against 'tout ce qui me rend absent et douloureux' (HR, 36), and he pins his faith on a future in which both he and his society will see clearly:

je sais que d'autres hommes forceront un peu plus
la transgression, des hommes qui nous ressemblent
qui vivront dans la vigilance notre dignité réalisée
c'est en eux dans l'avenir que je m'attends
que je me dresse sans qu'ils le sachent, avec toi
(HR, 45)

In 'Foyer naturel', his eyes are the eyes of a nocturnal creature whose vision pierces the colonial darkness:

Ma belle folie crinière au vent
je m'abandonne à toi sur les chemins
avec les yeux magiques du hibou
parmi les fous fins fils du mal monde
(HR, 87)

The most vigilant eyes, however, are those of 'l'homme agonique', who despite his torment preserves the painful lucidity that is his only means of salvation against unconsciousness and cultural death:

Jamais je n'ai fermé les yeux
malgré les vertiges sucrés des euphories
même quand mes yeux sentaient le roussi
même en butte aux rafales montantes du sommeil
(HR, 48)

Paradoxical and contradictory, he creates for himself an impossible role, seeking poetry yet cultivating didacticism and oratorical rhetoric. His deliberate, often prosaic, self-denunciation is a means of divesting himself of his linguistic-poetic colonialism. 'L'homme agonique' is not synonymous with 'le colonisé'; rather he is colonial man undergoing the painful process of transformation. As soon as he becomes aware of the contradictions of his colonial image, he seeks to destroy his former vacuous self. A process of self-immolation and derision is therefore the primary function of l'homme agonique' and a prelude to authenticity. He is initially a man on stage, fulfilling a time-honoured role:

- Tapi au fond de moi tel le fin renard
alors je me résorbe en jeux, je mime et parade
ma vérité, le mal d'amour, et douleurs et joies

Et je m'écris sous la loi d'émeute
je veux saigner sur vous par toute l'affection
j'écris, j'écris, à faire un fou de moi
à me faire le fou du roi de chacun
volontaire aux enchères de la dérision
mon rire en volées de grelots par vos têtes
en chavirées de pluie dans vos jambes
(HR, 48)

The role, however, is temporary; the fool and clown is to be destroyed, his world un-invented, so that the death of the 'colonisé', the Québécanthrope, 'ce garçon qui ne ressemble à personne' (HR, 86), should be the birth of a new man, who will start afresh the process of becoming himself:

Un jour de grande détresse à son comble
je franchirai les tonnerres des désespoirs
je déposerai ma tête exsangue sur un meuble
ma tête grenade et déflagration
sans plus de vue je continuerai, j'irai
vers ma mort peuplée de rumeurs et d'éboulis
je retrouverai ma nue propriété
(HR, 48)

Through self-derision and denunciation ('Les pharisiens ne me pardonneront jamais à ma poésie d'avoir eu honte AVEC tous, en esprit et en vérité, au lieu DE tous') (HR, 129), he abandons a poetry disengaged from the immediate political and social concerns:

> Mes camarades au long cours de ma jeunesse
> si je fus le haut-lieu de mon poème, maintenant
> je suis sur la place publique avec les miens
> et mon poème a pris le mors obscur de nos combats
>
> Longtemps je fus ce poète au visage conforme
> qui frissonnait dans les parallèles de ses pensées
> qui s'étiolait en rage dans la soie des désespoirs
> et son coeur raillait la crue des injustices
>
> Or je vois nos êtres en détresse dans le siècle
> je vois notre infériorité et j'ai mal en chacun de nous
> (HR, 61)

As in the earlier poems, when Miron writes his pastiches in the style of Mallarmé and Valéry, he is not bidding farewell to poetry; he is stating that until the demythologising of the colonial language has taken place, he will not claim to write poetry. His deliberate didacticism is rendering a service, not a disservice, to poetry:

> je ne chante plus je pousse la pierre de mon corps
>
> Je suis sur la place publique avec les miens
> la poésie n'a pas à rougir de moi
> (HR, 61)

Miron's 'recours didactique', the strongly interlocutory character of his appeals and denunciations, is an attempt to evince a collective response, to see evidence among his fellows of some awareness of their situation. The clown who mimics the follies of his society hopes ultimately to see their folly exorcised, and exorcism, the 'conjuration de mes manitous maléfiques' (HR, 36) is one of Miron's chief aims. He points out clearly the colonial spell that has been cast upon their political and poetic consciousness, while at the same time avoiding the temptation to seek any purely personal salvation:

- Car je trempe jusqu'à la moelle des os
jusqu'aux états d'osmose incandescents
dans la plus noire transparence de nos sommeils
(HR, 48)

Love, like poetry, can only flourish when the collective situation allows for the individual's creative freedom:

Je voudrais t'aimer comme tu m'aimes, d'une
seule coulée d'être ainsi qu'il serait beau
dans cet univers à la grande promesse de Sphynx
mais voici la poésie, les camarades, la lutte
voici le système précis qui écrase les nôtres
(HR, 44)

The word 'précis' suggests, as do the demonstratives, that Miron has begun - but it is a beginning fraught with intense struggle - the process of freeing subjectivity from the cloying effects of a given set of colonial values.

Miron, indeed, characterises himself as exemplary, both in his self-mockery and in his poetic and political activism; he acts as representative of a whole class in its struggle for authenticity:

ah sonnez crevez sonnailles de vos entrailles
riez et sabrez à la coupe de vos privilèges
grands hommes classe écran, qui avez fait de moi
le sous-homme, la grimace souffrante du cro-magnon
l'homme du cheap way, l'homme du cheap work
le damned Canuck
(HR, 55)

Such destructive violence is not only directed against the 'classe écran' that separates inner and outer worlds; he also condemns those Québécois whose acquiescence has contributed in large part to the alienation:

devant toutes les litanies
    de chats-huants qui huent dans la lune
devant toutes les compromissions en peau de vison
devant les héros de la bonne conscience
les émancipés malingres
    les insectes des belles manières
(HR, 57)

And in 'L'Octobre', he draws no distinction at all between self and collectivity as he associates his own sense of guilt with that of a society that has abandoned its humanity and its language:

> voici mes genoux que les hommes nous pardonnent
> nous avons laissé humilier l'intelligence des pères
> nous avons laissé la lumière du verbe s'avilir
> jusqu'à la honte et au mépris de soi dans nos frères
> nous n'avons pas su lier nos racines de souffrance
> à la douleur universelle dans chaque homme ravalé
> (HR, 62)

The poems of 'La vie agonique' constitute in some way a kind of *vox de profundis*, whose appeal is directed to those whose political and social response will determine the existence or disappearance of 'la terre de Québec'. Miron appeals to his society:

> Rien n'est changé de mon destin ma mère mes camarades
> le chagrin luit toujours d'une mouche à feu à l'autre
> je suis taché de mon amour comme on est taché de sang
> mon amour mon amour fait mes murs à perpétuité
> (HR, 53)

to his land:

> l'homme de ce temps porte le visage de la flagellation
> et toi, terre Québec, Mère Courage
> dans ta longue marche, tu es grosse
> de nos rêves charbonneux douloureux
> de l'innombrable épuisement de corps et d'âmes
> (HR, 62)

and to humanity in general. In this latter context the prehistoric Québécanthrope, the cro-magnon, becomes authentic through the recognition granted him by the international community, which permits him to see an image of himself that he has created in the eyes of others:

> les vents qui changez les sorts de place la nuit
> vents de rendez-vous, vents aux prunelles solaires
> vents telluriques, vents de l'âme, vents universels
> vents ameutez-nous, et de vos bras de fleuve ensemble
> enserrez son visage de peuple abîmé, redonnez-lui
> la chaleur
> et la profuse lumière des sillages d'hirondelles
> (HR, 49)

In 'Compagnon des Amériques', the appeal becomes stronger, and Miron celebrates the discovery not only of the outside world but of a humanity that the Québécanthrope had never possessed:

> mais donne la main à toutes les rencontres, pays
> ô toi qui apparais
>   par tous les chemins défoncés de ton histoire
> aux hommes debout dans l'horizon de la justice
> qui te saluent
> salut à toi territoire de la poésie
> salut les hommes des pères de l'aventure
>
> (HR, 57)

Self-destruction and derision have finally created a man 'hors de lui', who has exorcised his old identity and begun to speak and evolve a poetic territory that truly belongs to him.

Having thus 'un-invented' the world, detached himself from the semantically perverted language of colonialism, Miron begins to establish his cosmology, the significant space based upon the primal metaphors that reflect the physical and experiential world, the substantive Québec. There are a number of features of this naming of things that are important to Miron insofar as they reflect the relationship between poetry and a post-colonial world. The first is a sense of original history, of the naming of things in the beginning of time. As a preface to *L'Homme rapaillé*, Miron writes a short poem reflecting a return to his origins and the perhaps paradoxical notion of going into the past to discover the future. He has been 'absent', in the person of 'l'homme agonique', but has returned to his first landscapes, has cleared away the colonial notions which inhibited his free growth, and can then affirm:

> je ne suis pas revenu pour revenir
> je suis revenu à ce qui commence
>
> (HR, 5)

The image of the cultivator ('je pioche mon destin de long en large' (HR, 52)) and the evocation of a world of beginnings, take us back to the first clearing of land and, paradoxically, bring us to a future in which the naming and inventing of the world will signal the birth of an independent Québec and the birth of Québec poetry. It is the misty world of the beginning of time that he sees as truly poetic, a world outside the cultural fortress that has favoured the cultivation of the European garden and neglected the North American landscape:

> j'avance en poésie comme un cheval de trait
> tel celui-là de jadis dans les labours de fond
> qui avait l'oreille dressée à se saisir réel
> les frais matins d'été dans les mondes brumeux
> (HR, 77)

The world of origins is as important to Miron as it is to other Québec poets of his generation such as Paul Chamberland or Gatien Lapointe. Having un-invented the civilized colonial world of a European-centred culture, Miron rediscovers the language of his ancestors, the first images of the American landscape that were named but whose names have been hitherto declared regionalist or exotic by literary authorities. In his 'Art Poétique', Miron refers to this native language, threatened, yet always affirming itself and deriving its strength from the land:

> je suis malheureux ma mère mais moins que toi
> toi mes chairs natales, toi qui d'espérance t'insurges
> ma mère au cou penché sur ton chagrin d'haleine
> et qui perds gagnes les mailles du temps à tes mains
>
> dans un autre temps mon père est devenu du sol
> il s'avance en moi avec le goût du fils et des outils
> mon père, ma mère, vous saviez à vous-deux nommer
> toutes choses sur la terre, ô mon père, ô ma mère
> (HR, 79)

The process of naming is, in effect, a revaluation of two elements of the Québec cultural scene that traditionally have been rejected or neglected. One is the popular and oral tradition, which finds its natural extension in the rhetoric and didacticism of Miron's poetry, a tradition that only since the Second World War and the influx of the rural working class population to the cities, has begun to seek literary expression (we might add, en passant, that another major example of this phenomenon is Jacques Ferron, whose *contes* reflect a similarly established popular tradition). What Miron is seeking to break is the stranglehold of the old middle class on language. His desire is to establish the imagery of those who worked the land as the origin of the Québec language and sensibility.

The second neglected element is related to the first. We have seen that the colonial fortress attempts to preserve and control language, reflects the status quo, and fixes language within formal limits. Preserving an essentially European heritage against an American wilderness, the fortress ultimately breaks down since it cannot control the energy of the outside space. The dichotomy between form and energy is a mark of colonial language; when, as in Québec culture, the forms are preserved in order to repress and exclude natural energy (which for the colonial mentality is savage and demonic), then that energy will ultimately destroy form, break out of its repression and unequivocally reassert itself. In the 'poésie du pays' of the 1960's, this tendency is frequently associated with sexual imagery, or with the imagery of the resurgence from the depths of a popular unconscious; the 'abondance captive' (HR, 51) gives voice to its reality:

> Aujourd'hui sur la place publique qui murmure
> j'entends la bête tourner dans nos pas
> j'entends surgir dans le grand inconscient résineux
> les tourbillons des abattis de nos colères
>
> (HR, 61)

Pioneer language, that of the 'abattis', the clearing of the land, is allied to a conception of poetry as process, as the organic substantial growth of language that replaces the colonial language of form and order.

If, then, the language and character of 'l'homme agonique' is held to be vacuous and alienated, that of the new man beginning his discovery of self and poetry is substantive. Yet Miron does not affirm total victory; the images upon which he begins to build his world are revealed intermittently, subversive elements within the pervading darkness of his 'aliénation délirante':

> c'est l'aube avec ses pétillements de branches
> par-devers l'opaque et mes ignorances
> je suis signalé d'aubépines et d'épiphanies
> poésie mon bivouac
> ma douce svelte et fraîche révélation de l'être
> tu sonnes aussi sur les routes où je suis retrouvé
>
> (HR, 59)

It is in such primary, indeed almost primaeval, metaphors that Miron finds the origins of his new sensibility, a sensibility that he makes quite clear in 'Situation de notre poésie' (1957):

> C'est entendu, nous parlons et écrivons en français et notre poésie sera toujours de la poésie française. D'accord.
> Mais notre tellurisme n'est pas français et, partant, notre sensibilité, pierre de touche de la poésie; si nous voulons apporter quelque chose au monde français et hisser notre poésie au rang des grandes poésies nationales, nous devrons nous trouver davantage, accuser notre différenciation et notre pouvoir d'identification. Sans cesser d'écrire en un français de plus en plus correct, voire de classe internationale. Nous aurons alors une poésie très caractérisée dans son inspiration et sa sensibilité, une poésie canadienne d'expression française et, si nous savons aller à l'essentiel, universelle.
>
> (HR, 91)

Miron's poetry thus becomes shot through with fundamental imagery that begins the process of re-mythologizing Québec, once the old myths and structures have fallen apart. These fundamental metaphors vary from that of an intimate poetic response to a woman's myriad enticements:

> toi quels yeux as-tu dans les feuillages
> de bulles de hublots de pépites
> de geai bleu en jaseur des cèdres
> quel coeur effaré de chevreuse en fuite
>
> (HR, 52)

to the metaphorisation of the land itself, as, indeed, of a collectivity deeply aware of the existence and special beauty of this land:

nous te ferons, Terre de Québec
lit des résurrections
et des mille fulgurances de nos métamorphoses
de nos levains où lève le futur
de nos volontés sans concessions
les hommes entendront battre ton pouls dans l'histoire
c'est nous ondulant dans l'automne d'octobre
c'est le bruit roux de chevreuils dans la lumière
l'avenir dégagé
l'avenir engagé
(HR, 62)

Miron's appeal to the future is, however, paradoxically and simultaneously an appeal to the past, a renewal, or more precisely, a giving of literary voices to a process of naming and metaphorisation that had taken place during the first cultivation of the land, a process which had given birth to a clear identity, but which, through history, has been buried. The eradication of semantic confusion takes place under the guise of the insurrection of images that break through the fixity of the pre-ordained colonial signs and instigate the dynamism and energy of the organism:

Ce que la terre dans l'alchimie de ses règnes
abandonne et transmue en noueuses genèses
de même je l'accomplis dans l'homme concret
dans l'arborescence de l'espèce humaine
et le destin qui me lie à toi et aux nôtres
(HR, 67)

In Miron's love-poems the figure of the woman, Eve wandering in the wilderness, takes him back to the first times, the years in his native village. Around her are clustered images of his birthplace, the first irreducible signs that guarantee a sense of identity and structure. Miron's 'Marche à l'amour' is a paradoxical progress towards a future past, that pre-colonial time when names are given. He therefore evokes in the image of the woman a green world just discovered:

ma ravie
frileuse aux pieds nus sur les frimas
par ce temps doucement entêté de perce-neige
sur ces grèves où l'été
pleuvent en longues flammèches les cris des pluviers

harmonica du monde lorsque tu passes et cèdes
ton corps tiède de pruche à mes bras pagayeurs
lorsque nous gisons fleurant la lumière incendiée
et qu'en tangage de moisson ourlée de brises
je me déploie sur ta fraîche chaleur de cigale
je roule en toi
tous les saguenays d'eau noire de ma vie
je fais naître en toi
les frénésies de frayères au fond du coeur d'outaouais
puis le cri de l'engoulevent vient s'abattre dans ta gorge
terre meuble de l'amour ton corps
se soulève en tiges pêle-mêle

(HR, 39)

Similarly, the sexual act is another sign of unity and reintegration, an act in which is mirrored the relationship between poet and land:

du milieu de nous confondus sans confins
se lèvent et nous soulèvent
l'empan et le faîte de l'étreinte plus pressante
que la fatalité
noueuse et déliée, chair et verbe, espace
que nous formons largués l'un dans l'autre

(HR, 65)

Replacing the static, fixed, abstracted language of the colonial is the energetic language, the dynamic substantial vocabulary that derives its power from its particular and concrete reference. Movement, progression, the violent eruption of subterranean forces characterise the new man as Miron piles metaphor upon metaphor:

je me ferai porteur des germes de ton espérance
veilleur, guetteur, coureur, haleur de ton avènement
un homme de ton réquisitoire
un homme de ta commisération infinie
    l'homme artériel de tes gigues
dans le poitrail effervescent des poudreries
dans la grande artillerie de tes couleurs d'automne
dans tes hanches de montagnes
dans l'accord comète de tes plaines
dans l'artésienne vigueur de tes villes

(HR, 56)

Miron's experience of language is typical of the decolonizing process that has given birth, since the Second World War, to a literature of discovering and foundation. Evolving through several stages, revolt against the cloying forms of an empty tradition, revolt against self that creates the contradictory and destructive 'homme agonique', Miron strips his culture down to its essential elements. At this point the re-invention of the world can begin, the monologue of alienation is replaced by a dialogue with experience, and in an atmosphere not unlike that of Genesis, Miron's new Québécois begins the work of reconstruction. 'L'avenir est aux sources' (C, 49), he proclaims, and he sees the revival of a real Québec tradition in the revaluation of the first contacts with the land. Here is the first world:

> dans le temps plus nu
> que la plus que pierre opaque
>
> J'ai enfin rejoint mes chemins naturels
> les paysages les bordant depuis l'origine
>
> (C, 50-51)

a world into which the poet extends his presence:

> j'avance quelques mots ...
>
> (C, 51)

and begins not only to rebuild and revalue his identity but to infuse language with the irreducible physical experience of place.

In his essay 'Gaston Miron ou l'invention de la substance', Georges-André Vachon refers to Miron as 'le poète du recommencement perpétuel et total' (HR, 148). The process of new beginnings involves also a totemic identification, and in Miron's totem we see the return of a poet to his country. 'Me voici en moi comme un homme dans une maison/ qui s'est faite en son absence' (HR, 5), he says in the opening poem of *L'Homme rapaillé*. The poet who brings back a new life to Québec, however, is not yet triumphal and total; Miron is well aware that the Québécois is still ambiguous and the creature with which he identifies most closely is the curious harbinger of the Québec spring:

> Corneille, ma noire
> corneille qui me saoûle
> opaque et envoûtante

venue pour posséder ta saison et ta descendance
(HR, 78)

Yet it is this bird, 'parmi l'avril friselis' (HR, 78), that shows Miron the way to the first and essential physical contact with his space:

Avec l'alcool des chaleurs nouvelles
la peau s'écarquille et tu me rends
bric-à-brac sur mon aire sauvage et fou braque
dans tous les coins et recoins de moi-même
j'ai mille animaux et plantes par la tête
et cependant que tes larges battements
m'agitent en frondaisons de désirs
mon sang dans l'air remue comme une haleine
(HR, 78)

To infuse words with physical energy, with the dynamism of an organic life that is precious and particular, is perhaps Miron's chief poetic task. In this optic there can be little doubt that the raucous cawing of the crow is a bizarre cry of poetic triumph, a special, local sign of the beginning of a new and unique spring:

Tu me fais prendre la femme que j'aime
du même trébuchant et même
tragique croassement rauque et souverain
dans l'immémoriale et réciproque
secousse des corps
Corneille, ma noire.

NOTES:

1. 'Situation de notre poésie', originally published in *La Presse*, 22 June, 1957, reprinted in *L'Homme rapaillé*, p. 95. The following abbreviations are used throughout: HR: *L'Homme rapaillé*, Presses de l'Université de Montréal, 1970; C: *Courtepointes*, Editions de l'Université d'Ottawa, 1975.

2. In 1970 the Front de la Libération du Québec kidnapped British Trade Commissioner James Cross and Pierre Laporte, a Québec cabinet minister. Laporte was subsequently murdered. The Canadian Government invoked the War Measures Act on October 16, 1970, declaring a state of 'apprehended insurrection'. Civil liberties were suspended; 497 were detained on suspicion of illegal activites. The majority, including Miron, were released without charges being laid.

3. The term 'Quiet Revolution' is generally used to define the sixties, the decade that began with the defeat of the conservative Union Nationale, the party of Maurice Duplessis that had governed since 1944 and the election of the Liberal government of Jean Lesage. This decade saw the rapid decline of religious authoritarianism, the liberalisation of many Québec institutions and the rise of the independantist movement.

4. *La Barre du Jour*, 'Document Miron', octobre 1970, p. 25.

5. 'Joual', from the local pronunciation of 'cheval', is the term first used by André Laurendeau in 1959 to designate the local manner of speaking French. The term was taken up by Jean-Paul Desbiens in *Les Insolences du Frère Untel* (1960), a book severely critical of the prevailing education system, and quickly became common usage in Québec to denote a speech both grammatically incorrect compared to standard French and containing a high proportion of anglicisms.

6. *La Barre du Jour*, 'Document Miron', octobre 1970, pp. 35-36.

in periodicals, until *Le Parti pris des choses* (1942), since when his work has become increasingly well known. Most of it will be found collected in the following volumes: *Le Grand recueil* (3 vols: *Lyres, Méthodes, Pièces*; Gallimard, 1961); *Tome premier* (Gallimard, 1965); *Nouveau recueil* (Gallimard, 1967); *L'Atelier contemporain* (Gallimard, 1977). His other published volumes are *Pour un Malherbe* (Gallimard, 1965); *Le Savon* (Gallimard, 1967); *Entretiens de Francis Ponge avec Philippe Sollers* (Gallimard/Seuil, 1970); *La Fabrique du pré* (Skira, 1971); *Comment une Figue de paroles et pourquoi* (Flammarion, 1977); *L'Ecrit Beaubourg* (Centre Georges Pompidou, 1977).

DENIS ROCHE, born in Paris in 1937, spent much of his early childhood in the Caribbean and South America, returning to France in 1946 where he ultimately pursued medical and dental studies. His first poems appeared in 1961 in *Locus Solus* in 1961, with translations by John Ashbery. From 1962 on he was to establish liaisons of varying durability with the 'Tel Quel' group, as well as with a number of established literary reviews and the Editions Tchou. His first volume, *Récits complets* (1963), was followed by *Les Idées centésimales de Miss Elanize* (1964), which received the Prix Fénéon, and by translation of Pound's *Pisan Cantos* (1965) and *ABC of Reading* (1966). *Eros énergumène* appeared in 1968 during which year Roche's differences with the 'Tel Quel' group were heightened by the Prague invasion. More recently he has published *Le Mécrit* (1972), *Louve basse* (1976) and *Notre antéfixe* (1978).

LEOPOLD SEDAR SENGHOR was born in 1906 in Joal, about one hundred kilometres from Dakar. He received his education in Senegal and Paris, where he was the first African to be awarded the *agrégation*. In 1934 he founded with Césaire and Damas the review *L'Etudiant Noir*. Both prior to and after the war, during which he was captured, invalided and member of the Resistance, he taught in French *lycées*. His first volume of poetry, *Chants d'ombre* appeared in 1945 and was followed by *Hosties noires* (1948) and *Chants pour Naëtt* (1949). Various essays, texts and collections ensued, all of significance in the context of the emergence of black

African culture, politics and aesthetics. *Ethiopiques* (1956) and *Nocturnes* (1961) confirmed his poetic genius and 1960 saw Senghor elected first President of the Republic of Senegal. In 1964 a collective volume, *Poèmes*, appeared with Seuil, as well as *Liberté I*. Both the latter volume and *Liberté 2* (1971) present much of Senghor's socio-political thought.

TCHICAYA U TAM'SI was born in 1931 in Congo-Brazzaville. Educated in Paris from the age of fifteen, he worked in various odd jobs before turning to writing and radio production. His early volumes of poetry, *Le Mauvais Sang* (1955), *Feu de brousse* (1957) and *A triche-coeur* (1960), caught the attention of writers such as Senghor and Janheinz Jahn for their authenticity and intensity. *Epitomé* (1962), *Le Ventre* (1964) and *Arc musical* confirmed his place in African letters. In 1966 he received the *Grand Prix de Poésie du Festival mondial des Arts nègres de Dakar*. Today Tchicaya is on the permanent staff of UNESCO. His most recent writings include *La Veste intérieure, suivi de Notes de veille* (1976) and a full-length play.

NOTES ON CONTRIBUTORS

A. JAMES ARNOLD is Associate Professor of French at the University of Virginia. He has published various articles on modern francophone literature, is the author of *Paul Valéry and his Critics* and *Genèse critique d'une autobiographie: 'Les Mots' de Jean-Paul Sartre* (with J. P. Piriou), and is currently preparing a full-length study of the work of Aimé Césaire.

JOHN BEAVER was until recently Assistant Professor of French at the University of Manitoba and now teaches at Hillfield-Strathallan College, Hamilton. A contributor to various reviews and managing editor of Turnstone Press, he is presently preparing a book on French-Canadian poetry.

MICHAEL BISHOP is Assistant Professor of French at Dalhousie University. He has published essays on the work of Bernard Noël, André Frénaud, Pierre Reverdy, Michel Deguy, Jean-Pierre Burgart, Jacques Dupin and other modern poets, and is the author of *Pierre Reverdy: A Bibliography*. He is at present completing books on the contemporary poetry of France and the work of Pierre Reverdy.

PETER BROOME is Senior Lecturer in French at Queen's University, Belfast. Author of articles on Henri Michaux, Philippe Jaccottet, René Char, Julien Gracq and Robert Pinget, he has also published *The Appreciation of Modern French Poetry 1850-1950* and an accompanying anthology (with Graham Chesters), as well as *Henri Michaux* and a critical edition of Michaux's *Au Pays de la Magie*.

JAMES BROWN is Associate Professor of French at Dalhousie University. He has published various essays on French literature - Rousseau, Bernardin de Saint-Pierre, Flaubert, Rimbaud - and language and is currently completing books on the function of meals in the Nineteenth Century French Novel and semiotics as applied to foreign language pedagogy.

MARY ANN CAWS is Professor of Comparative Literature at the Graduate Center of the City University of New York. She has published numerous articles on modern French poetry and is the author of various books, amongst which the following: *Surrealism and the Literary Imagination: A Study of Gaston Bachelard and André Breton, The Poetry of Dada and Surrealism, The Inner Theatre of Recent French Poetry, The Presence of René Char, The Surrealist Voice of Robert Desnos*. She has also translated the poetry of René Char and will shortly publish translations of André Breton and Yves Bonnefoy, as well as a critical study of Pierre Reverdy and essays on art.

BRIAN GILL is Assistant Professor of French at the University of Calgary. He has published critical pieces in the area of modern French poetry and language and is the translator of John Lyons' *Chomsky*. He is currently preparing a Bibliography of Paul Eluard.

IAN HIGGINS lectures in French at the University of St. Andrews. He has published various essays on the work of Prévost, Emile Verhaeren, Francis Ponge and others, has edited the volume *Literature and the Plastic Arts 1880-1930*, and is the author of *Francis Ponge*, as well as a critical edition of Ponge's *Le Parti pris des choses*.

JAMES LAWLER is McCulloch Professor of French at Dalhousie University. Author of numerous articles on modern French poetry, he has also published various books, amongst which the following: *Lecture de Valéry. Une étude de 'Charmes', The Language of French Symbolism, The Poet as Analyst, Paul Valéry: An Anthology, René Char: The Myth and the Poem*. He is currently working on studies of Claudel and other modern poets.

ROGER LITTLE is Professor of French at Trinity College, Dublin. He has published various essays on modern French poetry and is the author of a number of books, amongst which the following: *Saint-John Perse: A Bibliography, Saint-John Perse, Apollinaire,* critical editions of Perse's *Exil* and Apollinaire's *Alcools*.

GRAHAM DUSTAN MARTIN lectures in French at the University of Edinburgh. He has published numerous articles and translations in the area of modern poetry, and is the author of various books, amongst which the following: *Paul Valéry: Le Cimetière marin, Louise Labé: Sonnets, Anthology of Contemporary French Poetry, Language, Truth and Poetry.*

GERALD MOORE was until recently Reader at the School of African and Asian Studies at the University of Sussex and is now Professor of English at the University of Ife, Nigeria. He has published numerous articles on francophone and anglophone literature and is the author/translator of various books, amongst which the following: *Modern Poetry from Africa, Wole Soyinka, Seven African Writers, Singer and Accompanist, Selected Poems: Tchicaya U'Tam'Si, Poor Christ of Bomba.*

INDEX

UNIVERSITY